THE
HORSE

An unusual head and neck study of the famous Greyhound 1:55¼.
Photo by J. A. McClasky.

THE HORSE

Third Edition

John M. Kays

ARCO PUBLISHING, INC.
NEW YORK

Published by Arco Publishing, Inc.
215 Park Avenue South, New York, N.Y. 10003

Copyright © 1969, 1982 by Arco Publishing, Inc.

Library of Congress Cataloging in Publication Data

Kays, John M., 1915–
  The horse.

  Includes index.
  1. Horses. I. Title.
SF285.K322 1982   636.1   82-11496
ISBN 0-668-05469-7

Printed in the United States of America

10 9 8 7 6 5 4 3 2 1

Look back at our struggle for freedom,
  Trace our present day's strength to its source;
And you'll find that man's pathway to glory
  Is strewn with the bones of a horse.

—ANONYMOUS

Contents

Preface to the Third Edition

The first edition of *The Horse*, published in 1953, was a balanced account of the many problems of horse production—selecting and judging, breeding, feeding, managing, and selling. In 1969 I retained much of my father's original text, but rewrote about one-third of the book for the revised edition.

This third edition presents a further reorganization and reworking of the book. I have made major additions to the chapters on the breeds of horses and smaller changes in all other chapters to make them more accurate and up to date. I have also added forty new photographs to show some horses and horsemen that have become prominent in recent years.

My father originally intended *The Horse* to be a textbook for college courses in horse production. It is my hope that the third edition of *The Horse* will provide useful, easily understood information to anyone who owns, breeds, or rides horses and want to learn more about them.

JOHN M. KAYS

Storrs, Connecticut

THE HORSE

1

Horse Judging

Horse judging consists of making a careful analysis of horses and of measuring them against a standard that is commonly accepted for their type, use, and breed.

To do an intelligent job of judging one must know what the standard is. One must be able to recognize the good and bad points of a horse and balance them against those of another as well as against the accepted standard.

IMPORTANT CONSIDERATIONS IN JUDGING HORSES

This brief discussion of the important considerations in horse judging may help the novice judge organize his thinking on the subject. In show-ring judging, the stress placed upon each of the qualities discussed will vary with the class specifications. In practical selection or buying of horses the emphasis varies according to the indicated use of the horse.

Type. Type refers to the sum total of those characteristics that make an animal efficient, valuable, and useful for a particular purpose. Type is a more inclusive term than conformation because it includes *all* of those qualities that are sought in the ideal animal for a particular job. The combination of characteristics that constitutes excellent type in the working cow horse differs from five-gaited saddle horse type. The ideal Thoroughbred hunter for riding cross country differs markedly from the draft type ideal. Yet some qualities are fundamental to all types.

Conformation. Conformation means the form or shape of the horse. In all livestock there is a correlation between the form and the function of the animal. Probably nowhere is this correlation more noticeable than in horses.

Since selection is on the basis of the entire horse, not on any one part of his conformation, the horse breeder and the show-ring

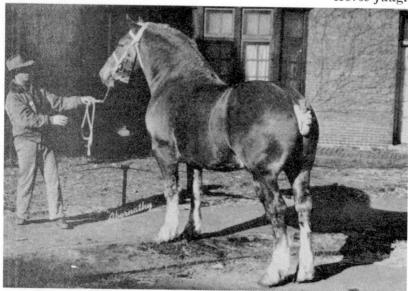

Jay Farceur 2nd 28147, grand champion Belgian stallion, Chicago International, 1948. Balanced in conformation, standing on legs that are correctly placed, with lean ankles, springy pasterns and big shapely feet, this stallion includes in his make-up the features sought in modern-day Belgians. Photograph courtesy J. F. Abernathy.

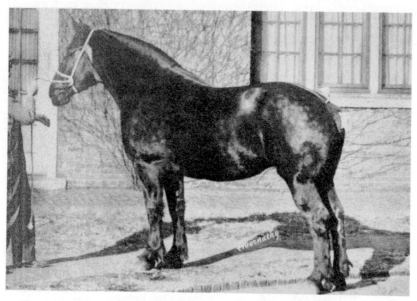

Muriel Ann Degas 244381, grand champion Percheron mare, the Ohio State Fair, 1947. Note her muscle and her bone. Also study her ankles, her pasterns, her feet, and the set of her legs. This mare was owned at The Ohio State University for a number of years and made a great classroom mare in training students. She was shown to her championship by The Ohio State University. Photograph courtesy J. F. Abernathy.

judge look for horses with symmetrical, balanced conformation. The blending of the individual parts in such a way as to make the horse most useful and efficient for his job contributes to the excellence of his type. Chapter 2 gives a detailed discussion of conformation as a factor in judging horses.

Soundness. A sound horse is free from any abnormality in the form or function of any part. A serviceably sound horse is one capable of doing his job although he may have some minor unsoundness or blemish not serious enough to incapacitate him. No other quality is more important than soundness in determining a horse's value. It matters little how fine his type, conformation, and breed character are, if he is unsound. Chapter 4 treats this important topic in more detail.

Way of going. Horses are valuable for what they can do. Beef cattle, sheep, and hogs merely have to produce a good carcass. But a horse's way of going, his ability on the move, is of fundamental importance to his usefulness and his value.

Size. Adequate size for age is an attribute of the best horses. Potential growth and promise of future development are sought in the young animal. A colt definitely small in his age group is penalized in show-ring judging and is criticised by the horse breeder in search of foundation breeding stock. Of course, some pony breeds, such as the Shetland, have definite height limitations for show ponies of various ages. Some horse-show classes are limited to horses of a certain height range. But, in general, adequate size and development for the age are wanted. Extremes, in either direction, are faulted.

Substance. Horsemen sometimes use the term substance to refer to bone and muscle. The ideal for all breeds and types actually is an intermediate condition. Horses should have all the substance and ruggedness possible without being coarse; they should have, at the same time, all the refinement possible without being delicate. A Belgian that is light-boned and light-muscled is off-type as a Belgian and as a draft horse. An Arabian lacking substance is off-type, also, even though not expected to have the heavy bone and muscle of the draft type. Usually horsemen seek somewhat more rugged bone in their prospective breeding stallions than in fillies selected to become brood mares.

Sex character. Stallions must have a bold, aggressive, masculine appearance to please most horse breeders. A greater crest to the neck than mares have, a heavier jaw, a proud and lofty carriage contribute to this look. Both the show-ring judge and the horse breeder disqualify any stallion without both testicles.

Mares and fillies should show a sweet, broody, refined, feminine character. Coarseness and stagginess about the front are faults in mares.

Sparkling Waters, American Saddlebred stallion in stud for many years at the Dodge Stables, Lexington, Ky. He was sired by Sparkling Firefly and was out of Dorothy Lloyd by Bourbon King. Photograph by John R. Horst, courtesy of Dodge Stables.

Constitution. Depth, width, and roominess through the chest and middle make for a rugged constitution. Such dimensions give ample room for the heart, lungs, digestive tract, and reproductive organs. The shallow-bodied horse lacks the stamina of a deep-chested horse. The slim-middled kind is always a "hard keeper." All types and all breeds of horses need the feeding and breeding capacity that go with a rugged constitution.

Quality. Quality refers to refinement as opposed to coarseness in the make-up of the horse. Horses of good breeding usually show quality as compared to horses of mixed, indeterminate blood lines. Refinement of underpinning, definition and leanness of pasterns, fetlocks, cannons, knees, and hocks, is associated with long time service and good wearing qualities. On the other hand, coarse joints and thick, meaty cannons are faults that good horsemen try to avoid when making their selections. Quality may also show in the features of the head. Fine ears, a fine throat latch, and a chiseled look about the face and jaw contribute to quality. Their opposite conditions detract.

Condition. When applied to horses the term condition may mean two things. Condition may refer to the degree of fat and fleshing. Thus a horse in poor condition would be thin, run-down, and perhaps in bad coat, while a horse in good condition would be in good flesh, sleek, and show a lot of bloom.

Condition may, at other times, refer to the horse's physical ability and fitness to do the job required of him. Thus a race horse is in condition when he has been brought through training to the stage where he has the speed, stamina, and ability to withstand the rigors of racing.

As is true with all kinds of livestock, fat may fool the beginner or the inexperienced judge. For this reason, old time horse traders, when asked what color horse sold best, said that fat was the best color. Fat gives a horse more crest to his neck. Fat makes a horse appear shorter in his back and coupling, and smoother over his hips and croup. Fat makes a horse seem deeper bodied. Therefore, the beginner must observe horses closely and analyze their conformation carefully, if he is not to be misled by their condition.

Breed character. Those characteristics that distinguish one breed from another may include body shape, features of the head, color, size, style, way of going, and many other traits. The term breed character refers to this distinctiveness of make-up. Some breeds are more distinctive than others, hence show more specific breed character. Intimate knowledge of breed character comes only with experience. Close association with good horesmen and their horses will broaden the novice judge's knowledge of the breeds.

SOME DIRECTION FOR JUDGING HORSES

In making a rating on a class of horses shown at the halter, it is a good plan to pose each one for individual analysis and inspection and then move each one at the walk and the trot.

1. Look at the eyes. Be sure to do this. Blindness or impaired eyesight disqualifies. If the foretop is draped over an eye, lift the foretop and look at the eye.

2. Note the position of the front legs and the front feet. Open

knees, knock knees, pigeon toes, toe-wide position, splints, width or fullness of feet at toes and quarters are observations to make from the front.

3. Look between the front legs at the base of the hocks for jack spavins. Normal hock joints should be smooth at the base on the inside.

4. View the horse from the side position. Note the position of the legs. Calf knees, buck knees, hocks that are too straight, and sickle hocks are observations to make from the side.

Thinking in terms of balanced conformation, note the symmetry of body lines. Observe the length of neck, the length and the slope of shoulder, the definition at the withers, the turn of the top from withers to tail, the length of the back and the coupling, the turn of the croup, the fullness of heart, and the depth at fore and rear flanks, the bulge of the hind quarters, and the strength of the stifle.

Study the underpinning carefully. Note the amount and quality

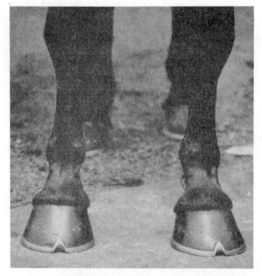

A splendid study in lean ankles, springy pasterns, and big, tough shapely feet. This picture also features Scotch-bottom show shoes, a winning entry in the Blacksmiths' Contest at the Ohio State Fair. Note the drawn toe clips and the even spacing of the nails. Photograph courtesy Cook and Gormley.

*THREE CHAMPIONS IN
THEIR RESPECTIVE
DIVISIONS DEMON-
STRATE THE TROT.*
From the top down:

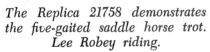

*Jay Farceur demonstrates the draft
horse trot. Earl Allen at the halter.*

*The Replica 21758 demonstrates
the five-gaited saddle horse trot.
Lee Robey riding.*

*Fiery Crags demonstrates the
three-gaited saddle horse trot.
Charles Dunn, riding.* Photographs
by Abernathy, Horst, and Rounds.

D.J. Kays, the author of the first edition of this book, at a job he loved—
judging a Futurity class for American Saddlebred weanlings at a horse show
in the Middle West. Photo by McClasky.

of bone, especially the strength of bone beneath knees and hocks, the cleanness of the hocks, the leanness and set of the ankles, the length and the slope of the pasterns, the fullness of the hoof heads, the size and the shape of the feet, and the texture of the hoof walls.

5. View the horse from the rear. Note width through the hind-quarters, width and depth of the heels in front and hind feet, and the crest of the neck to see if it is broken or straight. All horses should have sufficient muscle in their thighs to make them at least as wide through the quarters as they are at the points of their hips.

After having looked at the horse from the front, the side, and the rear, return to the front end where the inspection began.

6. Move the horse at the walk. Move him at the trot. Watch for lameness. On the turns watch for signs of stringhalt. If lameness is questionable, have the horse trot slowly. If stringhalt is questionable, back the horse or pivot him on his front feet, turning the rear end in each direction.

7. When the horse comes back to you at the trot, listen to detect wind unsoundness.

8. On the move, at the walk and the trot, note the style dis-

played and study knee and hock action, length of stride, and trueness and promptness of stride. Note whether the action is collected or sprawling and uncollected. The front feet should break over straight. The hocks should be carried close together. Prompt, true action with length of stride is desired at the walk and the trot in all kinds of horses.

2

Features in Horse Make-up

The Head
In all types of horses, the size of the head should be in proportion to the size of the body. As in other animals, the proportions of the head are considered a rather accurate index of the body proportions. Therefore, in judging horses one should always keep in mind the importance of balanced conformation.

In the case of foals, yearlings, and two-year-olds, a big head balanced in its proportions is an indication of growthiness and outcome. Of course, the terms "too big" and "too small," as applied to the head of any horse, are used advisedly. The head should not be so big that it appears coarse and plain and common. It should be big, with refinement as one of its essential features.

The small pony type of head in draft foals and yearlings is undesired because such heads are correlated with a tendency toward too early maturity, failure to grow out properly, and a consequent lack of size.

Therefore, in judging horses, the big coarse head in the case of all kinds of light-leg horses and the small pony type of head in the case of draft horses should receive sharp penalty. Somewhere between these two extremes discriminating judges make their choice.

The Features of the Head
Soundness of the head in all its features is a primary qualification in horses of all types. This requirement is emphasized in the market, in the show ring, and in the stud. Buyers of horses for these purposes are imperative in their demands for soundness. But the buyers for show and the buyers in quest of foundation stock also emphasize some features of the head which are of little interest from the standpoint of the open market.

Roadsters, saddlers, heavy harness horses, and all types of pleasure and show horses must be "breedy"—smart and trim about their heads and fronts—if they are to please the people who patronize the shows.

In all types of horses intended for breeding purposes, masculinity and feminity are important features of the head. Long, narrow heads with deeply dished faces or ugly Roman noses are undesirable because of their plainness. Width between the eyes and width of muzzle and jaws are taken to indicate capacity and growth possibilities. Straight-faced horses are preferred to the dished-faced and Roman-nosed types.

The Ears

The size, length, set, direction, and movements of the ear are important. Extremes in size of ear detract from the appearance of the head. The medium-sized ear, with proportions that help dress up the head, make the facial expression the most pleasing. Ears that are long, thick, and heavy—"mulish"—in their proportions make the head look plain. Ears that are short result in displeasing proportions. Such ears, however, are usually associated with the chunky type of horse, thick, closely and evenly made, and of prompt energetic manner on the move. A medium-sized ear, clean-cut in design, that shows the blood vessels clearly outstanding is characteristic of all horses in whose make-up quality and finish are well-marked features.

Set or location of the ear in no small way determines the beauty of the head. Ears set pretty well apart, not too low down over the eyes or too far back on the poll of the head, contribute to good looks. Ears set too low make a horse appear plain and unintelligent. Set too far back, they cause a horse to look sour and sulky, especially if such ears are accompanied by a Roman nose.

If the ears are carried in semihorizontal position, that is, if a horse drops his ears sideways, he is said to be lop-eared. Lop ears always make a head look common.

The direction and movements of the ear are important considerations. Horses that carry their ears at an angle of about 45 degrees with the axis of the head are directing their ears in pleasing fashion. Horses at work or posed and set for inspection always look well with their ears so directed. Such direction of the ears brings out the beauty of the head and results in a pleasing countenance.

The movements of the ear are indications of temperament. Ears kept in a constant state of unrest may indicate nervous temperament, impaired eyesight, or even total blindness. Motionless ears are indications of a slow, lazy, sluggish, phlegmatic disposition.

The set and carriage of the ear is most important in all types of light-leg horses for pleasure and show purposes, where finish and dressiness about the front contribute to good looks. In general, the ears are satisfactory if of proportionate size, properly set and directed, clean-cut and trim in appearance, with a minimum of long coarse hair protruding from the inside and fringing the borders.

The Eyes

Big, full, prominent eyes, of a dark, rich hazel color are desired in all types of horses. Eyes that are distinctly blue are considered weak eyes because such color is associated with eye unsoundness. In buying horses or in judging horses the examination of the eyes is a first consideration. This is because blindness seriously depreciates value on the open market, and in the show ring constitutes a disqualification. This is true of stallions, mares, or geldings. Therefore eyes that are characterized by clearness, deep coloration, and intensity of reflection are preferred.

Walleyes, sometimes called glass eyes, watch eyes, or Clydesdale eyes, are those in which the iris is of a pearly white color, destitute of pigment. Such eyes are objectionable on the basis of looks, but nevertheless are functional and are not considered disqualifications.

The bovine eye is one characterized by excessive convexity. Its bulging tendency has resulted in the name "popeyed." Such eyes are objectionable because they depreciate good looks and predispose to myopia or nearsightedness. Horses having such eyes quite commonly shy.

"Pig's-eye" is the term applied if the eye is too small, narrow, and squinty. Such eyes usually have thick eyelids and are commonly associated with coarseness and a sluggish, phlegmatic temperament.

The Nostrils

Good-sized nasal passages are considered indications of good breathing apparatus throughout. Small nostrils, on the other hand, are usually associated with short, flat ribs and consequently a chest that lacks capacity.

Just as the color of skin in sheep is an indication of health, so is the color of the mucous membrane or lining of the nostrils in horses. In buying horses, therefore, it is a good plan to examine the nostrils. The normal nostril discharge is transparent, resulting from the continuous discharge of tears. It is also odorless. Colored discharges of any kind from the nostril suggest sickness or disease.

The normal nostril should be large, the skin clear, the mucous membrane rosy at rest, more or less deep red after exercise, the liquid discharged should be clear and transparent, the breath should

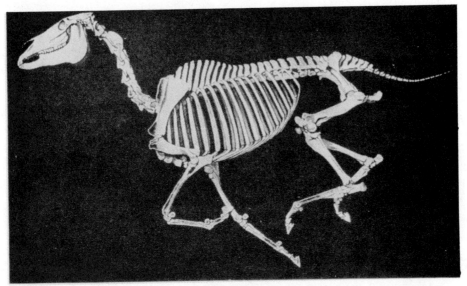

The famous American race horse Sysonby, showing action and sequence of hoofbeats at the run. This illustration shows plainly the way in which the bones act as levers as the hind legs are drawn up beneath the body, and moved forward again preparatory to straightening out and propelling the horse forward with a long stride typical of great running horses.
Photograph courtesy American Museum of Natural History.

be odorless or at least not unpleasant, and breathing should be noiseless. The nostrils should be large because the nasal passages are the only avenues of air intake to the lungs.

The Mouth

The jaws of the mouth should meet evenly. Protruding or receding lower jaws—synonyms of monkey mouths or parrot mouths—are undersirable because they are unsightly and may also interfere with eating and good doing ability.

The parts of the mouth are the lips, the teeth and the gums, the bars, the lingual canal, the tongue, and the palate.

The lips, like the jaws, should meet evenly. They function as organs necessary to the prehension of food and also aid in mastication. The lower lip in part supports the bit and the impulses or directions of the bit are in a degree received by it.

To avoid a continuous escape of saliva the lips should meet closely. This is not always possible if the head is reined too high or if the lower lip is actually paralyzed. In the first case, the lower

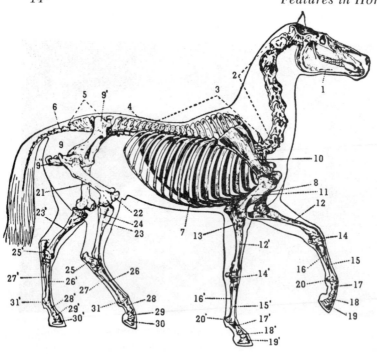

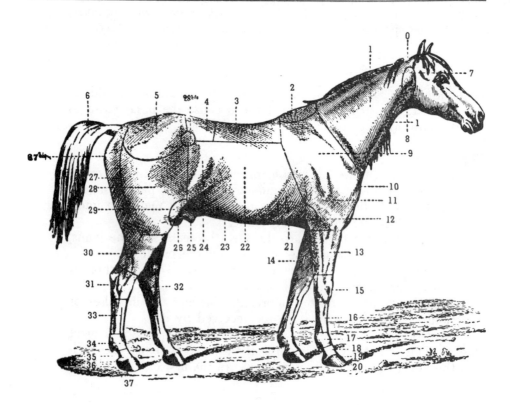

Opposite, upper: *Skeleton of the horse, showing the vetebral arch and the bone columns, one pair of the legs supporting, the alternate pair partially flexed, in a stride.* 1, *bones of the head;* 1', *lower jaw;* 2, *cervical vertebrae;* 3, *dorsal vertebrae;* 4, *lumbar vertebrae;* 5, *sacral vertebrae* (*sacrum*); 6, *coccygeal vertebrae;* 7, *ribs;* 8, *sternum* (*breastbone*); 9, *pelvis;* 9', *ilium;* 9″, *ischium;* 10, *scapula* (*shoulder blade*); 11, *humerus;* 12, *radius;* 13, *ulna;* 14, *carpus* (*knee*); 15, *large metacarpal bone* (*cannon*); 16, *small metacarpal bones* (*splint bones*); 17, *first phalanx* (*long pastern*); 18, *second phalanx* (*short pastern*); 19, *pedal bone* (*hoof bone*); 20, *proximal sesamoid bones;* 21, *femur;* 22, *patella* (*knee-pan or -cap and stifle joint*); 23, *tibia;* 24, *fibula;* 25, *tarsus* (*hock*); 26, *large metatarsal bone* (*cannon*); 27, *small metatarsals* (*splint bones*); 28, *first phalanx* (*long pastern*); 29, *second phalanx* (*short pastern*); 30, *pedal bone* (*coffin bone*); 31, *proximal sesamoid bones. This illustration does not show the navicular bone, either front or rear legs. Other illustrations in this chapter show the location of the navicular or distal sesamoid bone.* From Gay, *Productive Horse Husbandry,* courtesy J. B. Lippincott Company.

Lower: *A scorecard terminology study of the horse. Regions of the horse seen in profile.* 0, *poll, or nape of the neck;* 1, *neck;* 1', *jugular gutter;* 2, *withers;* 3, *back;* 4, *loins;* 5, *croup;* 6, *tail;* 7, *throttle, or throat latch;* 8, *throat;* 9, *shoulder;* 10, *point of the shoulder;* 11, *arm;* 12, *elbow;* 13, *forearm;* 14, *chestnut;* 15, *knee;* 16, *cannon;* 17, *fetlock;* 18, *pastern;* 19, *coronet;* 20, *foot;* 21, *xiphoid region;* 22, *ribs;* 23, *abdomen;* 24, *flank;* 25, *sheath;* 26, *testicles;* 27, *buttock;* 27, *bisection of buttock;* 28, *thigh;* 28, *bisection of haunch;* 29, *stifle;* 30, *leg;* 31, *hock;* 32, *chestnut;* 33, *cannon;* 34, *fetlock;* 35, *pastern;* 36, *coronet;* 37, *foot.* From Gay, *Productive Horse Husbandry,* courtesy J. B. Lippincott Company.

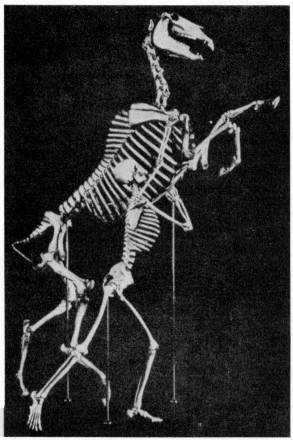

This illustration pictures clearly the skeletal structure of the horse and the man and shows how bones act as levers in supporting and propelling the body. The hock joint in the horse is the counterpart of the ankle joint in man. The knee joint in the horse is the counterpart of the wrist in man. The tuber calcis, the short bone protruding at the rear of the hock joint, like the heel in man, is the lever upon which the muscles act to lift the body upward and forward. Photograph courtesy American Museum of Natural History

lip drops down after becoming tired by the unnatural position of the head. In the second case, in addition to difficulty in the prehension of food, the appearance is unsightly. Unilateral paralysis draws the lip to one side. Bilateral paralysis causes the lip to drop on both sides and become pendulous. This defect may be congenital but usually it is acquired.

Some horses have the annoying habit of lip slapping or beating the lower lip against the upper by a series of convulsive movements. Usually it is a vice of idleness.

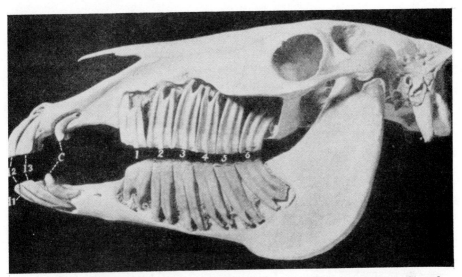

Skull of adult horse, sculptured to show embedded parts of teeth. The jaws are separated for the sake of clearness. I1, I2, I3, incisor teeth; C, canines. The cheek teeth are numbered without reference to the first premolar teeth (wolf teeth), which are not present in this specimen. This is the skull of a stallion or gelding, for the canine teeth are present. In the case of stallions and geldings, the bars of the mouth (the interdental space) extend from the canine teeth to the premolars. The lower jaw is hinged. Sometimes it protrudes beyond the lower limits of the upper jaw and the defect is termed "monkey mouth." Sometimes the lower jaw recedes and the defect is termed "parrot mouth." The distal extremities—the incisor teeth—of upper and lower jaw should meet evenly. From Sisson, *The Anatomy of the Domestic Animals,* courtesy W. B. Saunders Company.

The Teeth

The teeth are classified as incisors, canines, and molars. They are organs of mastication. Age is estimated by inspection of the incisors.

The bars of the mouth occupy the space on each side of the lower jaw between the incisor and the premolar teeth or between the canine and the first molar teeth. The bars are covered only with mucous membrane.

In the mare the canines, or tushes, are undeveloped, and the bars extend from the corner incisors to the molars. In stallions and geldings, however, they are developed; hence the bars of the mouth are shorter, extending only from the canines to the molars.

It is against the bars of the mouth that bit pressure is brought to bear in the control of horses by the reins. Horses are said to be hard-mouthed when the mucous membrane of the bars becomes toughened and thickened and the sensibility of the mouth is deadened because of the calloused condition of the bars.

The lingual canal is the space between the branches of the lower jaw in which the tongue is situated.

The tongue is an organ of prehension, mastication, gustation, and deglutition. It is located in the lingual canal and practically fills the mouth when the jaws are in proper position. The tongue helps to support the bit and, like the lower lip, receives impressions from the reins.

The hard palate forms the anterior or superior wall of the oral cavity. It is limited in front by the incisor teeth and in the back by the attachment of the soft palate.

Sometimes the hard palate becomes congested and inflamed, pouches and projects downward below the edges or tables of the incisor teeth and interferes seriously with mastication. This condition is termed "lampas," commonly but incorrectly called "lampers." Horses thus afflicted will go off feed until the tissues recede to normal position.

The Neck

The anterior limits of the neck are the poll, the parotid region, and the throat. The posterior limits are the withers, the shoulders, and the breast.

In all types of horses, proportionate length of neck is desired. Cleancutness about the throat and width between the mandibles of the lower jaw indicate minimum interference with the wind passages. Crest of neck in both mares and stallions is needed to break up the plainness that always accompanies a neck which is straight along the top.

"Arch" and "crest of neck" are synonymous terms. In mares the neck is not so strongly crested as in stallions. The neck of the mare is leaner, less bulging, not so heavily muscled. Its proportions suggest femininity, broodiness, and maternal refinement. In stallions, the crest of neck is stronger because of height and thickness. The lateral muscles of the neck are more bulging. Such bulky muscling contributes to the masculine make-up of the stallion front.

Mares are said to be strong-fronted, too strong, or "studdy" about their fronts when their head and neck suggest stallion proportions. Stallions are dubbed weak-fronted, gelding-fronted, or mare-fronted when they lack typical stallion proportions of head and neck. Stallionlike features, style, and boldness of carriage should characterize the stallion front.

THE FORM OF THE NECK   The neck is straight when the superior border from the poll of the head to the withers approaches a straight

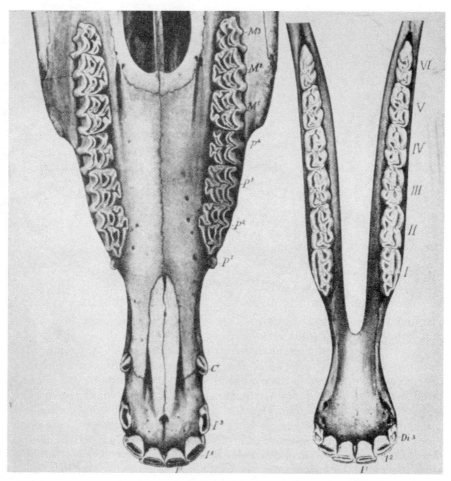

Left: *Upper teeth of horse about four and a half years old. I1, I2, I3, permanent incisors; C, canine teeth or tushes; p1, small vestiges of premolar teeth known as "wolf teeth"; P2, P3, P4, true premolars; M1, M2, M3, true molars. A typical rising five-year-old mouth.*

Right: *Lower teeth of horse four years old. I1 and I2, middle and intermediate permanent incisors. Di3, deciduous or baby incisors. I, II, III, premolars; IV, V, VI, molar teeth. The interdental space, incisors to first premolars, is known as the bars of the lower jaw. The bit rests here when in proper position. From Sisson,* The Anatomy of the Domestic Animals, *courtesy W. B. Saunders Company.*

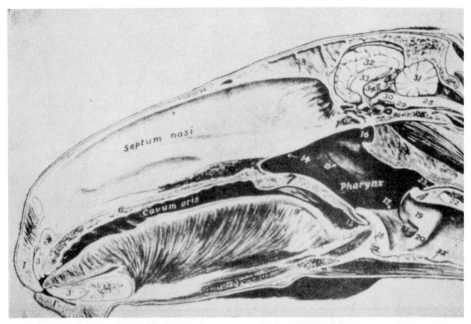

Sagittal section of head of horse. This illustration shows why horses do not breathe through their mouths as do cattle, sheep, swine, and dogs. The soft palate is a musculomembranous curtain which separates the cavity of the mouth from that of the pharynx except during swallowing. The soft palate is greatly developed in horses, its average length, measured medially, being about six inches. Its length and contact with the epiglottis, plus the fact that the horse does not have voluntary control of his soft palate, may account for the fact that, in horses, mouth breathing does not occur under normal conditions and for the fact that when a horse vomits the ejected matter escapes usually through the nasal cavity. This explains why horses even on the hottest days, at the end of a race or at work in the field, do not run their tongues out. The air supply for horses is furnished through their nasal cavities. They inhale and exhale through their nose. Study especially the following: 6, hard palate; 7, soft palate; 13, the epiglottic space; 18, the epiglottis. Note the relative positions of the soft palate, the trachea, and the esophagus. From Sisson, The Anatomy of the Domestic Animals, courtesy W. B. Saunders Company.

line. The neck is arched when the superior border is convex from poll to withers. "Swan-neck" is the term applied when the anterior portion of the neck is strongly convex and the whole neck imitates in form and carriage that of the bird from which it takes its name.

"Ewe-necked" is the term used when the superior border of the neck shows a distinct depression just in front of the withers. The ewe-neck is the reverse of the form desired; hence horsemen refer to it by the expression "set on upside down."

"Lop-neck," "fallen neck," and "broken crest" are terms applied when the crest of the neck becomes invaded with adipose tissue, resulting in so much weight that the neck cannot sustain itself and it breaks over or falls to one side.

Ewe-necks and broken crests are unsightly and undesired. The straight neck always means a plain front because arch or crest of neck is needed to make the front look imposing and attractive. Therefore crest of neck is demanded in all types of horses where impressive fronts are a requirement.

Length of neck is an important consideration and varies with the type of horse in question. Length is one of the outstanding features of the swan type of neck which characterizes gaited saddlers. More or less shaped like a letter S, this type of neck, although long, places the weight of the head closer to the body, thereby enabling a saddler in action to shift the weight from the front end rearward to his hind legs. This lightens the forehand and contributes to the finish of the horse's performance.

Proportionate length of neck is required in all horses, because long muscles mean more contraction, and this in turn results in a longer, more sweeping stride of the fore foot. The swan necks of saddlers therefore have two advantages. The long muscling makes possible grace and brilliancy on the move and permits rapidity and extended action of the fore legs. At the same time, the S design brings the head close to the body and lightens the forehand.

Short necks, bulky, thick, and staggy in proportions, are undesirable in saddle horses because they mean a lack of suppleness and mobility. Quite commonly a short neck makes a horse heavy-headed and less subject to control. In race horses, short, bulky necks mean short elevator muscles in the shoulders and less length of stride.

Thick, bulky necks are least objectionable in draft horses, because they do most of their work at slow paces and can use to advantage the weight that comes from big, heavy muscles. Such necks are not desired in light harness horses, heavy harness horses, or saddlers. They contribute to plainness of make-up and depreciate performance.

The Withers

These comprise the region between the two shoulders on top, behind the crest of the neck, and in front of the back. The height of a horse is measured from the highest point of the withers to the ground. Equine stature is stated in hands and inches, four inches constituting a hand.

Withers that are fairly prominent are desired because they ensure maximum length of spinal and shoulder muscles, also a longer stride to the fore foot. Horses with low, thick, rounding withers

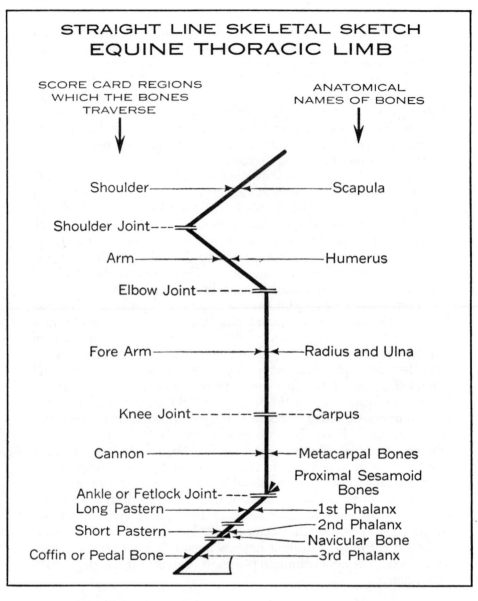

STRAIGHT LINE SKELETAL SKETCH
EQUINE THORACIC LIMB

SCORE CARD REGIONS
WHICH THE BONES
TRAVERSE

ANATOMICAL
NAMES OF BONES

Shoulder————————Scapula

Shoulder Joint———

Arm————————Humerus

Elbow Joint—————

Fore Arm————————Radius and Ulna

Knee Joint——————————Carpus

Cannon————————Metacarpal Bones

Proximal Sesamoid
Bones

Ankle or Fetlock Joint————
Long Pastern————————1st Phalanx
Short Pastern————————2nd Phalanx
                              Navicular Bone
Coffin or Pedal Bone————————3rd Phalanx

which lack definition move out awkwardly and clumsily in front. Such horses are usually low-headed, too heavy on the bit, predisposed to forge and interfere, and unfit for movement at rapid paces.

"Mutton withers" is the term applied to coarse, flat, rounding conformation over the shoulder top. In saddle horses such withers are objectionable, not only because they affect performance but also because they fail to provide a good seat for the saddle and do not furnish the proper purchase for the saddle upon the back. Consequently it is difficult to keep a saddle in place.

The Back

The back is limited in front by the withers, behind by the loin, and laterally by the ribs. In saddlers it is the part of the top which receives the weight of the rider. In all horses its function is to transmit to the front end of the body the efforts of propulsion which are communicated to it from the back legs through the loin.

A straight back of proportionate length is most desired. It is always a sign of strength and provides for the greatest freedom of movement of the legs. A convex back is termed a "roach back." Such backs are shorter than straight backs and do not permit sufficient extension and flexion of the legs in taking long and rapid strides. Roach backs and long legs are a combination which results in forging.

The back that is concave or hollow is referred to as sagging or as a swayback. It is objectionable because it depreciates appearance and suggests weakness. The short, straight back supported by ribs that are well sprung, long, and deep provides a middle that has ample breathing and digestive space. Such proportions indicate good wind as well as good feeding and staying qualities. Short, flat ribs are characteristic of horses that are poor feeders and have poor wind and staying power as well as poor shipping qualities.

The Loin Region

The loin includes the portion of the top which extends from the last ribs to the hips. Short, heavy loin muscles are demanded because they furnish the chief means of support for the lumbar vertebrae. Shortness of the loin is necessary to the best functioning of this part in the transmission of power from the hind legs forward.

All types of horses should have an abundance of muscling over the loin. "Coupled up good and close" describes ideal muscling on the loin. Horses that break across the top in front of the hips and that are long, narrow, and weak in loin conformation are spoken of as being slack in their coupling. Other terms applied are light over the kidney, long in the coupling, wasp-waisted. Quite commonly such horses are long-middled, shallow-middled, racy-middled, short in the back rib, cut up in the flank or hound-gutted.

The Croup

This includes the region from the hips back to the buttocks. In direction, the croup may be too steep, it may be too nearly level, or it may even incline upward from hips to tail. If a horse is too steep in the croup, the top line looks plain. Furthermore, the steep croup tends to displace the hind legs too far forward beneath the body, causing them to bear too much of the body weight. If the

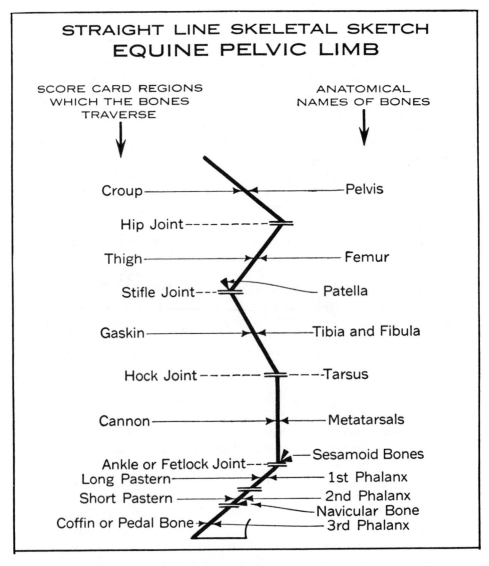

STRAIGHT LINE SKELETAL SKETCH
EQUINE PELVIC LIMB

SCORE CARD REGIONS
WHICH THE BONES
TRAVERSE

ANATOMICAL
NAMES OF BONES

Croup ——————————— Pelvis

Hip Joint —————————

Thigh ———————————— Femur

Stifle Joint —————— Patella

Gaskin ——————————— Tibia and Fibula

Hock Joint ———————— Tarsus

Cannon ———————————— Metatarsals

Ankle or Fetlock Joint ——— Sesamoid Bones
Long Pastern ——————— 1st Phalanx
Short Pastern ——————— 2nd Phalanx
                                   Navicular Bone
Coffin or Pedal Bone —— 3rd Phalanx

croup is too nearly horizontal or is set up a bit at the tailhead, the hind legs are displaced rearward. In the latter case the back is not so well supported because the front and rear bases are spread farther apart.

The croup should carry the width as uniformly as possible from the hips rearward. "Goose-rumped" is the term applied to horses that taper from the hips to the tailhead, displaying peakedness and angularity in this region. Horsemen like to see the croups of their horses deeply creased. They associate this feature with heavy muscling and with easy-keeping and good feeding qualities.

The Flanks

To give balance to the middle, horses of all types should be deep in the fore and rear flanks. Depth of flank in front and behind contributes to the symmetry of conformation. The best flanks are seen in horses that are well fleshed and highly fitted.

The flank movements, which are indicative of a horse's wind and breathing, should be slow and regular without any signs of jerkiness. The normal number of movements when at rest is twelve to fourteen a minute.

The Breast

The breast is limited above by the inferior border of the neck, behind by the axillae or armpits, and on the sides by the arms.

Proportionate width is demanded in all types of horses. Too much width, even in draft horses, where width is greatly emphasized as a feature in conformation, constitutes a real defect. When the front legs are set too far out on the corners, a rolling, rocking, laboring, ungainly gait results. With front legs so placed, horses are unfit for work at speed. This is the reason why the draft horse, whose business is to work at slow paces, can be proportionately wider in front.

The narrow-breasted horse whose front legs appear to have the same point of junction to the body is spoken of as being pinched or too close in front. A narrow breast commonly accompanies a lack of muscling and constitution.

The Chest

The chest or thorax, the bony frame which houses the important organs of circulation and respiration, functions in three important ways: it protects the organs of circulation and respiration; it serves as one of the most important parts of the respiratory equipment; and it serves as a base of attachment for many muscles that function in locomotion.

Height, width, and length of chest are important features. Height is measured from the summit of the withers to the floor of the chest. Width is the transverse dimension. Length or depth is measured from front to rear. This dimension is taken from the angle of the shoulder to the middle of the last rib. Length of chest depends upon the distances between the ribs and upon the projection of the ribs backward.

Backward projection of the ribs makes it possible for a horse to have a short back or top and still have a long or deep chest. The measure of the projection of the ribs backward gives the measure of the projection of the ribs forward during inspiration.

The arch of rib, the depth of rib, the distances between the

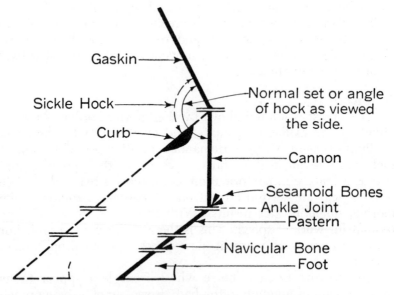

WHY ARE SICKLE HOCKS OBJECTIONABLE IN HORSES?

Gaskin

Sickle Hock

Curb

Normal set or angle of hock as viewed the side.

Cannon

Sesamoid Bones

Ankle Joint

Pastern

Navicular Bone

Foot

Sickle hocks result in displacing the hind feet
so far forward beneath the body that there is
a predisposition to curbiness.

ribs, and their degree of projection backward are all features which
contribute to chest capacity. Ribs that are flat, short, close together,
and slightly inclined rearward diminish chest capacity and are
objectionable.

The Shoulder

The scapula is the skeletal base of the shoulder. The chief
duties of the fore legs are to support weight, to preserve the sta-
bility and balance of the body, to aid the hind legs in propelling the
body forward, and to resist the injurious effect of wear and tear on
their own structures. Listed below are reasons why the shoulders
should be long and sloping, rather than short, straight, and steep.

1. A long, sloping shoulder makes possible a greater extension
of the forearm.

2. The front leg can be raised higher, allowing the stride to be fully completed before the foot strikes the ground.

3. A long shoulder gives power and strength to the swing of the fore foot.

4. A long, sloping shoulder contributes to ease, freedom, and style of action.

5. Long, sloping shoulders help to disperse the evil effects of concussion.

STRAIGHT SHOULDERS, ON THE OTHER HAND, ARE OBJECTIONABLE FOR SEVERAL REASONS:

1. They depreciate looks.

2. They are commonly accompanied by short, straight pasterns, resulting in a stilty set to the front leg, a conformation predisposing to shorter steps and harder concussions.

3. Straight shoulders do not furnish so desirable a collar bed.

4. Straight shoulders retard the rotation of the scapula, and horses commonly work their front legs with less freedom. Shoulders are sometimes referred to as pegged when shoulder action seems retarded rather than free.

The Arm

The humerus traverses the arm region. To permit a sufficient extent and rapidity of action of the thoracic limb, the bone of the arm should be short in comparison with that of the shoulder.

If the length of the arm be excessive in comparison with the shoulder, especially if the shoulder be short and straight, the foot will cover less ground at a single stride, and action will not be so reachy, free, and easy.

A long shoulder, a short arm, plus a long forearm makes possible maximum extension of stride and speed. The arm should operate in a plane parallel to the plane occupied by the horse's body. If the arm deviates inward too much, a horse will stand toe-wide at the ground. If the arm deviates outward too much, a horse will stand toe-narrow or pigeon-toed.

The Forearm

This is the name given to the region between elbow and knee joints. Length of stride depends very largely upon the length of the forearm because the forearm carries the knee forward and upward. Hence the longer the forearm, the longer the stride.

Short forearms in comparison with the cannon regions are objectionable because they result in shorter strides. They augment height rather than extension as a feature of the stride. Long forearms and short cannons not only favor speed but contribute to sta-

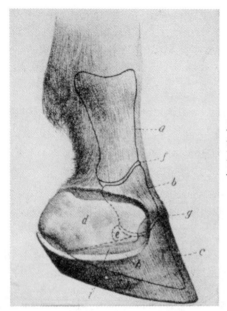

Digit of horse showing surface relations of bones and joints. From Sisson, The Anatomy of the Domestic Animals, *courtesy W. B. Saunders Company.*

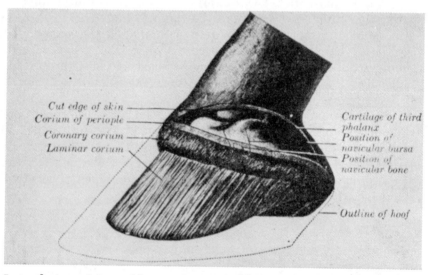

Lateral view of foot of horse after removal of hoof and part of the skin. From Sisson, The Anatomy of the Domestic Animals, *courtesy W. B. Saunders Company.*

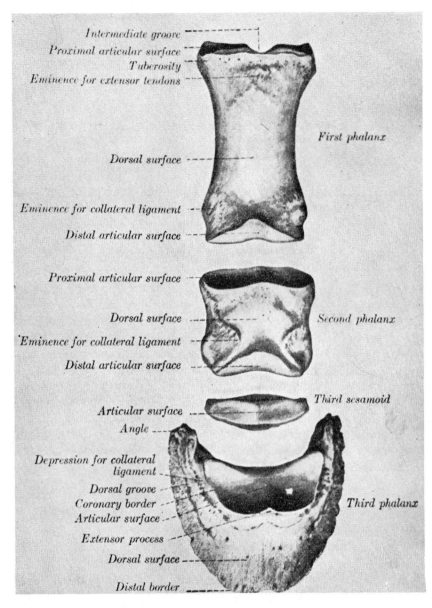

Phalanges and distal sesamoid of horse, dorsal aspect. From Sisson, *The Anatomy of the Domestic Animals,* courtesy W. B. Saunders Company.

bility on feet and legs. The knees are brought closer to the ground, making the support of the body easier during contact.

A heavily muscled forearm is most appropriate in draft horses. Slender, "weedy" forearms in drafters are correlated with angularity of appearance throughout and a general lack of draftiness.

The Chestnuts

These are semihorny formations varying in size with the type of horse in question. On the front legs they are located upon the inside face of the forearm a few inches above the knee. On the hind legs they are located on the lower inside face of the hock. They are not nearly so well developed in light-leg types as in draft horses. They are thought to be the rudiments of the internal digit which once characterized the species.

The Knee

This joint should be wide, thick, deep, and clean-cut in outline, properly placed and directed. Thickness of the knee is measured from side to side, width from front to rear. Width and thickness are desirable features because they increase the supporting area of the joint and furnish a more stable support for the body.

To distribute wear and tear properly, the knee must be correctly placed. If the joint breaks or deviates forward, a horse is termed knee-sprung, over on the knees, easy on the knees, or buck-kneed. If length of toe accompanies this knee-sprung conformation, there is a strong disposition to stub the toes, stumble, and fall.

If horses stand back on their knees, they are termed calf-kneed. Such horses on the move usually bring their feet down hard, increasing concussion. Furthermore, a calf-kneed horse stands and goes up hill all the time.

If knees break inward, they are termed knock-kneed. If his knees break outward, a horse is said to be bow-kneed or to stand open in his knees.

The Hind Leg and the Front Leg Compared

The arm of the front leg corresponds to the thigh of the hind leg. The femur is the anatomical base of the thigh. The elbow, the forearm, and the knee of the front leg are the counterparts of the stifle, the gaskin, and the hock behind. Heavy muscling through thigh, stifle, and gaskin is demanded. The hind legs are the propellers; hence this muscle requirement.

Horses that are turned out a trifle in the set of the stifle are preferred. This permits maximum extension of the hind leg, augments freedom of action, and turns the hocks inward beneath the body, permitting a horse to work his hocks close together and go

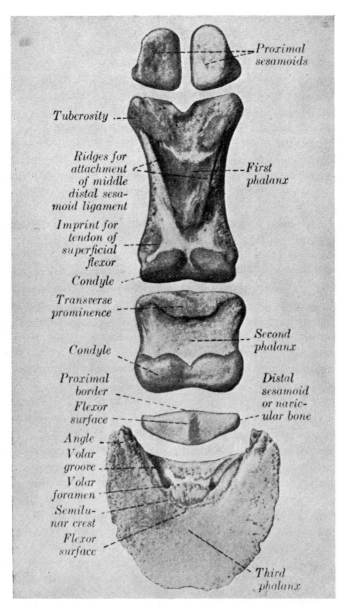

Digital bones of fore limb of horse, volar aspect. From Sisson, *The Anatomy of the Domestic Animals,* courtesy W. B. Saunders Company.

collectedly. The gaskin should equal the forearm in length and, like the forearm, should be heavily muscled.

The Hock Joint

The hock joint is referred to as the pivot of action in a horse. It plays an important part in propulsion and aids in the work of decreasing and dispersing the evil effects of concussion. It is called the pivot of action because it is the region upon which the extensor muscles concentrate their propulsive efforts. As the feet carrying the body forward at a great rate of speed strike the ground it is mostly upon the hock joint that the reaction from locomotion bears. It is the hock joint that bears the burden of the weight when a horse rears from the ground.

The hock joint presents a satisfactory make-up when it is clearly outlined, appears lean in quality, is wide and deep in its proportions, is well opened as viewed from the side, and is properly directed as viewed from the rear. A hock is lean and dry in appearance when its prominences and depressions are well marked and when the skin in fine and close fitting.

In the preferred direction of the hock joint as viewed from the rear the points of the hocks are slightly deviated inward. In some breeds, the Clydesdale, for example, the hocks typically deviate inward at their points. The hind cannons occupy parallel planes. The hind toes turn slightly outward.

Horses that stand with the points of the hocks turned inward and basewide at the ground are termed cow-hocked. Horses with hocks that turn outward are dubbed open in the hocks. Such hocks predispose to a twisting, rotating action on the move and are also termed rotating hocks.

If the angle formed by the hock as viewed from the side is too acute, a horse is called crooked in his hocks, is said to have too much set to the hocks or is called sickle-hocked. If hocks are rounding on the back side they are called curby or saber-hocked. A hock may lack set and be too straight. This condition is objectionable because it tends to shorten the stride. Improper set of the hock joint results in improper distribution of body weight and predisposes to early unsoundness of the part.

The Cannon Region

The cannon region extends from knee and hock to fetlock joints. The three bones, one large and two small, which traverse each front cannon are the metacarpals. The small metacarpals are commonly termed "splint bones." The three corresponding bones in each of the rear cannons are the metatarsals. In general form and arrange-

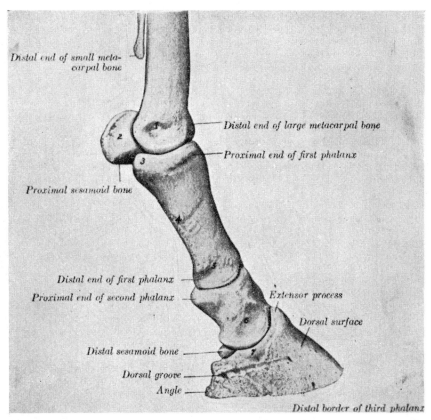

Skeleton of digit and distal part of metacarpus of horse. From Sisson, *The Anatomy of the Domestic Animals,* courtesy W. B. Saunders Company.

ment, the metacarpals and the metatarsals resemble each other rather closely. The metatarsals, however, are longer.

The size of the cannons depends not only upon the size of the metacarpal or metatarsal bones, but also upon the size and the set of the tendons that traverse the region. Horses that are constricted, "chopped away," or "tied in" beneath the knee are criticized by horsemen as lacking bone. Bone is an indication of substance and contributes to ruggedness and draftiness of make-up. Furthermore, big cannon bones and strong, well-set tendons are required to furnish ample support to knees and hocks. Clean-cutness and definition should characterize the cannons. Round, meaty cannons suggest staleness, secondhandedness, and a lack of quality.

The Fetlock Joint

The fetlock joint is the connecting link between cannon and

pastern bones. It functions as an elastic support of the body weight and aids greatly in dispersing concussion.

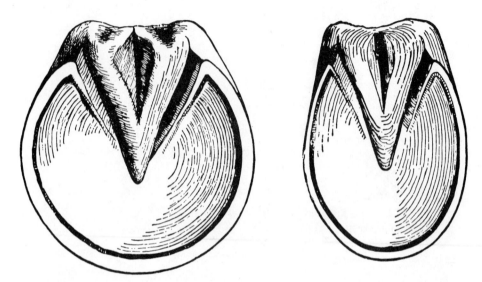

A wide fore hoof and a narrow fore hoof. From Lungwitz and Adams, *Horse Shoeing*, courtesy J. B. Lippincott Company.

Ankles set well back on springy pasterns are desired. Straight, stilty ankles mean hard concussions. They also predispose to knuckling or cocked ankles. "Up on the ankles" and "over on the ankles" are terms referring to the same conformation of this joint. Clean-cut fetlock joints are desired in all types of horses. Thick, coarse, round ankle joints characterized primarily by fullness rather than leanness contribute to the plainness and coarseness of the underpinning.

Feather, Footlock, Ergot

"Feather" is the term given to the hair which fringes the posterior border of the cannon and fetlock joints. Among the draft breeds Clydes and Shires have it in greatest abundance; hence they are termed the "feather-legged" breeds.

The footlock refers to the tuft of hairs which grows from the posterior base of the fetlock. This tuft surrounds and hides from view the ergot, a semi-horny projection which protrudes from the posterior base of the fetlock joints. Usually it is completely surrounded by the footlock.

The Pasterns

Springy length and set of pasterns are primary requirements in both light and heavy horses. Extremely long, low pasterns are weak pasterns. Such pasterns in company with shallow heels characterize horses that are termed "coon-footed." Short, straight pasterns increase concussion, produce stilty action, and rob the gait of spring and freedom, important features of the stride.

Straight pasterns and small, boxy feet with their narrow heels and their straight, upright hoof walls hasten the formation of sidebones. The pasterns serve as a base of attachment for extensor and flexor tendons; hence they function in locomotion as agents of extension and flexion. Snap, as a feature of the stride, is due in no small part to the working of the pastern joints.

The Foot

Three bones constitute the bony base of a horse's foot about which the other supporting structures are arranged. The largest one of these bones is the pedal bone, resembling in shape a miniature foot and so porous in structure as to resemble pumice stone in appearance and density.

The navicular bone is the smallest of the three bones of the foot. It is located at the posterior junction of the pedal and coronary bone, resting slightly on the pedal bone, but held in place largely by the deep flexor tendon.

The third bone, called the short pastern or coronary bone, belongs partly to the foot and partly to the leg.

The pedal bone is located mainly toward the anterior and lateral portions of the foot, the back portion of the foot containing but very little pedal bone. In this posterior portion of the foot, the deficiency of pedal bone is made up by the introduction of two large plates of cartilage. The presence of these lateral plates of cartilage in this region is due to the lateral movements which the foot is called upon to perform. These movements could not take place if the pedal bone in extent completely filled the hoof wall within which it fits.

The pedal bone is not placed parallel to the ground, but it fits within the hoof, with the toe slightly lower than the heel.

The Foot Joint

The foot joint is formed by the articulation of the three bones, pedal, navicular, and coronary.

FUNCTIONS OF THE NAVICULAR BONE The navicular bone increases the articulatory surface of the pedal bone and supplies or provides a yielding articulation, thus saving a direct concussion and lessening wear and tear on the structures. It is not held in place by

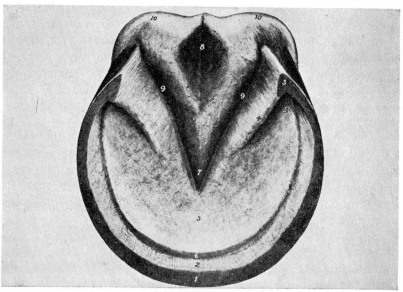

Right fore hoof of horse, ground surface. From Sisson, *The Anatomy of the Domestic Animals,* courtesy W. B. Saunders Company.

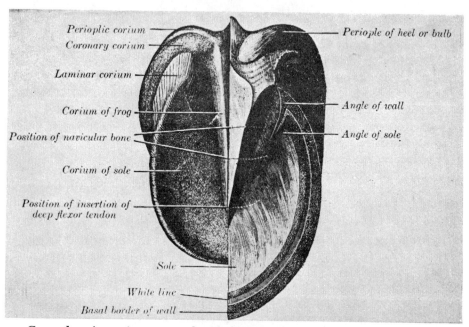

Ground surface after removal of half of hoof to show corium. From Sisson, *The Anatomy of the Domestic Animals,* courtesy W. B. Saunders Company.

ligaments alone. Its chief support is the flexor tendon. A close fit occurs between the tendon and the bone, a synovial apparatus or bursa between them preventing friction.

Held in place largely by the flexor tendon, the navicular bone is permitted to function as a yielding articulation. To this ability to function as a yielding joint is due in large degree the springiness of stride which features a horse's gait. If the navicular bone fails to function properly, a short, stilty, peggy gait results.

Lateral Cartilages

Attached to each wing of the pedal bone is a large, curved plate of cartilage. In extent it reaches upward beyond the coronary band, extends backward to the heel, and in forward location embraces two thirds of the lateral circumference of the foot. These cartilages function in the following ways:

1. They form a yielding and elastic wall to the sensitive foot.

2. The elastic movements of these cartilages assist the circulation of the blood in the foot.

3. They render the internal foot elastic and permit a change in shape which occurs under the influence of the weight of the body. The weight bears upon the frog and this in turn presses upon the bars of the foot. The pressure on the frog is also transmitted to the plantar cushion, which likewise flattens and spreads under pressure. Both of these factors cause the cartilages to bulge slightly outward.

When these elastic cartilages ossify their function is destroyed and lameness may occur. When sidebones result in lameness, however, there are usually other defects of the feet accompanying the sidebones which help to account for the lameness. If lameness occurs, the pressure which causes it may be due to the compression of the sensitive laminae between the ossified cartilages and a contracted hoof wall at heel and quarters.

Causes of Sidebones

1. Concussion. Sidebones are thus common accompaniments of straight shoulders, short pasterns, and narrow, contracted feet. This combination of characteristics increases concussion.

2. Improper shoeing. The feet may not be allowed to spread and expand at the heels normally because a shoe that is too small or one in which the nail holes are punched too far back holds the heels in too rigid a position.

3. Treads from other animals or treads inflicted by the animal itself with the calks of an opposite shoe.

4. Dropping the pole or the shafts of a vehicle carelessly upon the hoof head.

5. In severe cases of laminitis, ossification of the cartilages may result.

Plantar Cushion
This is a fibrofatty mass located in the posterior part of the foot between the lateral cartilages and filling in completely the hollow of the heels. Its inferior face is a complete counterpart of the face of the frog above which it lies. The back portion of the cushion is softer than the front, where at its apex it is dense and fibrous.

The Hoof Wall
The division of the hoof wall into toe, quarters, and heels is for convenience of reference and discussion only; no natural division exists. On the outside of the wall, at the point of junction of hair and hoof proper, is a rim of rather soft, nonpigmented horn known as the periople. It functions in cementing the skin to the hoof and in providing the wall with a thin covering resembling a light coat of varnish, which prevents undue evaporation from the horn.

The wall is thickest and longest at the toe, thinnest and shortest at the heel. Thickness of hoof wall at toe and quarters is necessary because of the wear at these points. Thinness of the wall at the heels makes the foot yielding instead of a rigid, horny box.

At the heels, the wall is inflected and continued beneath the foot as the bars. They extend forward, forming a V-shaped structure to receive the frog.

The wall, therefore, is an incomplete circle of horn designed to provide and permit spread at the heels. The bars give the wall additional strength as a supporter of weight and prevent a rupture between the wall and the frog during the expansive movements of the foot. They afford a solid bearing to the back portion of the foot.

The Sole
This portion of every normal foot is concave. The sole of a hind foot is more concave than that of a fore foot. This concavity is proof that the general surface of the sole is not primarily to bear weight, although the thin edge of the sole in contact with the wall is a weight-bearing surface. The union between the sole and the wall is indicated by a white line which encircles the entire junction of sole and wall. The chief function of the horny sole is to afford protection to the sensitive parts above.

The Frog
The foot pad or frog is a semisoft elastic structure, shaped

somewhat like a pyramid and molded or fashioned upon the surface of the plantar cushion. The horn of the frog contains more moisture than any other portion of the foot, and it is this moisture, aided by the secretion of the glands of the plantar cushion, which explains the soft, fluctuating characteristics of the frog.

The depression on the undersurface of the frog is called the cleft of the frog. Above the cleft on the side of the frog next to the sensitive foot is a projection of horn known as the frog-stay or peak. This peak functions in preventing the displacement of the frog, it also acts as a wedge which is forced upward under pressure when the foot comes to the ground. It thereby exerts pressure on the plantar cushion, which bulges outward and assists in the expansion of the foot.

The frog-stay also stimulates the nerve endings in the plantar cushion, thereby permitting the frog to function as an organ of touch. The frog is an anticoncussion mechanism to prevent jar. In conjunction with the posterior wall the frog receives the impacts of the foot when it comes in contact with the ground. These impacts are imparted to the plantar cushion and through the lateral cartilages to the hoof wall, which expands.

Sometimes when a foot has been kept shod for a long period and the frog is kept off the ground too long, the part atrophies, the heels contract, the foot gets smaller, and the pad is rendered functionless.

The Anticoncussion Mechanism of the Foot

Several characteristics in the design of the equine foot tend to reduce wear and tear, batter and jar. When a horse is in standing position the weight carried on each fore foot is somewhat more than one fourth of the weight of the body. On the move, the weight borne by a single foot varies from half the weight on the trot or the pace, to the entire weight in certain phases of the canter, the rack, or the gallop. The mechanisms to save concussion and to protect the structures of the foot and the limb are as follows:

1. The yielding articulation in the pedal joint.
2. The increase in the width of the foot, known as expansion, when the feet are in contact with the ground.
3. The frog and the plantar cushion.
4. The slight descent of the pedal bone and the slight yielding tendency of the sole of the foot.

The Determination of Age

There is nothing mysterious or empirical about the determination of the age by the teeth. Up to five years it is simply a matter of the eruption of the teeth, which in the normal individual follows

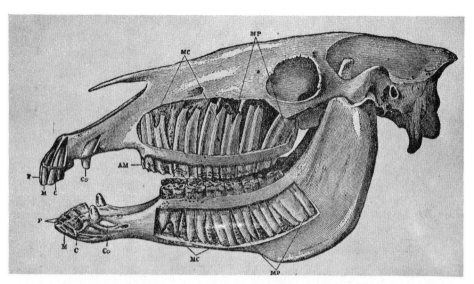

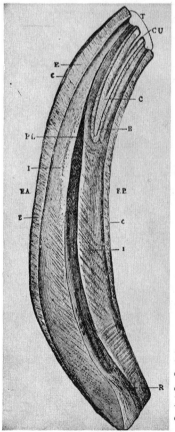

Above: *The whole dentition of the horse. P, pincers; M, intermediates; C, corners; CA, canines; AM, supplementary premolars; MC, deciduous molars or premolars; MP, permanent molars. The bars of the mouth in this specimen are the interdental spaces between the canine teeth and the premolars. Note that the lower jaw is hinged and hence is mobile. The upper jaw is fixed or immobile. If the lower jaw extends beyond the lower limits of the upper jaw, a horse is called monkey mouthed. If the lower jaw recedes, a horse is called parrot mouthed.* From Sisson, *The Anatomy of the Domestic Animals,* courtesy W. B. Saunders Company.

Left: *Longitudinal and median section of a permanent inferior pincer (enlarged). FA, anterior face; FP, posterior face; C, cement; E, enamel; I, ivory; PL, pulp cavity; CU, cup; T, table; R, root.* From Gabaux and Barrier, *The Exterior of the Horse.*

the same regular course that characterizes all other physiological processes. After the permanent teeth are all in, the indications are the result of wear, which is uniformly accomplished in the normal mouth on account of the extreme durability of the individual teeth and their arrangement.

Certain general features must be understood before any attempt is made to differentiate the appearance of the mouth at various years. After their eruption the permanent teeth may be distinguished from the milk teeth, which are shed as the permanent teeth come through, by greater size, by a broader neck showing no constriction, by perpendicular, parallel grooves and ridges on their face, and by a darker color.

The incisor teeth, which are the ones depended upon because they are the most easily exposed to view, are originally oval-shaped at the table or wearing end, gradually becoming triangular toward the root. The longitudinal dimensions of the teeth are curved, with the convexity forward toward the lips and the concavity toward the mouth. The table itself is cupped out in the center by a depression, into which the enamel of the tooth dips.

As wear commences, the surface enamel is worn off, leaving two distinct enamel rings, one around the margin of the table and the other around the cup.

The cup itself becomes gradually more shallow until it is finally worn almost completely away. As wear on the table removes more and more of the end of the tooth, the level of the pulp cavity in the center of the tooth is finally reached, and the exposed tip of this canal appears between what is left of the cup and the front of the tooth.

Other sequences of the continued wearing away of the tooth are the changes in outward outline of its transverse diameter, becoming, first, more oval from side to side, then more distinctly triangular as wear continues toward the root. Also, as the mouth end of the tooth is worn away, the levels of the tables and their contact are maintained by the tissues which close in behind the root and force the tooth forward. This gives the angle of the incisors less curve and more slant, at the same time rendering the margin and the outline of the jaw sharper and flatter. As the arch becomes more slanting, the surfaces of the teeth meet at a different angle. In the case of the corners, the lower teeth do not wear clear to the back margin of the uppers, so that a hook or notch is gradually formed, worn away, and formed again at different years. These, with the eruption of the canines which occurs in males at four to six years, are the principal changes upon which the age is reckoned.

It remains now to indicate just what changes are characteristic of the different yearly periods. Charts and actual inspection of mouths are helpful visual aids in making such determinations.

Helpful Information in Making Age Determinations

The teeth of the horse function as organs of prehension and mastication. They also serve as weapons of combat. Horses have two sets of teeth. The first set of teeth is referred to by the names "baby," "milk," "temporary," or "deciduous." These are replaced during the period of growth by the second set known as the permanent teeth.

Classification of teeth is based upon their form and position. The front teeth are called incisors. The central incisors or nippers are the first pair of incisors to erupt. The next pair lateral to the central incisors are called the intermediates. The third and outside pair are called the corner incisors. Permanent incisors may be distinguished from the milk incisors as follows:

1. They do not have a well-defined neck joining root and crown as do the milk teeth.
2. They are larger, longer, and more nearly rectangular.
3. They are not so white in color.
4. They are more flat in curvature.

THE INCISORS AS SIGNPOSTS OF AGE

1. The milk teeth are shed at regular intervals and replaced by permanent teeth. The dates at which these changes occur are helpful in age determination.
2. The angle formed by the incisor teeth of the two jaws is called the angle of incidence. This angle decreases as the horse gets older.
3. As a horse ages there is a distinct difference in the length of the teeth, the gums appearing to recede.
4. With age, permanent teeth lose their oval shape, becoming much more cylindrical.
5. The disappearance of the cups indicates age. The cups in the tables of the upper incisors are deeper than in the lower. Therefore the lower cups disappear before the upper.

The canine teeth, also referred to as tushes or tusks, are located in the interdental space between the incisors and molars. In mares the canine teeth rarely erupt, as is shown by an examination of the mouths of eight thousand mares. Of these, only 2 to 3 per cent had canine teeth erupted in both jaws; only 6 to 7 per cent in the upper jaw; and only 20 to 30 per cent in the lower jaw.

Sisson gives four to five years as the date of eruption for the canine teeth.

The molars or the large back teeth are sometimes called the grinders.

TABLE SHOWING NUMBER OF DECIDUOUS TEETH—INCISORS, CANINES, AND PREMOLARS

$$2 \ DI \dfrac{3}{3} - DC \dfrac{0}{0} - DP \dfrac{3}{3} - \ = 24$$

TABLE SHOWING NUMBER OF PERMANENT TEETH—INCISORS, CANINES, MOLARS, AND PREMOLARS

$$2 \ I \dfrac{3}{3} - C \dfrac{1}{1} - P \dfrac{3\text{-}4}{3} - M \dfrac{3}{3} - \ = 40\text{-}42$$

Note on above tables: In the mare the canines usually do not erupt, thereby reducing the number of teeth to 36.

The number of teeth in the upper jaw may be increased by the presence of so-called "wolf" teeth. Such teeth are much-reduced vestiges of teeth, situated just in front of the first well-developed premolar. There is one on each side of the upper jaw. Often these teeth are not more than half or three quarters of an inch in length. They may erupt during the first six months and be shed about the same time as the milk teeth behind them. They may remain, however, indefinitely. The occurrence of similar teeth in the lower jaw, which rarely erupt, increases the number of teeth to 44.

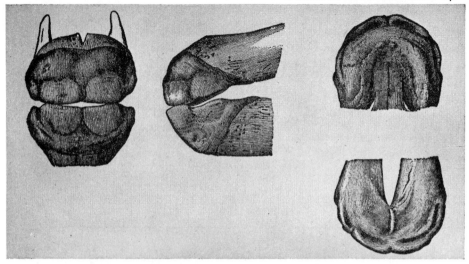

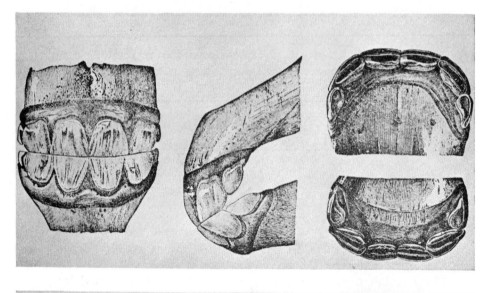

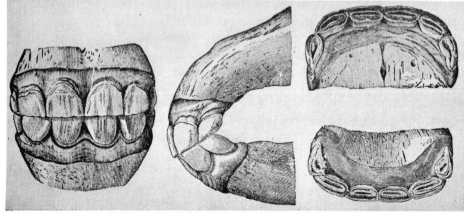

BIRTH: Top Left. *None of the incisor teeth has penetrated the gums. The buccal mucous membrane still covers those which were to appear first. In front, under the gums, the two pincers are perceived above and below. In profile, we distinguished the intermediates, less developed than the pincers. The jaws are very round at their extremity and but little separated from each other. On each side of the median line the dental tables show the prominence formed by the anterior border of the pincers and, external to these, but less developed, the borders of the intermediates. The internal side of these teeth is the more prominent, and it is this side which would have first pierced the mucous membrane.* From Gabaux and Barrier, *The Exterior of the Horse.*

ONE YEAR: Middle Left. *Viewed in front, all the milk incisors are visible; the pincers and the intermediates are well penetrated through the gums. In profile, the superior corners are not yet in contact with the inferior. The tables show that the posterior border of the pincers and the intermediates is worn more. Nevertheless, this character is liable to vary, according to the mouths which are examined, because of the unequal height of this border. However, it will be easy to avoid too great an error by recognizing the degree of wear of the anterior border. Ordinarily, at this period, the latter presents a yellow line, elongated transversely, which is surrounded by the remainder of the dentin; this is the dental star. We must also compare the degree of wear of the pincers and the intermediates. If the latter are the more worn off, it will tend to make the young animal older rather than younger. The corners are still virgin. The incisive arcades are wider transversely and less round in their middle.* From Gabaux and Barrier, *The Exterior of the Horse.*

TWO YEARS: Bottom Left. *Contrary to the preceding illustration, these jaws belonged to a colt of a lymphatic type, since the period of his weaning, having been fed almost entirely on forage. Also, to judge of the age from the state of the dental tables alone would be to make this animal only about twenty months old. The subject, nevertheless, was two years and twenty-six days old. The mouth, however, presents some special characters which tend to modify the inferences that would be formed at first sight. Viewed in front, the pincers and the intermediates are quite free from the gums at their base, the superior pincers especially. This fact indicates that the permanent teeth should have accomplished their eruption in seven or eight months. In profile, the neck of the corners is visible. The tables of the latter show decided wear; the dental star is distinctly visible in these teeth, and the wear slightly involves their external border. The central enamel of the superior intermediates forms a complete circle. Finally, the incisive arcades, much elongated transversely, are greatly depressed in the region of the pincers and the intermediates. If to these signs be added the information obtained from the nature of the ailment, the period of the year, the general development, and so on, one will easily be able to arrive at an accurate determination.* From Gabaux and Barrier, *The Exterior of the Horse.*

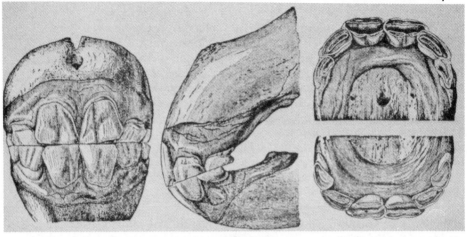

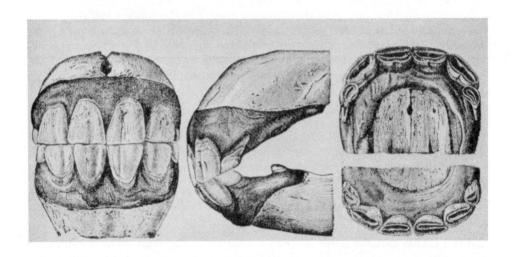

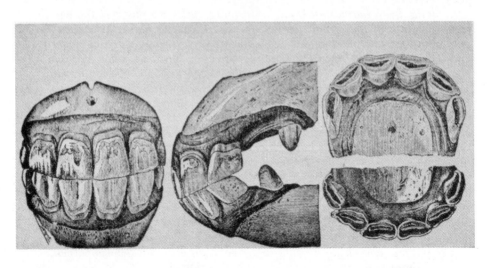

THREE YEARS: Top Left. *Viewed in front, the four permanent pincers are seen to be much wider and larger than the neighboring teeth. The anterior border of the superior pincers is slightly oblique; as a result, its external part is not in contact with the corresponding border of the inferior. In profile, the milk intermediates are much pushed out and very short; the corners are constricted at their base and shortened; their table is worn off squarely. Between the corner and the intermediate, on the left, is found a prominence due to the protrusion, under the gums, of the permanent intermediate, whose eruption was about to take place. The dental tables of the inferior intermediates are very much worn; above they are somewhat less so. The inferior corners are almost destitute of the central enamel. As to the permanent teeth, the wear is not the same in both jaws; the inferior are the more worn, because they come out before the superior.* From Gabaux and Barrier, *The Exterior of the Horse.*

FOUR YEARS: Middle Left. *Viewed in front, all the permanent superior teeth are in contact with the inferior; the jaws, in the part which corresponds to the pincers and the intermediates, have acquired so much width, from one side to the other, that the deciduous corners can scarcely be seen. In profile, the latter appear very small; the superior had commenced to be pushed from their sockets; behind the inferior is seen the extremity of the canine tooth. The tables of the intermediates are much worn, especially those of the superior, which come out first. The central enamel in the pincers forms a distinct oval only in the superior incisors; if this character is absent in the others, the absence is due to the fact that the external dental cavity is more or less fissured in the vicinity of its external border. The inferior corners are almost leveled, and the superior are more so. Moreover, they are stripped around their base and a portion of their root is seen.* From Gabaux and Barrier, *The Exterior of the Horse.*

FIVE YEARS: Bottom Left. *The mouth is entirely made. All the permanent teeth are on the same level in their respective jaws. Viewed in front, the jaws appear very convex in both directions. In profile, they have a similar disposition; the canines are completely out. Upon the tables it is seen that the corners were already commencing to wear at their anterior border. The pincers are almost leveled, but the infundibulum, or cup, is still very much elongated transversely, and narrow from before to behind; it is closer to their posterior border. This form of the infundibulum indicates that the external dental cavity was not very deep in consequence of the abundance of the central cement; these teeth are also soon leveled. Almost the same disposition, as regards the external dental cavity, exists in the inferior intermediates. In order, therefore, not to misinterpret the significance of the leveling, it is necessary to consider the form and dimensions of the central enamel. In this way alone can the degree of wear of the tooth be inferred. The incisive arcades form an almost regular semicircle in each jaw.* From Gabaux and Barrier, *The Exterior of the Horse.*

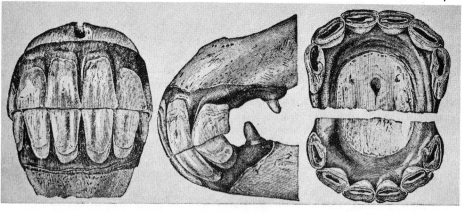

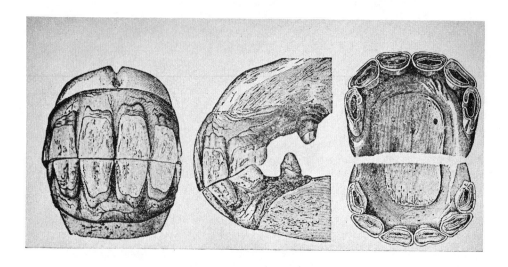

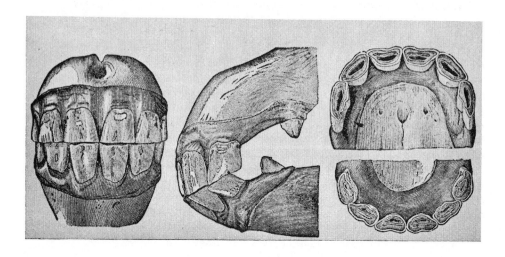

SIX YEARS: Top Left. *Viewed in front, the jaws present almost the same characters as at five years. In profile, we see here a retarded eruption of the canines; these teeth had not yet reached their full length; they are therefore incapable of giving any exact information as to the age. The tables furnish by far the best indications. The posterior border of the inferior and superior corners is notably worn. The pincers are ordinarily leveled, and the table tends to take an oval form. In the figure, the leveling of the inferior pincers is not altogether complete. Nevertheless, the central enamel is wider from before to behind, and narrower from one side to the other, than at five years; it is also closer to the posterior border of the table. The same remarks apply to the intermediates. It will be noticed that the external dental cavity is fissured upon its posterior face in the two superior corners. This irregularity of form, somewhat common, amounts to little in the determination of the age.* From Gabaux and Barrier, *The Exterior of the Horse.*

SEVEN YEARS: Middle Left. *No marked change is shown by the jaws viewed in front except that the teeth appear whiter because the layer of cement, which at first covered their anterior face, is worn off. In profile, it is found that the table of the inferior corners is narrower from side to side than that of the superior; this results in the formation of a notch upon the latter. The incidence of the incisive arcades is always less perpendicular than at six years. As to the tables, they are leveled upon the pincers and upon the intermediates; the ring of central enamel is wider anteroposteriorly and shorter from side to side. The surface of friction in the corners is larger; sometimes the central enamel forms a complete ring, and sometimes it is incomplete. These differences often result from an irregular form of these teeth. In some subjects, their posterior border is almost absent. It then requires a longer time for the table to be completed behind. The pincers are oval; the intermediates tend to become so. The superior corners are fissured at their posterior border.* From Gabaux and Barrier, *The Exterior of the Horse.*

EIGHT YEARS: Bottom Left. *The direction of the incisors is noticeably changed; the superior and inferior teeth are opposed obliquely. Hence, viewed in front, the jaws project at the level of their line of meeting. In profile, this fact is more apparent, for the anterior face of the incisive arcades has no longer the form of a regular semicircle, as at five years. Their arc appears broken at the place where the tables of the superior and inferior incisors meet, and it acquires more and more the curve of an ogive. The base of the corner is cut squarely by the gum. The incisive arcades are still regular, but narrower than at five years; the surfaces of friction represent, in fact, sections closer to the summit of the cones constituted by the teeth. All the inferior teeth are leveled. The pincers and intermediates are oval; the corners were becoming so. Finally, the dental star appears upon the pincers and intermediates, between the anterior border of the table and the corresponding border of the central enamel.* From Gabaux and Barrier, *The Exterior of the Horse.*

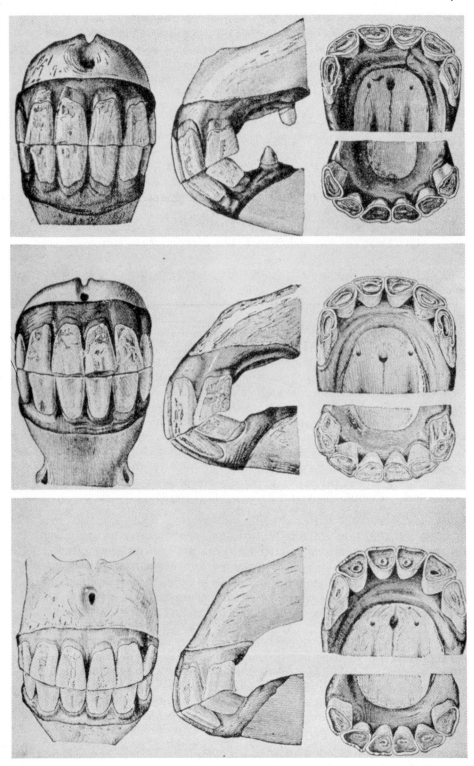

NINE YEARS: Top Left. *No marked change is to be seen upon the jaws viewed in front or in profile. The teeth are ordinarily more oblique and less fresh looking than at eight years of age. The notch on the superior corner has often disappeared. The characters furnished by the tables are more positive. The pincers are round; their central enamel has a triangular form; their dental star is narrower but more distinct, and occupies almost the middle of the dental table. The intermediate teeth are becoming round, and the corner teeth are oval. At this age, the superior pincer teeth are leveled in most jaws. The inferior incisive arcade is narrower transversely and depressed in the center.* From Gabaux and Barrier, *The Exterior of the Horse.*

TEN YEARS: Middle Left. *In consequence of the more marked obliquity of the teeth, the jaws become prominent in front when they are examined from this point, and it is necessary to raise the head of the horse higher in order to have a good view of the inferior incisors. In profile, this character is still more apparent. The ogive formed by the contact of the two arcades is smaller, the inclination of the corners augments, and the interspace which separates them from the intermediates is larger. Upon the tables, the inferior pincers are still more round; their central enamel is smaller, distinctly triangular, and closer to their posterior border. Finally, their dental star, more visible, encroaches upon the middle of their surface of friction. The intermediates are round, and the corners tend to assume this form. In the illustration the latter have an irregular table because they as well as the superior corners are fissured on their posterior border; this border has been checked in its development and hence is but slightly prominent. The inferior incisive arc is more depressed in its middle.* From Gabaux and Barrier, *The Exterior of the Horse.*

FIFTEEN YEARS: Bottom Left. *Viewed in front, the inferior teeth appear shorter than the superior because the jaws are viewed without being elevated. In profile, the incisors are found to be of almost the same length. The notch in the superior corner always exists. The inferior tables all present in their center a rounded and very distinct dental star. The pincers are almost triangular; the intermediates were becoming so. The central enamel, in the superior pincers, is much smaller than at thirteen years. The incisive arcade is greatly depressed in front and narrow transversely.* From Gabaux and Barrier, *The Exterior of the Horse.*

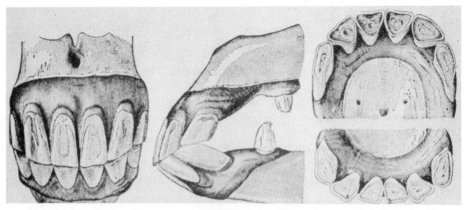

TWENTY-ONE YEARS: *The teeth have become so horizontal that, when viewed in front, it is difficult to see their anterior face, unless the head of the horse be raised. The triangular interstices, situated at the base of the superior incisors, augment more and more; this shows the convergence of the intermediates and the corners at their free extremity. In profile, the jaws are thin. The inferior corner, almost horizontal, has caused the disappearance of the notch on the superior corner. This disposition causes the formation, in these two teeth, of a surface of friction which is elongated from before to behind or, rather, from the external to the internal side, instead of remaining triangular. The superior tables, in the pincers and the intermediates, are wide from their anterior to their posterior borders, they are regularly triangular, and the central enamel, in most instances, is absent. The inferior tables tend to become flattened from one side to the other and more and more divergent in front. From Gabaux and Barrier, The Exterior of the Horse.*

TABLE SHOWING ERUPTION OF THE TEETH

Deciduous Incisors:
Middle incisors: Erupt at birth or from first week to 10 days.
Intermediate incisors: Erupt between 4 and 8 weeks.
Corner incisors: Erupt between 6 and 9 months.

Permanent Incisors:
Middle incisors: Erupt at 2½ years.
Intermediate incisors: Erupt at 3½ years.
Corner incisors: Erupt at 4½ years.

Horsemen often say that the milk incisors erupt in pairs at 8 days, at 8 weeks, and at 8 months. This easy rule should help one to remember the dates of eruption for the milk incisors. The permanent incisors will be full grown six months after eruption; hence at five years of age a horse should have a full mouth. In other words, at five years of age all permanent incisor teeth should be down, squared off, and in wear.

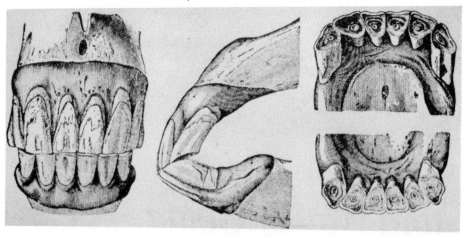

THIRTY YEARS: *The characters of this period are those of extreme old age. In front, the superior arcade overlaps the inferior, which is considerably narrowed; the convergence of the corners and the intermediates becomes more and more distinct. In profile, the inferior incisors are very horizontal, especially the corners; the jaws are thin and separated from each other at the level of the bars. The inferior tables are flattened from side to side, or biangular; the peripheral enamel having tended to disappear from their posterior border. The superior tables are flattened in the same sense, and their peripheral enamel has a similar disposition. Sometimes in one of the incisive arcades, and at times in both, the teeth have acquired an excessive length; then the central enamel has not yet disappeared. At other times, on the contrary, they are worn down almost to the gums and surrounded by a thick layer of radical cement, directly applied upon the dentine, which is deprived of its peripheral enamel. Finally, the incisive arcs are very narrow and rectilinear from one side to the other.* From Gabaux and Barrier, *The Exterior of the Horse.*

A green mouth is any mouth which features all or some deciduous incisors.

A full mouth is one which features all permanent incisors.

A smooth mouth is the term applied when horses are ten years old or older.

In a typical six-year-old mouth, the corner incisors are up and in wear at both the anterior and the posterior borders of the teeth, and the grinding edges are on a level with the intermediate and central incisors. Usually the cups of the lower central incisors show considerable wear or are completely gone.

In a seven-year-old mouth, the upper corner incisors are commonly characterized by a hook on the posterior borders. The cups of the lower intermediate incisors show considerable wear or are completely gone.

For information concerning eight-year-old mouths, nine-year-old mouths, ten-year-old mouths and older, see the cuts in this chapter and the accompanying legends.

3

Form, Function, and Way of Going

The author of a bulletin entitled "Market Classes and Grades of Horses and Mules," a publication prepared many years ago at the University of Illinois, made the following statement in his opening paragraph: "Horses on the open market are classified according to their jobs."

Utility—the use to which a horse is put, the job at which he works—is therefore the basis for the market classification of all horses.

Since horse judging consists largely of a study of the relationship of form to function and since a horse's value is based largely upon what he can do, it is most important that we as students of horses have an intelligent understanding of the relationship between form and function.

Some structural features in the make-up of the horse place definite limits upon his usefulness in any specific field of service. Other structural features greatly enhance his usefulness in a specific field. In judging horses, therefore, we should keep in mind constantly this matter of relationship of form to function because horses have to do as they are designed to do.

EXAMPLES OF CORRELATED FEATURES INVOLVING THE RELATIONSHIP OF FORM AND FUNCTION

1. The proportions of the head in all kinds of horses are a rather accurate index of the body proportions to be expected. That is to say, long, narrow heads are commonly correlated with long, shallow, narrow bodies.

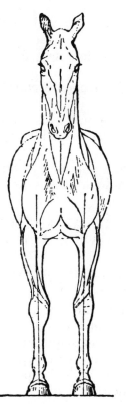

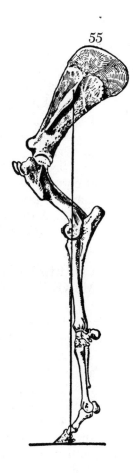

Left: *The correct standing position of the front leg as viewed from in front.*

Right: *The correct standing position of the front leg as viewed from the side.*

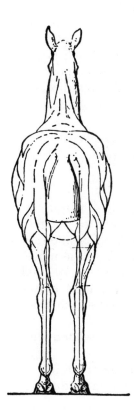

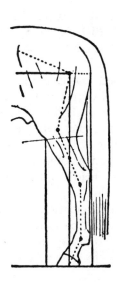

Left: *The correct standing position of the hind leg, viewed from the rear, as determined by the plumb line.*

Right: *The correct standing position of the hind leg, viewed from the side, as determined by the plumb line. Drawings from Gabaux and Barrier, The Exterior of the Horse.*

2. Small heads in draft foals and yearlings are correlated with too early maturity and an ultimate lack of scale or size.

3. Long, sloping shoulders are correlated with long, sloping pasterns.

4. Short, straight shoulders are correlated with short, straight pasterns.

5. A small, narrow, squinty eye, known as pig's-eye in horses, is correlated with coarseness in quality and a lazy, sluggish, phlegmatic disposition.

6. A deeply creased croup as a feature in horses is correlated with easy-keeping, good-doing, and satisfactory feeding qualities.

CORRELATED STRUCTURAL FEATURES IN HORSE MAKE-UP WHICH ENHANCE ACTION

1. Long forearms as features of the front legs are correlated with long strides.

2. If horses stand toed straight away on their front feet, they are likely to have trueness of action or directness of stride.

3. Sloping shoulders and sloping pasterns are features of the front leg which are correlated with a springy stride.

4. When horses stand with the points of their hocks turned slightly inward, with their hind toes turned slightly outward, and with their hind cannon bones occupying parallel planes, their hocks will be carried close together instead of wide apart. Such a position on the hind legs is therefore correlated with collected action instead of spraddled action behind.

CORRELATED STRUCTURAL FEATURES IN HORSE MAKE-UP WHICH PREDISPOSE TO DEFECTIVE GAITS OR TO UNSOUNDNESS

1. The calf-kneed position on the front legs is a feature in horse make-up that is correlated with hard concussion of the feet at the completion of the stride. That is, the calf-kneed position on the front legs tends to make a horse pounding-gaited on the move.

2. Low, rounding withers are features which are correlated with the defect in gait known as forging. Thick-withered horses commonly hang in the bridle, go low-headed, and handle their front legs awkwardly and clumsily.

3. The pigeon-toed position on the front feet is correlated with a defect in gait known as paddling or winging out.

4. The toe-wide or splay-footed position on the front feet is correlated with the defect in gait known as winging in or dishing.

5. If horses stand with the points of their hocks turned outward, this faulty position on the hind legs is correlated with a defect in stride known as limber hocks or rotating hocks.

6. Stilty ankles and pasterns are correlated with a stilty stride, hard concussions, and a predisposition to cocked ankles or even unsoundness at an early age.

7. Front legs, set way out on the corners of the body, constitute a structural defect which is correlated with rolling, laboring action in front.

8. Short, thick, bulky necks are features of saddle horse make-up which are correlated with a lack of suppleness and mobility of neck.

9. Short, straight shoulders and short forearms are features of the front legs that are correlated with short strides.

10. Buck knees and long toes are features of the front legs that are correlated with stumbling as a defect in action.

11. An extremely straight hock is a defect in position on the hind leg, as viewed from the side, which is correlated with the unsoundness known as stringiness or crampiness of the hind legs when the horse is on the move.

12. Nervous and continuous movements of the ears may be correlated with impaired eyesight or actual blindness.

13. Protruding, bulging, bovine eyes sometimes called pop-eyes are correlated with a defect in vision known as myopia, a synonym for nearsightedness.

14. Short, straight shoulders, short, straight pasterns, narrow, contracted heels are correlated with the unsoundness known as sidebones.

15. Long, low, weak pasterns and shallow heels are correlated with the unsoundness known as ringbone, a bony deposit or exostosis which appears on the pastern bones.

16. "Sickle hocks," a term which applies to hocks that have too much set as viewed from the side, are correlated with the hock unsoundness known as curbiness.

17. A thick, discolored, mucous discharge from a horse's nostrils is correlated with sickness or disease.

18. Very steep croups often accompanied by displacement of the hind legs too far forward beneath the body are correlated with sickle hocks and a predisposition to curbiness.

WAY OF GOING HELPS TO DETERMINE FUNCTION

The term "way of going" is self-defining. The pace refers to the rate at which a horse moves. Action implies flexion of knees and hocks.

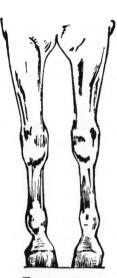

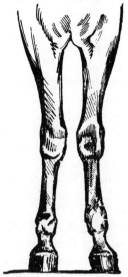

Base-narrow   and
splay-footed, or toe-
wide

Toe-narrow or
pigeon-toed

Knock-kneed

From Gabaux and Barrier, *The Exterior of the Horse.*

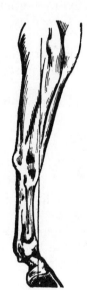

Knee-sprung or over
on the knees

Calf-kneed

Pastern too straight

From Gabaux and Barrier, *The Exterior of the Horse.*

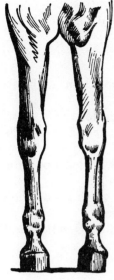  

| *Bow-kneed* | *Too close at the ground* | *Too wide at the ground* |

From Gabaux and Barrier, *The Exterior of the Horse.*

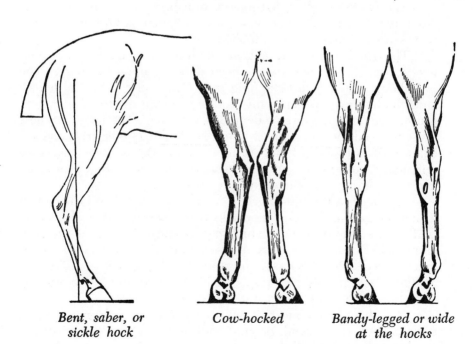

| *Bent, saber, or sickle hock* | *Cow-hocked* | *Bandy-legged or wide at the hocks* |

From Gabaux and Barrier, *The Exterior of the Horse.*

The stride presents for study the following features:

1. Length, the distance from the point of breaking over to the point of contact of the same foot.

2. Directness or trueness, the line in which the foot is carried forward during the stride.

3. Rapidity or promptness, the time consumed in taking a single stride.

4. Power, the pulling force exerted at each stride.

5. Height, the degree to which the foot is elevated in the stride, indicated by the radius of the arc described.

6. Spring, the manner in which the weight is settled upon the supporting structures at the completion of the stride.

7. Regularity, the rhythmical precision with which each stride is taken in turn.

8. Balance, the ability of a horse to coordinate his action and go in form.

THE GAITS

A gait is a term which refers to a definite way of going, characterized by distinctive features regularly executed.

The *walk* is a slow, flat-footed, four-beat gait; it is one of the most useful gaits, whether in harness or under saddle, if executed with snap and animation, as it should be.

The *trot* is a two-beat gait, in which the diagonal fore and hind legs act together. The rate of speed depends upon the horse. The road horse trot is a fast-stepping trot, characterized by the length and rapidity with which individual strides are accomplished, and is executed with an extreme degree of extension. The heavy harness horse trot and the Hackney pony trot are high-stepping trots and are characterized by height and spring of stride, the horse setting himself, going collectedly, and executing each step with an extreme degree of flexion and the utmost precision.

The *pace* of the light harness horse is a rapid, two-beat gait in which the lateral fore and hind legs work together. It is characterized by the readiness with which pacers can get away at speed, a minimum of concussion, more or less side motion (pacers are sometimes called side-wheelers), the absence of much knee fold (although some pacers are trappy gaited), and the necessity for smooth, hard footing and easy draft for its execution.

It is difficult for most pacers to go in deep or heavy footing, such as fresh snow, sand, or mud, and they have a jerky, unsteady way of pulling a rig if any pull is necessary. The increased draft caused by an extra person up behind or a rough bit of road will

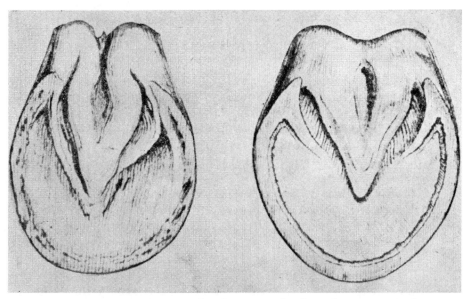

Contracted vs. wide heels. The figure on the left shows a foot that is narrow and contracted at the heel. The figure on the right shows a foot with ample width at the heel. From Lungwitz and Adams, *Horse Shoeing,* courtesy J. B. Lippincott Company.

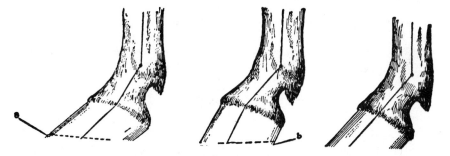

How the foot axis may be broken forward or backward by the trimming of the hoof wall. Left: An untrimmed hoof with an excess of horn (a) at the toe, which breaks the foot axis backward. Middle: An untrimmed hoof with an excess of horn (b) at the heel, which breaks the foot axis forward. Right: Hoof dressed and foot axis straightened by removing excess of horn below dotted lines in the two preceding illustrations. From Gay, *Productive Horse Husbandry,* courtesy J. B. Lippincott Company.

swing most pacers into a trot if they can trot at all. Jogging down hill will force some trotters to pace, while an upgrade will set pacers to trotting. The pace is essentially more a speed gait than a road gait.

The *amble* is a lateral gait usually distinguished from the pace by being slower and more broken in cadence. It is not a show gait as is the stepping pace, which is the *slow gait* required of gaited saddlers in competition. The *stepping pace* is a lateral four-beat gait done under restraint in showy animated fashion, with the chin set and with the folding of knees and flexing of hocks which contributes to showiness of performance. There is a break in the impact of the feet on the same side of the body, thereby actually making the gait a stepping pace or a four-beat gait done at slow speed.

The *rack* is a fast, flashy, four-beat gait more clearly defined by the discarded name "single-foot." It is rarely executed voluntarily, but under compulsion of hand and heel and is characterized by quite a display of knee action and speed. While very pleasant to the rider, it takes a lot out of a horse and should therefore be called for with judgment and discretion.

The *gallop* is a fast, three-beat, natural gait. A hind foot makes the first beat; the other hind foot and its diagonal forefoot make the second beat simultaneously; the remaining forefoot makes the third beat. Then the body is in suspension, all four feet off the ground, until the hind foot begins a new series. A horse is said to gallop on the right lead when his left hind makes the first beat and his right fore makes the last beat of the series. He is galloping on the left lead when his right hind makes the first beat and his left fore the last. For ease, comfort, and safety, a horse should gallop on the right lead when turning to the right, and he should be on the left lead when going to the left.

The *canter* is a slow, restrained gallop. The horse goes in a more collected manner, with his head set, his neck arched, and more of the weight sustained on the hind quarters than in the gallop. A horse should canter on either lead at command. Show ring judges discriminate against horses cantering on the wrong lead and penalize horses that canter too fast.

The *run*, or *racing gallop*, is the gallop extended to the greatest possible speed. However, the run is a four-beat gait because the paired diagonal of the gallop becomes dissociated, the hind foot striking the ground before its diagonal forefoot.

The *running walk* is a slow single-foot or four-beat gait.

Since the running walk is a gait that can be maintained all day, it is the business gait in the South and Southwest, where plantation horses are ridden extensively. It is good for six to eight miles an hour, with the greatest ease to both horse and rider. Walking horses,

A sharp contrast in draft horse type. The Belgian mare on the left is short-legged, deep-bodied, and thick-stifled, stands correctly on her legs, with sufficient muscle wrapped up in her hide to have balanced proportions, thin or fat. The gray gelding is too leggy, too shallow, and too narrow—a hard-keeping kind. Note also his straight ankles and pasterns. Photograph courtesy Photography Department, The Ohio State University.

running walkers, plantation horses, plantation "nodders" (sometimes so called because these horses keep time to their paces by the nodding of their heads)—all these terms refer to the same type of horse. At the shows, plantation horses are required to do a flat-foot walk, a running walk, and a canter.

The *foxtrot* is a short, broken, nodding, somewhat uncollected trot, a gait sometimes used as a substitute for the running walk. It is rougher to ride and is therefore not as popular as the running walk, a gait which does contribute to the comfort of the rider.

SOME FACTORS WHICH DETERMINE THE WAY OF GOING

The factors determining a horse's way of going are either

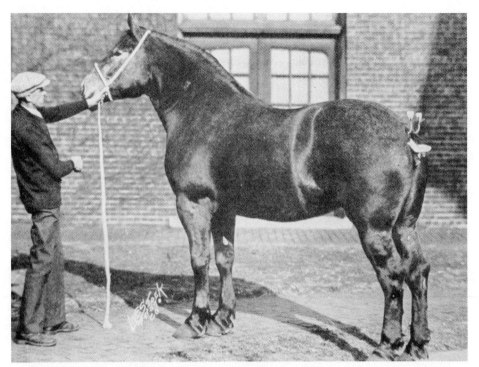

Miss Annatation 203115, a good type study in Percheron mares. Note her strong back, short coupling, heavy muscling, and rugged bone. Balanced in conformation, she stands on lean ankles, springy pasterns, big, shapely feet, all of which contribute to the correctness of her underpinning. Photograph courtesy Cook and Gormley.

natural or acquired. The former consist of type, conformation, direction of leg and form of foot, and breeding. The latter are schooling, handling, and mechanical appliances.

Type

On account of the correlation between form and function, a horse must do as he is made to do. His capabilities in the way of performance will be limited in some respects and extended in others, according to the plan of his structure. A short, thick, low-set horse will have more power than speed, the reverse being equally true. A cobby horse has a trappy stride, while the stride of a tall, rangy horse is characterized by reach.

Conformation

A horse low in the forehand—that is, round and flat over the withers—is likely to forge because such horses move their front legs out poorly and the front feet get in the way of the rear feet.

The racing gallop, or run, shown here on the right lead. The third horse is just landing on his left foot. The second horse is on the right hind and left fore foot. The winning horse is on the right fore foot. Thus three distinct phases of the gait are shown, and all three horses are on the same lead. The winning horse, Mr. Busher, a son of War Admiral, is pictured here winning the 1948 Arlington Futurity at Arlington Park, Chicago. Photo courtesy Arlington Park.

Long, rangy-bodied horses, slack in the coupling, usually have a tendency toward an uncoordinated way of going.

Direction of Leg and Form of Foot

The relation that the direction of the leg bears to the form of the foot is most intimate; each is an important factor in determining the directness of the stride. The form of the foot fixes the point at which the leg breaks over—the center of the toe, or the outer or inner quarter, depending upon whether the foot is symmetrical or the inner or outer quarter is higher.

The direction of the leg determines the course of the foot during its stride, whether advanced in a straight line or describing the arc of a circle inward or outward, dependent upon the deviation in the direction of the leg. The form of the foot and the direction of the leg are correlated, usually, so that their combined influence on the way of going may be considerable.

Breeding

Hackney foals at the trot show great flexion of knee and hock joints and go with great height of stride. Tennessee Walking Horse foals move at a running walk. In the Standardbred breed, some bloodlines produce trotters; others produce pacers. In each of these examples, breeding was responsible for the way of going.

Heredity

All Morgans and Arabians can trot. However, in each breed, certain bloodlines are known to produce horses that trot exceptionally well. All Thoroughbreds can run. Some family lines produce very fast sprinters, while others produce horses that can stay a distance. Heredity does affect the way of going.

Schooling and Training

No race horse, show horse, or pleasure horse becomes a high class horse without an education. No matter how perfect his type and conformation, no matter how fine his breeding, a horse must be schooled and taught to do his job if he is to reach his full potential. He must be trained carefully to the physical condition that will enable him to do his job well. Skillful schooling and conditioning will enhance the way of going.

Handling

The well-made, well-bred, well-trained horse will perform up to his ability only if he is well handled. A heavy-handed, awkward rider can ruin a good horse's performance. A jockey with a poor sense of pace can lose a race even when riding the fastest horse. On the other hand, the rapport between horse and rider in high-level dressage competition is a joy to behold. Handling has a very definite bearing on the way of going.

Mechanical Appliances

Mechanical appliances are chiefly accessories to the handling and schooling of horses. They consist of the bit, shoes, weight, and hopples.

BIT   The bit is for purposes of control and also for the use of the rider to indicate to the horse the gait required.

SHOES The style of the shoe and the dressing of the foot for its application have considerable influence on the way of going. By shortening or lengthening the toe, the breaking over is either facilitated or retarded, with a consequent shortening or lengthening of the stride; by raising or lowering the inner or outer quarter, the point at which breaking over takes place may be regulated within limits.

WEIGHT By putting weight on or by taking weight off the foot, the stride may be lenthened or shortened, heightened or lowered. Weight may be secured either by permitting an abnormal growth of the foot itself or by adding it to the shoe. Weight fixed at the toe promotes extension on the principle of the pendulum, the weight coming into play toward the end of the stride to carry the foot out.

On the other hand, weight well back in the shoe, toward the heel, is believed to be conducive to action by calling for extra flexion in order to lift the foot. Whatever alterations are made in the matter of shoeing or weighting must be gradual in order not to unbalance the horse in his stride.

HOPPLES By uniting a hind leg and a fore leg by means of hopples, a horse is held to his stride and prevented from breaking, mixing, or going any other gait. The straps are crossed or straight, depending upon whether the horse trots or paces. Hopples about the pasterns are sometimes put on harness horses to develop action. "Rattlers" or links of light chain are often fastened about the pasterns of saddle horses in training to increase both knee and hock action. Weighted boots are also used to enhance action.

Going Surface

Although not of a mechanical nature, the character of the surface on which the horse steps has a marked influence on the kind of stride he takes. As a general rule, heavy, soft, or deep going causes a high stride, while a hard, smooth surface is more conducive to speed. Of the speed horses, trotters and pacers require the hardest, smoothest track. Heavy going frequently induces double-gaited horses to trot instead of pace and seriously interferes with pacing performance. Runners do best on the turf or on a dirt track that has had the surface loosened with a scratch harrow, thereby providing footing that has some cushion.

DEFECTS AND PECULIARITIES IN WAY OF GOING

Forging, or striking the end of the branches or the undersurface of the shoe of a fore foot with a toe of the hind foot.

A COMPARISON OF TROT-
TERS AND PACERS IN AC-
TION

*The top photograph
shows a trotter in mo-
tion. If a trotter forges
or speedy-cuts himself,
legs on the same side of
the body are guilty of
interference. If a pacer
forges or speedy-cuts
himself, diagonal legs
are guilty of interfer-
ence.* Photographs cour-
tesy *Horseman and Fair
World* and Department
of Photography, The
Ohio State University.

Interfering, or striking the supporting leg usually at the fetlock
with the foot of the striding leg. Commonly interference occurs between a supporting front leg and a striding front leg or between
a supporting hind leg and striding hind leg.

Brushing, the term used when the interference is slight, pos-
sibly just roughing up the hair.

Striking, the term used when the interference results in an
open wound.

Paddling, an outward deviation in the direction of the stride
of a fore leg, the result of a toe-narrow or pigeon-toed standing
position.

Winging, exaggerated paddling, very noticeable in high-going
horses.

Winding, a twisting of the front leg around in front of the
supporting leg as each stride is taken. This defect in gait is sometimes called threading, plaiting, or walking the rope.

Cynthiana, noted gaited mare, owned at one time by Dixiana Farms, Lexington, Kentucky, and shown very successfully in ladies' classes some years ago by Miss Mary Fisher. This picture demonstrates perfectly the sequence of hoofbeats when a horse is working at the rack, a four-beat gait done at speed and in form. Photograph by Haas, courtesy Dixiana Farms.

Honey Gold 451147, one of the top walking mares of the country. This picture shows the sequence of the hoofbeats at the running walk. Photograph by Tom Hill, courtesy Mr. Wood.

A roller-toe shoe and a heavy weighted-toe shoe, both of them front shoes that are in common use on saddlers. The roller-toe shoe aids and hastens the breakover of a front foot. The weighted toe helps the front leg to function like the pendulum of a clock, increasing the length of the stride in front. The roller-toe shoe weighs sixteen ounces; the weighted-toe shoe weighs twenty-one ounces.

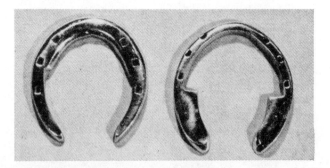

Two shoes that differ in design, each of them in common use on saddle horses, but used for altogether different purposes. The shoe at the left, with additional weight at the toe, is designed to increase the length of the stride. The shoe at right, with additional weight at the heel, is designed to make a horse break or fold his knees and go with a higher stride. The shoe on the left weighs twelve ounces; the shoe on the right weighs eleven ounces.

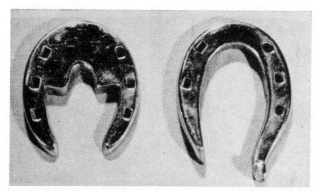

Harness show pony shoes, front and rear. The front shoe on the left weighs twelve ounces; the hind shoe on the right weighs ten ounces.

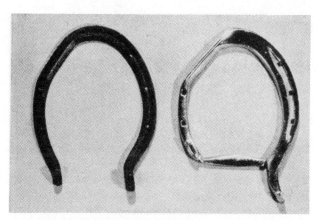

Common types of hind shoes for cross-firing pacers. The shoe on the left is an oblique toe, half-swedged shoe for use on the left hind foot of a pacer that cross-fires. The oblique toe furnishes a margin of difference which keeps the pacer from hitting the inside rear toe of a hind foot against the inside of a breaking-over diagonal fore foot. The half-swedged feature of this hind shoe, plus the use of an outside heel calk on the shoe, gives to the hind foot a retarding grip on the ground, making it possible for the diagonal fore foot to get out of the way. The shoe on the right is an oblique toe, half-swedged shoe which has a longer trailing heel calk and a light bar connecting the extremities of the shoe. This bar strengthens the shoe, thereby increasing the life of the shoe. The shoe on the left weighs 3 ounces; the shoe on the right weighs 5 ounces. Photographs courtesy Department of Photography, Ohio State University.

Creation's King 2663, Hackney pony stallion, demonstrates knee and hock action requirements for Hackney ponies. This pony was the grand champion Hackney pony at the Chicago International in 1949. Owned and shown by Heyl Pony Farm, Washington, Illinois. Harley Heyl driving. Photograph by Freudy Photos, courtesy Mr. Heyl.

Scalping, or hitting the hind foot above or at the line of the hair (coronet) against the toe of a breaking over fore foot.

Speedy-cutting, which occurs when a trotter or pacer at speed hits a hind leg above the scalping mark against the shoe of a breaking over fore foot. In trotters, legs on the same side are involved. In pacers, diagonal legs are involved.

Cross-firing, essentially forging in pacers, in which they hit the inside of the near fore and off hind foot, or the reverse, in the air as the stride of the hind leg is about completed and the stride of the fore leg is just begun.

Pointing, a stride in which extension is much more marked than flexion. Pointy-strided horses break their knees very little and are low-gaited in front. Thoroughbreds in the use of their front legs at the trot are pointy-gaited.

The term "pointing" is also used to indicate the pose in standing position where a horse stands on three legs and points with the fourth; that is, he rests or saves a leg.

Dwelling, a perceptible pause in the flight of the foot, as though the stride had been completed before the foot strikes the ground. A horse may be guilty of dwelling with either his front or his rear legs. Dwelling as a defect in gait is quite common in heavy harness horses, heavy harness ponies, and some saddlers.

Trappy, a quick, high, but comparatively short stride.

Pounding, a heavy contact usually accompanying a high, laboring stride.

Rolling, a defect in gait due to excessive lateral shoulder motion, as in wide-fronted horses. Excessively wide-fronted drafters have the rolling-gaited tendency at the trot.

THE IMPORTANCE OF ACTION IN JUDGING

The value of a horse depends largely upon what he can do. Horses earn their living on the move, not by standing still. Therefore, horse judging consists in large part of a study of form in relation to function.

Good Looks vs. Performance Requirements

Good looks may enhance value. But a good-looking horse unable to meet performance requirements in a special field is never a top horse in his field. A saddle horse posed for inspection at the end of the bridle reins may be as good-looking as saddle horses ever are. But if this same saddle horse fails to give a good account of himself in motion, he will be inspected and found wanting by those who are in quest of a high-class pleasure horse or a top show horse. To satisfy the trade in any division of the industry horses must be able to do something.

The performance of a horse depends a great deal upon the way in which he is put together. There is a definite relationship between form and performance. If a horse is defective in the set or position of his legs, there will be a predisposition to defect in gait. If a horse stands toe-wide on his front feet, he cannot break his feet over at the toe and carry them straight forward. Such horses will swing their front feet inward on the move and are guilty of the defect in gait known as winging in or dishing. If a horse stands both toe-wide and base-narrow in front, the winging-in tendency may result in striking a supporting leg with a striding leg. Quite commonly, horses that stand toe-wide in front will hit their ankles when in action. If the horse in question happens to be a toe-wide trotter performing at speed, he may hit his ankles, his shins, his knees, or his elbows and have to wear ankle boots, shin boots, knee boots, and elbow boots for protection. With the exception of quarter boots, this list of boots for a toe-wide, base-narrow trotter includes all of the boots that are made for the front legs of a horse.

The Trainer's Point of View

I heard a top trainer of saddle horses say one day, when we were inspecting a toe-wide, splay-footed, base-narrow gaited gelding, that he would just as soon someone else owned all the five-gaited saddle horses that stood in a splay-footed position on their front legs. Needless to say, that trainer had learned from experience that splay-footed horses are likely to hit a supporting front leg with a striding front foot.

FAULTY POSITION ON THE LEGS AN INDICATOR OF FAULTY ACTION

If a horse stands pigeon-toed in front, he cannot carry his front feet straight forward. He will wing out, or paddle. The splay-footed horse will wing in, and, if he is narrow chested, he may interfere, or hit the supporting front leg with the striding front foot. The calf-kneed horse is likely to pound, or bring his front feet to the ground with undue force. The buck-kneed horse may be inclined to stumble and to be less stable. The horse with short, steep, upright pasterns has less spring to his stride.

The set of the underpinning is an indicator of performance. There is a close correlation between the form and the function. Horses move as they are made. Hence it is necessary for anyone who hopes to be a discriminating judge of horses to have an intelligent understanding of the parts of a horse in their relationship to the function these parts are supposed to perform. A defective set of underpinning almost inevitably results in a defective way of going.

In summary, horses earn their living on the move. They are valued for what they can do. Therefore, in the judging of horses, their action or way of going should be given careful consideration, because a horse's ability on the move determines in large part his usefulness on the job.

Moreover, a horse's way of going depends largely upon the way he is put together. Faulty conformation of the feet and legs predisposes to faulty action.

4

Common Horse
Unsoundnesses and Ailments

The single most important factor in determining the value of any horse is his degree of soundness. The veterinarian considers any abnormality in the form or function of any part an unsoundness. Not many horses can be certified as 100 per cent sound according to this interpretation. The practical horseman seeks serviceable soundness. He regards the more minor troubles—those that do not incapacitate a horse for his job but only mar his looks—more as blemishes than as true unsoundnesses.

Anyone who hopes to do an intelligent job of buying or judging horses must know at least the location, character, and importance of the various unsoundnesses and blemishes. The diagnosis and treatment of these troubles are in the realm of the professional veterinarian and the groom caring for the horses.

COMMON UNSOUNDNESSES AND BLEMISHES
OF THE FORELEGS

Horses bear more than half of their weight on their forefeet. Carrying weight and working at speed increase the concussion suffered by the forefeet. Therefore, many of the unsound and blemished conditions that horses develop involve their front feet and legs.

Fistula of the withers. A fistula of the withers is an ulcerous sore at the withers connected to the surface by ducts. During the time that pus is running from the fistula the horse is lame and cannot be used. Hence, this serious condition would never be encountered in show-ring or college livestock judging sessions. Some-

75

times after a fistula has been healed following proper treatment, a thickening at the withers may be observed as well as a crease or depression at the site of the former opening.

Sweeney. A sweeney is a shrinking or atrophy of the muscles of the shoulder region of the horse. This condition renders the horse definitely unsound. Recovery is somewhat uncertain, and, when it occurs, usually takes over two months.

Capped elbow. A capped elbow, or shoe boil, is a swelling at the point of the elbow. In most cases a capped elbow is a blemish, not an incapacitating unsoundness. However, a very bad case may require surgery.

Splint. A splint is an exostosis or bony enlargement located on the side of the cannon. Usually splints are on the inner side of a fore cannon, though they are sometimes on the outside of the leg or even on a hind leg. The observant judge will see many splints because they are common blemishes. During the formative period a splint may cause severe lameness and at that time is a true unsoundness. However, once the inflammation has subsided and the bony growth has stopped the horse goes sound. He has the splint as a little sign that he is "second-handed" and has been used considerably.

Bowed tendon. A bowed tendon appears as a thickening and swelling of the back side of the cannon of a foreleg. This condition is not often seen except among Thoroughbreds or other horses that may be used at great speed under saddle. When the flexor tendons and tendon sheaths are first affected the horse is extremely lame. After recovery the tendon area remains thickened and the leg is seldom as sound as it was before injury. However, the horse might be serviceably sound for hacking, but unsound for strenuous training for racing. Bowed tendons are seldom seen in the show-ring but should be recognized by all horsemen.

Wind gall, road puff. A wind gall, or road puff, is a soft, puffy swelling located just above the fetlock joint on either the inner side or outside of any leg. Sometimes a horse will develop road puffs on all four legs. Such swellings usually are not associated with lameness. However, they indicate a certain lack of refinement. The horse with wind galls does not have that degree of leanness and cleanness of joints associated with the best wearing quality. Hence, most judges prefer to place clean-legged horses in top positions. Horses decorated with wind galls do not usually occupy the blue ribbon place in class nor do they win championships, if the competition is keen.

Ringbone. A ringbone is a hard, bony enlargement on and sometimes encircling the pastern. Horsemen regard a ringbone as a serious unsoundness because it so often results in severe lameness and inability to do any job. Horse breeders do not select horses with ringbones for breeding stock because the short, steep pasterns that predispose to ring bone formation may be inherited.

Sidebone. A sidebone is a hard bony prominence at the hoof head or coronet and back toward the heels. Sidebones result from the ossification or turning to bone of the lateral cartilages of the feet. Sidebones are found much more frequently in draft horses than in light horses. They develop more often at the hoof heads of the forefeet than the hind. Except in the formative stages, sidebones usually do not cause lameness. In the days when many draft horses were bred, used, and shown, judges preferred horses that were clean at the hoof heads and free of sidebones for their champions and first place winners.

Navicular disease. Navicular disease is an inflammation followed by an exostosis on the navicular bone in a forefoot. The horse with navicular trouble "points" the affected foot when standing and dose not bear his weight equally on both forefeet. Navicular disease causes varying degrees of lameness.

Laminitis. Laminitis, or founder, is an inflammation of the sensitive laminae of the feet. In its severe form, founder renders a horse permanently unsound. The sole of the foot sinks, the texture of the hoof becomes softer, the hoof wall becomes ringed with ridges, the toes turn up, and the horse is quite lame. If the attack of laminitis is comparatively light and if treatment is begun early, the horse, after the initial lameness, may recover to be serviceably sound.

Quarter crack. A quarter crack is a break in the hoof wall that begins at the side of the coronet and parallels the horn tubules. Cracks are most common in the quarter of a forefoot and in the toe of a hind foot. Quarter cracks may be caused by trauma of the coronet, excessive work on hard surfaces, excessive drying, or other factors. Horses with quarter cracks frequently are lame. Treatment is almost entirely in the field of surgery and corrective shoeing to change the distribution of the weight borne by the hoof, followed by measures to promote the secretion of new horn.

COMMON UNSOUNDNESSES OF THE HIND LEGS

The hock joint of the horse is put to great strain when the horse runs, jumps, turns, and pulls. The following paragraphs point up the fact that a large proportion of the hind leg troubles involve the hock joint.

Stifled. Stifled is a condition in which the horse's stifle joint becomes dislocated. As long as the patella bone of the joint is out of

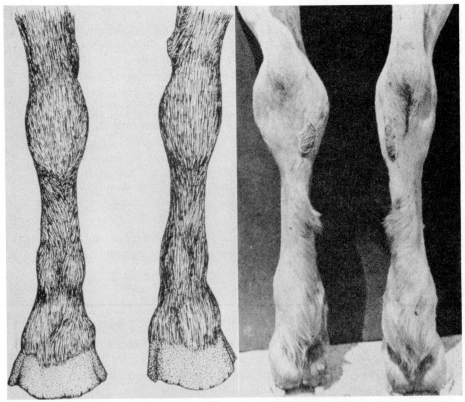

Chipped or split hoofs. | *Anchylosis of the hock joint. This horse swung his left hind leg from the stifle because the hock joint was immobile.*

Left: A normal pedal bone. Right: A pedal bone with ossified lateral cartilage.

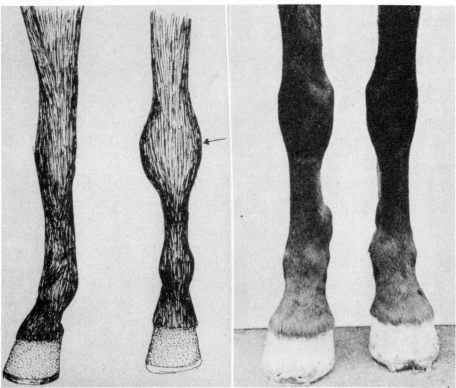

Above Left: *Knee spavin.* Above Right: *Splints, low down.* Photograph courtesy the Veterinary Clinic, The Ohio State University.

Above: *Sidebone unexposed. Sidebone exposed.* This drawing and that shown on the right were adapted from Holmes, *Principles and Practices of Horse Shoeing.*

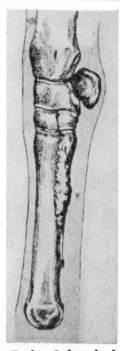

Right: *Splint, high up.*

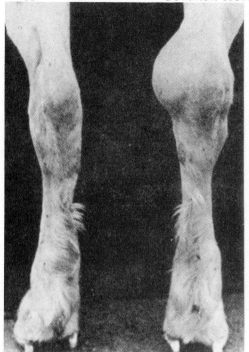

Thoroughpin and bog spavin combined.

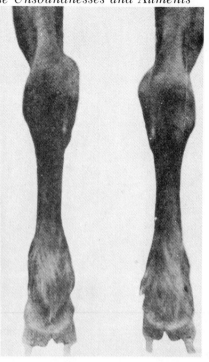

Thoroughpins.

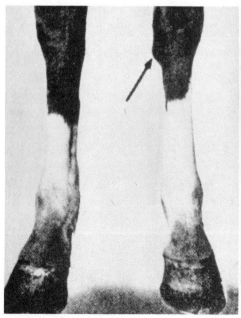

A large jack spavin.

Sickle hocks with curbs.

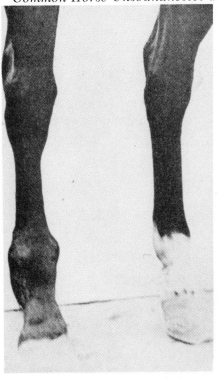

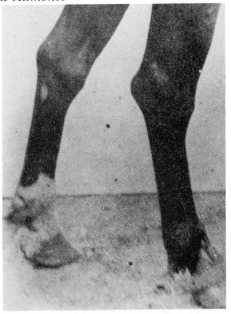

A capped hock.

Road puffs or wind puffs.

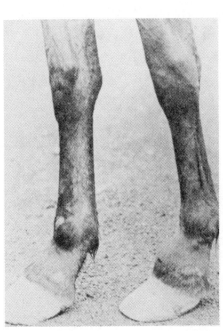

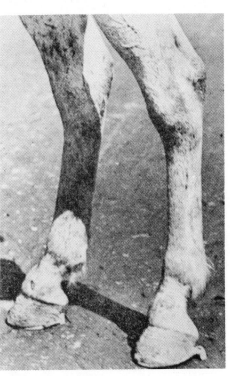

Long, low, weak pasterns, shallow heels with ringbone formation on front pasterns.

Crooked hind legs, ringbone formation on rear pasterns.

A typical pose in a case of laminitis or founder.

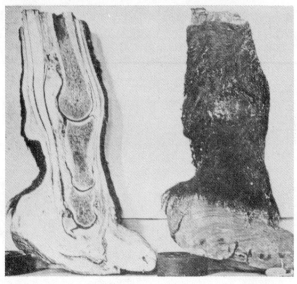

A sagittal section of the lower limb, showing the effects of acute founder, or laminitis.

A typical pose in a case of navicular disease.

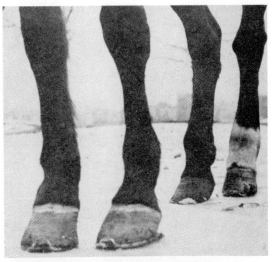

Pigeon toes, a cocked ankle, a bog spavin, a thoroughpin, a stocked hind leg, a thick rear ankle and coarse pasterns are all visible in this picture.

Crampy or stringhalt.

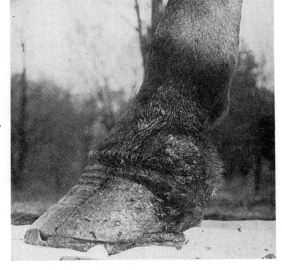

A quittor.

Milk leg or elephantiasis.

Contracted tendons.

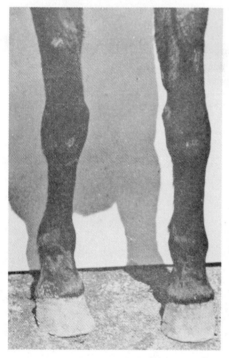

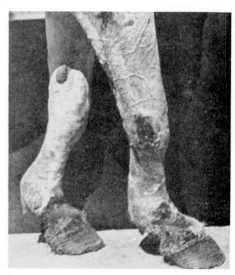

Pigeon-toed and forward on the knees.

Buck knees and dermatitis.

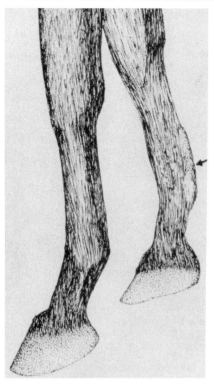

A bowed tendon.

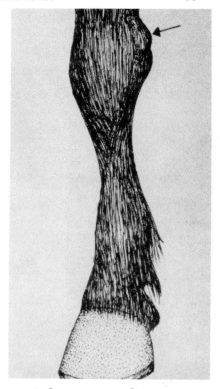

A knee joint enlargement.
A distended tendon sheath.

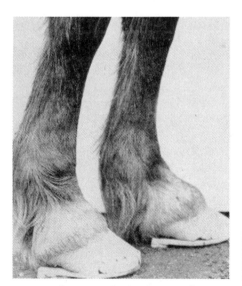

Long, low, weak pasterns and very
shallow heels. Coon-footed.

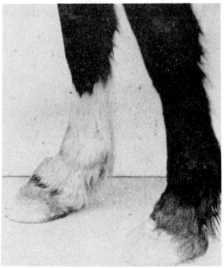

Long, weak pasterns, thin or flat
front feet, with ringbone on pastern
of off fore foot.

Above, *Location and the extent of a lateral cartilage. When a lateral cartilage ossifies, a sidebone is the result.* From Dollar, *Horse Shoeing.*

Left, *Sickle hocks which reveal a curb at the base of the hock on the left leg. Sickle hocks predispose to curbiness.*

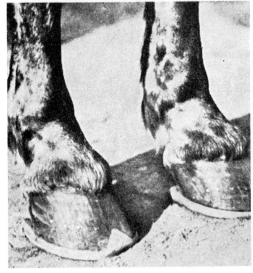

An exceptional study in ankles, pasterns, hoof heads, and feet. Note the depth at the heels and the fullness at toe and quarters. These feet are shod with Scotch-bottom shoes that have a brazed toe clip.

A large sidebone on the left fore foot.

UNLESS OTHERWISE CREDITED, ALL PHOTOGRAPHS APPEARING ON THIS AND PRECEDING EIGHT PAGES courtesy, The Veterinary Clinic, The Ohio State University.

place, the horse is very lame and cannot use his hind leg properly.

Bog spavin. A bog spavin, resulting from an over-secretion of the joint fluid, is a soft, puffy swelling located at the anterior face of the hock joint. A horse with a slight indication of a bog spavin is said to be "a little full in the hocks." Bog spavins usually do not cause lameness, and constitute more of a blemish than an unsoundness.

Bone spavin. A bone spavin, or jack spavin, most usually appears as a hard, bony protuberance at the inner, lower edge of the hock joint. In its formative stage a bone spavin causes severe lameness, and even after inflammation subsides may cause some occasional irregularity in gait. For this reason and because the spavined hock is subject to further troubles, horsemen consider a bone spavin a serious unsoundness.

Thoroughpin. A thoroughpin is a soft, puffy swelling in the hollows of the hock, just forward of the large Achilles tendon. Thoroughpins are regarded as blemishes because they usually do not affect a horse's way of going.

Capped hock. A capped hock is one with a swelling at the point of the hock. This swelling is a blemish. Sometimes the capped hock is permanently enlarged, especially if it has been repeatedly bruised by the horse in kicking at the stall partitions.

Curb. A curb is an enlargement five or six inches below the point of the hock and on the posterior edge of the hock joint. Curbs are most likely to develop on sickle-hocked horses. Once formed, curbs do not generally cause trouble, but the affected hock is apt to be a weaker hock because of its malformation.

Michigan pad. A Michigan pad, or Pennsylvania jack, is a soft, puffy swelling located on the outside of the hind leg at the lower edge of the hock joint. Such swellings do not cause the horse any trouble and are regarded as blemishes.

Stringhalt. Stringhalt is a nervous-muscular disorder characterized by a spasmodic jerking and abnormal flexing of the hocks. Some horses show this condition only when started up suddenly from a halt; others show it only when turned sharply. Some horses may appear stringhalt when backed. Horses in show-ring competition under saddle and in harness are asked by judges to back up for this reason, as well as to test their manners and training. Horses badly afflicted with the stringhalt condition show the jerking of the hock with every step.

Cocked ankle. A cocked ankle is one where the fetlock joint is forced forward by abnormally shortened flexor tendons. This condition is most commonly found in the hind legs. Cocked ankles are not encountered in show-ring judging because afflicted horses cannot move as do normal horses. Horse breeders reject for breeding stock all horses that have cocked ankles.

UNSOUNDNESS OF THE EYES AND WIND

Since horses are valued chiefly for what they can do, any loss of vision and any impairment of their ability to breathe normally constitutes serious unsoundnesses.

Blindness. Blindness is an unsoundness that results in disqualification in the show-ring. The commonly accepted ideal horse can see; he is not blind. Very occasionally a blind mare may be kept as a brood mare, but she causes special management problems. One or two blind Standardbreds have been successful in harness racing. A very few Thoroughbreds, blind in one eye, have had successful turf careers. But, in general, blind horses are too unsound to be used safely.

Periodic ophthalmia. Periodic ophthalmia, or moonblindness, is a recurring inflammatory disease of the eyes that leads ultimately to blindness. During an attack the eyes are very sensitive to light, become cloudy, and water freely. Attacks may leave a light-colored spot in the eye before total blindness occurs.

Heaves. Heaves, or chronic alveolar emphysema, is an unsound condition of the wind characterized by a wheezy cough, labored breathing, and a lift in the flanks when the abdominal muscles are used to complete exhalation of air from the lungs. The horse with heaves can inhale normally but cannot exhale properly because of the breakdown and loss of elasticity in some parts of the lungs. A horse so afflicted is unsound for anything that requires either strenuous or fast work.

Roaring. Roaring is a less serious unsoundness of the wind caused by a paralysis of the intrinsic muscles of the larynx. The roaring or whistling sound characteristic of this trouble is made when the horse inhales. Affected horses are unable to do the usual amount of work, and tire quickly as a result of the difficulty in breathing.

SOME COMMON AILMENTS

Azoturia. Azoturia, or Monday morning disease, is characterized by a sudden onset of a semi-paralysis of the horse's legs due, it is thought, to a toxic condition caused by overfeeding on idle days. The hind legs become stiff and useless, the croup muscles stiffen and harden, and the horse oftentimes knuckles over in front. When a horse accustomed to regular exercise is allowed to rest for several days on full feed, an attack may be precipitated when exercise is resumed. Attacks usually appear during the first hour of exercise, often during the first 15 minutes.

Colic. The term colic is commonly misused. It is simply a symptom of some difficulty and not a disease in itself. Colic is the outward sign or evidence of some abdominal pain. The pain may be due to indigestion, an impacted caecum, poisons, intestinal worms, a twist in the intestines, or to other causes.

Corns. Corns are bruised and discolored areas of the sole of the foot, usually located in the angles between the bars of the foot and the hoof wall.

Nail punctures and wire cuts. Nails and barbed wire are common sources of injury to horses. When a horse's foot is punctured by a nail there is always the danger of tetanus. A shot of antitoxin by a veterinarian to prevent lockjaw is always good management in the case of nail punctures. The tetanus organism may also be introduced by way of wire cuts. Prompt attention should be given to wire cuts to prevent the development of proud flesh. A skilled veterinarian should treat deep, ugly wounds.

Quittor. A quittor is a festering sore anywhere along the border of the coronet or the top of the hoof wall. Quittors may result from a calk wound, a neglected corn, or a penetrating wound through the sole by means of which disease organisms were introduced.

Scratches or grease heel. Scratches is the name of a low-grade infection or form of eczema affecting the hair follicles and skin at the posterior base of the fetlock joint, the posterior region of the pasterns, and the base of the heels. The hairy-legged breeds are more susceptible to scratches than are the short-haired breeds.

An infection in the blood stream may cause scratches, but more common causes are filthy stables and muddy paddocks that may result in chapped skin and breaks in the skin through which infection can enter. Good feeding, clean stable management, and application of standard antiseptic solutions to arrest infection will clean up most cases of scratches.

Thrush. Thrush is an inflammation of the frog of the foot, accompanied by a characteristic, blackish, purulent, foul-smelling discharge. The predisposing causes are unhygienic conditions which require the horse to stand in mud, urine- or feces-soaked earth or bedding, failure to clean the hoofs at regular intervals, and the atrophy of the frog as found in contracted hoofs. A number of organisms are involved. Removal of diseased tissue, application of various astringent lotions, and a clean, dry stall will effect a cure.

5

Miscellaneous Problems in Judging Horses

In this chapter are gathered together and expanded some of the earlier discussions of the most common problems which arise in connection with the judging of horses or, indeed, in connection with any phase of horse production.

Lameness

As noted before, horses earn their living on the move, not standing still. The worth of any horse is enhanced because of his ability to do the job that he is supposed to be able to do. This statement is true of work horses, heavy harness horses, light harness horses, saddle horses, or ponies. Inability to do the job depreciates value. Lameness is one of the most common reasons why a horse's value may be suddenly impaired. A work horse that is lame is greatly handicapped, although he may be asked to work only at the walk.

Any show horse or show pony that is lame on show day is doomed if in competition with good sound horses because lameness is not one of the requirements sought in a good show horse. To the contrary, it is a disqualification. Not only is it proof of the pain to which a horse is subjected at each stride; it introduces into the stride the feature of irregularity, which destroys rhythmical precision of stride and makes impossible a balanced, coordinated performance.

Before spending their money, all prospective buyers of horses for work, for pleasure, or for show should make it a point to inspect these animals on the move as well as in standing position. If horses move out lame, the best plan is leave them in the hands of their owner—at least until they move sound. Buyers who ride the country in quest of horses are not looking for lame horses. They are in search of sound horses which they hope will not go lame after they are purchased.

The common method of handling the lame-horse problem at the shows is therefore to excuse lame horses from the ring.

Blindness or Impaired Eyesight

Good vision is a primary requirement in horses and ponies of all types. Blindness or impaired vision handicaps horses in all areas of horse production. A blind horse is a special management problem, whether the horse is in stable, paddock, or pasture. Of course there have been instances where blind brood mares have been the dams of good, sound foals and where blind stallions have proved to be satisfactory sires. But blind stallions and blind mares are not commonly sought as seed stock because they are a special problem for anyone who owns them.

In the breeding classes at the shows, blind stallions and blind mares are commonly disqualified. Show managements do not provide classes for blind horses. Therefore, disqualification of horses because of blindness is the common practice and is considered sound judgment.

Glass Eyes

"Glass eye" is the term applied to a horse's eye, the iris of which is devoid of pigment. Such an eye is just as functional as the dark, hazel-colored eye, which is the kind of eye that is sought in all horses and ponies.

Glass eye, watch eye, walleye, and Clydesdale eye are synonymous. The term "Clydesdale eye" is used because glass-eyed horses appear with so much frequency in that breed.

Glass eyes are objectionable, chiefly on the basis of looks. Since they are just as functional as dark, hazel-colored eyes, there have been many instances at leading shows where glass-eyed horses, both mares and stallions, not only topped their class but have been made grand champions of their divisions.

Splay-footed

"Splay-footed" is the term applied when a horse stands on his front feet with his toes turned outward. With such a defect a horse cannot rock his front foot upward from the heel, break it over at the toe, and carry it straight forward. Splay-footed horses on the move will swing the striding foot inward toward the supporting leg and be guilty of a defect in gait known as winging in or dishing.

In such cases interference is almost inevitable. Even a work horse, doing most of his work at the walk, if he stands splay-footed

WHY IS THE SPLAY-FOOTED POSITION OBJECTIONABLE IN HORSES?

All horses at the walk and trot should be able to rock their front feet upward from the heel, break them over squarely at the toe, carry them forward in a straight line and set them down again. It is impossible for a splay-footed horse to carry his front feet straight forward. Study the adjacent diagram and learn why the splay-footed or nigger-heeled position in horses is objectionable. The following statements supply the answer.

1. The splay-footed position on the front feet predisposes to faulty action and results in a defect in gait known as dishing or winging in.

2. Winging in is a defect in gait that predisposes to interference. Toe wide horses quite commonly hit their ankles, their shins or their knees.

3. Interference predisposes to blemish or unsoundness.

4. Blemishes and unsoundnesses depreciate the value of a horse, thereby affecting the economics of the horse business. Hence the reason why there should be sharp discrimination against splay-footed horses.

◄—Diagram showing course taken by a front foot in case of toe-wide or splay-footed horses.

on his front feet, will wing in sufficiently to brush or strike the fet-lock of a supporting leg with the striding foot.

If the splay-footed horse be a trotter at speed or any other type of horse whose gaits call for speed, he may strike not only his ankles, but his shins, his knees, and his elbows. A bold, high-going, splay-footed trotter might have to wear quarter boots, ankle boots, shin boots, knee boots, and elbow boots. That is, he might have to be rigged with all of the boots that are made for the front legs of a light harness horse.

The most intelligent horsemen discriminate sharply against splay-footed horses. In such cases, faulty position on the legs pre-disposes to a defect in gait known as dishing, which in turn predis-poses to interference. Interference results in blemish or unsound-ness; in turn, blemishes and unsoundnesses depreciate value. Ex-perienced buyers of horses for use in areas where the competition is keen will therefore not spend their money for horses whose splay-footed position in front is almost a sure guarantee that they will pound a supporting front leg with a striding front foot.

Pigeon Toes

Horses that stand pigeon-toed in front are predisposed to swing their front feet outward when on the move. This defect in gait is known as paddling. Exaggerated paddling is sometimes referred to as "winging out."

There is definite correlation between the pigeon-toed position on the front feet and the defect in gait known as paddling, just as there is a correlation between the splay-footed position in front and the defect in gait known as dishing.

The horse that paddles, however, cannot pound a striding front leg against a supporting front leg, as does a splay-footed horse that wings in. The objection to the pigeon-toed horse that wings out arises from the fact that his spraddling, winging tendency in front results in uncollected action.

A straight line is the shortest distance between two points. Therefore, the best-going horses are those which can fold their knees and carry their front feet straight forward without any ten-dency to wing in or out.

Calf Knees

If a horse's knees as viewed from the side break backward, the horse is said to be calf-kneed. "Breaks back at the knees," "stands back at the knees," "calf-kneed" are synonymous. Calf knees in all horses are objectionable, because a calf-kneed horse stands and goes up hill all the time. Also, in horses whose calf-kneed po-sition constitutes a glaring defect, there is a predisposition to whip the front feet to the ground at the completion of the stride, thereby increasing concussion to a maximum.

Buck Knees
      "Over on the knees" and "easy on the knees" are synonymous expressions for "buck-kneed." Buck-kneed horses are less stable on their front legs than are horses whose knees as viewed from the side are perfectly straight and squarely placed beneath the body for purposes of support. If buck knees are accompanied by long toes, the predisposition in such horses is to stumble, particularly if the going is a little soft.

Knock Knees and Bow Knees
      Knock-kneed horses are sometimes referred to as horses that stand "in at the knees" or are "too close at the knees." "Bow-kneed" and "bow-legged" are synonymous terms. Knock-kneed horses, especially if worked at speed, are predisposed to interfere. Bow-kneed horses quite often stand over on the outside of their front feet. This faulty position brings undue weight upon the outside portions of the front feet, especially upon the outside lateral cartilages of the feet, with a predisposition to the early formation of sidebones.
      A primary function of the front legs of a horse is to support weight. If the front legs are straight as viewed from the front and from the side, the chances for an early breakdown of these legs in service are reduced to a minimum. The way in which a horse sets on his legs determines in large part the kind of service of which he is capable, as well the length of that service.

Sickle hocks
      "Sickle-hocked" and "too much set to the hocks" are expressions that are applicable when a horse's hind legs as viewed from the side are altogether too crooked. The hind legs of a horse are referred to as the propellers because the efforts of propulsion which are necessary to move the body forward are centered primarily in the hindquarters. Of course the hind legs of a horse also function as pillars of support for the body.
      Balanced conformation is a goal sought in the make-up of all types of horses. Sickle hocks do not contribute to balanced conformation; on the other hand, they help to destroy symmetrical form. There is a well-marked correlation between steep croups and sickle hocks as features in horse make-up. Steep croups destroy trueness of top line from withers to tail and thereby destroy the symmetry of form which is always a well-marked feature of the best horses. Since there is a correlation between sickle hocks and steep croups, sickle hocks help to destroy balanced conformation.

But there is a second and much more important reason why sickle hocks are objectionable features in horses. When the hocks of any horse or pony, as viewed from the side, have too much set to them, the hind feet are displaced too far forward beneath the body, and the hock joint has to bear a disproportionate share of the body weight.

Spavins and curbs, especially curbs, may be the result of sickle hocks because the cuneiform bone of the hock and the curb ligament are called upon to bear more than their normal share of the work assigned to the hind legs of a horse. On account of the deflection of the line of the leg upon which weight is borne and power applied, a curb may result. Hence sickle hocks are objectionable features in all kinds of horses and ponies because they predispose to curbiness.

Bandy Legs

When a horse stands pigeon-toed on his hind feet, with the points of his hocks turned outward, he is said to stand bandy-legged behind. There are several objections to this faulty position on the hind legs.

First, such horses are predisposed to go wide at the hocks, thereby making the most collected performance impossible. Horses and ponies of all types should work their hocks fairly close together instead of wide apart, because the goal of performance in the case of all horses is collected, coordinated action. Fairly close hock action with the hind legs working beneath the body makes collected action possible, whereas spraddle-gaited hock action makes it impossible.

A second objection to the bandy-legged horse is that it is impossible for a horse so stationed on his hind legs to rock his hind feet upward, break them over at the toe, and carry the hind legs forward with the hocks working fairly close together. On the contrary, the bandy-legged horse rocks his heel upward, and as the foot breaks over at the toe, he gives a lateral twist to his hock, a defect in gait known among horsemen as "rotating hocks." Some horsemen in describing the hock action of a bandy-legged horse refer to such horses as limber-hocked horses.

Since the action of a horse depends upon the way in which he is made, any bandy-legged horse is predisposed to rotate his hocks. This limber-hocked tendency is objectionable because rotating hocks cannot withstand maximum strain; hence early unsoundness of the hock joint is to be expected. Even a bandy-legged work horse, working at the walk, will rotate his hocks when he lifts with his hind legs and exerts the effort necessary to move a load.

Flat Feet vs. Contracted Feet

In the best days of the horse business the feet of draft horses on city streets commonly went wrong in one way, while the feet of light-leg horses in their various areas of service quite commonly went wrong in a distinctly different way. Flatness has always been the prevailing ailment of the draft horse's foot in service, whereas contraction and navicular disease have been prevailing foot ailments of light-leg horses.

Mr. James Johnstone, who for years wrote a draft horse column for the *Breeders' Gazette,* describes the ideal foot for the drafter as follows: "The ideal foot for a drafter should be big in proportion to body bulk, wide and deep at the heel, full and rounding at toe and quarters with enough arch of sole and strength of hoof wall to oppose flatness."

A horse's weight is borne chiefly upon the hoof walls of his feet. When the hoof wall draws inward and sinks downward, and when the sole of the foot drops, then to the latter, which is not primarily a weight-bearing surface, is assigned the task of supporting body weight. This, of course, results in sole bruises and lameness. By experience horsemen have learned that the flat-footed work horse needs shoes all of the time and that his feet are the most difficult to shoe and shoe properly.

Because the feet of light-leg horses are much smaller and much more narrow at the heels than are the feet of draft horses and because many light-leg horses are used at speeds at which the feet are subjected to maximum concussion, the prevailing ailments of light-leg feet are contraction and navicular disease.

Navicular disease is an inflammation of the sesamoid sheath, induced by repeated bruising or laceration and complicated in many cases by inflammation, ulceration, and partial disintegration or chipping of the navicular bone itself. Of course, this navicular condition results in lameness and if it is accompanied by contraction of the heels, the navicular difficulty becomes even more aggravated.

The old saying that "an ounce of prevention is worth a pound of cure" is most applicable in the case of navicular trouble because such cases rarely recover, although they may show temporary improvement.

When the feet become dry and hard, the tissues contract. Therefore, any management procedure that helps to retain the moisture in the foot tissues will aid in preventing contraction. Packing the feet with puddled clay helps to retain the moisture in the tissues of the feet. In the case of a saddle horse whose feet have been packed with clay to retain the moisture, a foot pick is used to remove the clay when the horse is worked. The feet are then repacked when the horse goes back to his stall.

Chico Chief, one of the greatest parade horses to appear before the show-going public in recent years. Study the set of his legs. He stands back on all of his ankles; and he has ample length of pastern and feet that are shapely in their proportions. Owned by Mr. John Costello of Bentwood, Missouri. Photograph courtesy Mr. Costello.

Leather pads or rubber pads beneath the wings of the shoe oftentimes help to prevent contraction. Usually, some oakum with tar or with Corona wool fat is smeared on the bottom surface of the foot before the pad and the shoe are nailed into position.

Flat feet and contracted feet in horses are a source of great annoyance to both horses and owners. Horses with flat or contracted feet should therefore be sharply discriminated against by prospective purchasers and by judges whose assignment it is to make a rating on them at the shows.

The Underpinning as a Factor in Judging Horses

Too much stress cannot be placed upon the importance of underpinning as a determining factor in appraising the worth of a horse. Like the chassis of an automobile, the supporting structures are subject to constant wear and tear.

The many unsoundnesses which may affect a horse's underpinning and impair his value justify the statement that much of the grief in the horse business occurs from the elbows and the stifles down, that the minimum worries occur above the elbows and the stifles.

Scottish breeders, in developing the Clydesdale, have believed so thoroughly in the importance of good underpinning that their slogan, which accentuates the need of good underpinning beneath a real draft horse, has been passed on from generation to generation:

> Feet, ankles, pasterns, feather,
> Tops may come, but bottoms never.

Scottish horsemen learned a long time ago that the body of a horse may be improved a great deal by feeding and that the underpinning of a horse is largely a matter of breeding.

Anyone selecting or judging horses should always do three things. First, he should study the set or position of the feet and legs. Second, he should study the quality of the underpinning. Third, he should determine the soundness of the underpinning. If he does these three jobs intelligently, and then closely observes the horses in motion, he will be well on the way to making a sound decision about the comparative rating of the horses.

6

Types, Breeds, and Show Classes of Horses

According to their uses, the principal types of horses are work horses, heavy harness horses, light harness horses, and saddle horses. Different breeds within each type may serve rather specialized purposes. Show-ring classes make still further subdivisions as indicated in the outline and discussion that follow. (For a more detailed discussion of types and breeds see Chapter 7, The Hackney; Chapter 8, The Standardbred; and Chapter 9, The Breeds of Saddle Horses and Ponies.)

I. Work Horses

Horse numbers in the United States were at their peak in 1915. Work horses then made up the greatest part of the horse population of 21,431,000 head. Over the next 40 years, as American agriculture became mechanized, the number of work horses decreased steadily. In 1955 there were 3,106,000 horses in this country. The boom in the horse business since then has been in light horses used for sport and recreation. Work horses today comprise only a small part of our horse population. Because horses have not been counted for several years in the census, their present number is unknown, but it is believed to be between 8 and 10 million head.

A. *Drafters.*   Drafters are work horses that stand at least 16 hands in height and weigh at least 1,600 pounds. In the heyday of the work horse the drafter was the highest-priced work horse on the market. He was a city horse used on short-haul assignments in congested areas. Discriminating city users of drafters wanted horses that served as walking advertisements for their firms.

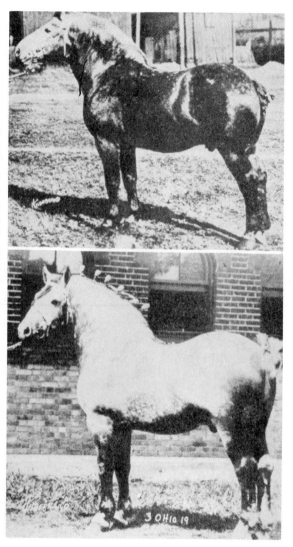

This pair of pictures shows how the pigment fades out of the coat of a gray horse as he grows older. Above is the Percheron stallion Libretto 121447 (97907) as a six-year-old weighing 2,100 pounds. Below is the same horse, four years later, weighing about a ton. Note how the pigment has faded from his hair coat. Photographs courtesy Hildebrand and Photography Department, The Ohio State University.

Soundness was a prime consideration in buying work horses for the city streets. In the United States we have had five breeds of draft horses:

1. Percherons. The first improved work horses imported to America were Percherons; for years they were the most popular of our work horses. This breed was developed in northwest France in an area known as the Perche, some 80 miles west of Paris. Originally of Flemish origin, these horses had some admixture of Arabian blood. They were used by armored

Jay Farceur 17628, one of the most noted show stallions and one of the most noted sires in the history of the Belgian breed in America. He has been champion at the Chicago International, at the American Royal, and at all the leading state fairs in the Middle West. Photograph courtesy J. F. Abernathy.

knights in the Middle Ages and later were used as heavy-duty freight and coach horses. They were selected for greater draft horse qualities during the mid-nineteenth century when they were first exported to America.

Percherons are usually grey or black. They stand 16 hands or higher; purebred Percherons weigh about a ton. Of the draft breeds they have the best combination of size, scale, quality, and a good way of going.

2. Belgians. These horses were developed over many centuries in Belgium as true draft horses with no mixture of other blood. They usually are some shade of chestnut or roan, but there are some bays. Belgian horses are noted for their roomy middles, heavy muscling, rugged bone, and their easy keeping qualities. They are extremely drafty in their make-up,

stand 16 hands or higher, and weigh about a ton. Belgians were not brought to America in large numbers until after 1900. They became the most popular farm and city work horses in many parts of the United States in the days when draft horses were used widely as a source of power.

3. Clydesdales.   Developed in the valley of the River Clyde in Scotland, Clydesdales are best known to Americans as the horses that pull the Budweiser beer wagon in parades and on television commercials. They most often are bay or brown in color. Blazed faces and white stockings are common markings. Abundant feathering on the cannons and fetlocks is a distinctive feature of Clydesdales. Of the draft breeds, Clydes have the most quality in their underpinning, lean, clean, well-defined joints, flat bone, and big, wide feet. At the walk and trot they go with snap, height, style, and animation. Hence, they were always popular with commercial firms. Their feathered legs and somewhat taller, less drafty conformation limited their popularity with American farmers in the old days. However, the six- and eight-horse show teams of Clydesdales have been made up of big, drafty, muscular geldings that averaged 17 to 18 hands and weighed over 2,200 pounds.

4. Shires.   Shire horses are native to central England. They are the biggest, most massive, and coarsest of the draft breeds. Used as war horses in the Middle Ages, they had the size, substance, strength, and stamina to carry the heavy armor then worn by both horse and rider. Shires are usually solid colors, but there are some greys. White markings are common. Like Clydesdales, they have abundant feathering on their legs. Purebred Shires stand 17 hands high and weigh over a ton. They never were numerous in the United States; however, in some parts of the Midwest, Shire mares were bred to Standardbred stallions to produce a medium-sized, active, free-walking farm work horse.

5. Suffolks.   The smallest of the draft breeds is the Suffolk, developed in the county of that name in east central England. All Suffolk horses are chestnut in color. For years they were the principal farm horse in the agricultural parts of Suffolk, but never achieved popularity in the United States.

B. *Loggers.*   Loggers are work horses of draft-horse size and scale, but often are lacking in similar quality. They are used for timber- and logging-camp operations. For such work looks are unimportant, but the horses must be serviceably sound, tractable, strong, and rugged.

C. *Chunks.*   Work horses of drafty conformation but small size are known as chunks. Many farm work horses would be in this

Captivation 3954, one of the greatest Hackney mares ever produced in America. A liver-colored chestnut mare, with white markings, she was always easy to look at when posed for inspection. Few indeed are the horses that have ever been able to imitate her matchless action. She was shown very successfully by Longview Farms, Lees Summit, Missouri. David Smith driving. Photograph by Rounds, courtesy Mrs. Loula Long Combs.

category. Ranging on the average from 1,300 to 1,500 pounds in weight and from 14.2 to 15.2 hands in height, chunks are often prompt and active at the walk and are able to stand the heat better than very large draft horses.

II.   Heavy Harness Horses

The Heavy Harness horse that was the coach and carriage horse of olden times is seen today in some large horse shows and in some driving competitions. This type is represented in the United States by the Hackney breed that was developed in England. Hackneys are usually bay, brown, or chestnut. They are driven with some type of curb driving bit (Liverpool, elbow, or

Invasion demonstrates the heavy harness horse trot. Mrs. Loula Long Combs driving. Photograph courtesy Mrs. Combs.

THREE CHAMPIONS IN THEIR RESPECTIVE DIVISIONS DEMONSTRATE THE TROT.

Cadet's Crystal Gazer demonstrates the heavy harness pony trot. Mrs. R. C. Flanery driving. Photograph courtesy Mr. R. C. Flanery.

President Lincoln demonstates the roadster trot. Kenny Mauer driving. Photograph courtesy J. A. McClasky.

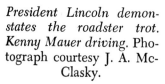

Buxton bit) and a side check rein attached to a check bit. They may be driven singly, in pairs, in tandem, or in a four-in-hand, according to class specifications. They may be hitched to a phaeton, a gig, a viceroy buggy, or a road coach, depending on the class requirements.

There is an implication about the term "Heavy Harness horse" that is not generally understood. Harness horses are of two classes: heavy and light. The adjective in each case describes the harness—not the horse. Since Heavy Harness horses draw vehicles of dignified, elegant design and heavy construction, the harness by which the horses are put to the vehicles must be correspondingly heavy.

Heavy Harness horses today are used almost entirely for show purposes. To be capable of both acting and looking the part the horses must be close and full-made with extreme finish, style, and action. They must be able to set their heads, fold their knees, flex their hocks, and trot with a high, balanced, collected stride at a park pace or be able to step on at greater speed and still maintain their form.

Although relatively few in number in the United States, Heavy Harness horses are featured at the Royal Winter Fair in Toronto, Canada.

III. Light Harness Horses

Before the automobile age, Light Harness horses hitched to light vehicles were used for rapid road transportation. Today these horses have a sporting use only. The only important Light Harness horse in the United States is an American breed—the Standardbred. Standardbreds are usually one of the dark solid colors. A few may be grey and others roan. They have two major uses:

1. Trotters and pacers in harness races. Harness race horses are driven with a snaffle driving bit and an overdraw check rein attached to a check bit, and are hitched to a racing sulky. In recent years pacers have greatly outnumbered trotters at the big harness race tracks. Since most pacers race while wearing pacing hopples, they are less likely than trotters to break stride during a race. Hence they have been favored by the betting public, and more pacing races than trotting races have been offered on each race program.
2. Roadsters in horse shows. Only trotters appear in roadster classes. Old-time horsemen regarded the pacer as a kind of counterfeit roadster because pacers are greatly handicapped in the mud, sand, snow, or on rough ground. To do their best, pacers must have smooth, level footing that is reasonably firm.

Kate Shriver 43606, champion fine harness mare, sired by Anacacho Denmark and out of Reverie's Desdemona, winner of the Junior Fine Harness Stake at Louisville in 1949. She came back as a five-year-old to win the $10,000 Fine Harness Stake at the Kentucky State Fair in 1950. She had good looks and a fine harness trot. She was owned by Mr. and Mrs. R. C. Goshorn, Jefferson City, Missouri, and was shown by Garland Bradshaw. Photograph by John R. Horst.

In roadster classes the horses are shown in light harness with a snaffle driving bit and overdraw check rein. They are hitched to either a road wagon (light, four-wheeled) or a bike (light, two-wheeled cart similar to a sulky) according to class specifications. There are also classes for roadsters under saddle.

In all roadster classes the horses enter the ring at a jog trot and circle the ring in a clockwise direction. After the judge has asked the horses to reverse, they are trotted counterclockwise at a road gait and then at speed. At all speeds they should work in form at a balanced trot. Animation, brilliance, and show-ring presence should characterize roadsters at the jog trot and road gait. When asked to drive on, they must show as much speed as possible within the show ring

Emerald Sweet Sue 46757, sired by American Ace, and out of Janet Sue.
As a junior mare in 1949, she won the junior stakes at Dayton, Cincinnati,
and the Ohio State Fair. She was reserve at Lexington, Louisville, and
Harrisburg. Photograph courtesy J. A. McClasky.

and still go in form. Pacing or racking the turns or breaking
and running are penalized. Many roadsters have been former
racing trotters that happen to have the good looks, quality,
and manners to make creditable show horses when they were
retired from racing.

IV. Saddle Horses

  A. *Thoroughbreds*
    1. Race horses on the flat
    2. Steeplechasers
    3. Polo ponies
    4. Hacks
    5. Hunters

Hunters are ridden to hounds cross-country and often must carry
considerable weight. All hunters, in addition to being able to carry

THREE CHAMPIONS IN THEIR RESPECTIVE DIVISIONS DEM- ONSTRATE THE TROT.

The Auctioneer demon- strates the three-gaited saddle pony trot. "Bob" Whitney riding. These pho_ tographs courtesy J. A. McClasky.

Vanity demonstrates the fine harness horse trot. Mrs. Victor Weil driving.

G. I. Joe demonstrates the harness show pony trot. Louis Robinson driving.

Runancarry, one of the best types ever to appear in the hunter classes in the shows of this country. Winner one year at Devon of six blue ribbons and the green hunter championship. Sired by Runantell and out of Graceful Carrie, this champion mare was owned by Bryn Du Farms, Granville, Ohio, and was shown by Mrs. Sally Jones Sexton. Study this photograph. Note the balanced conformation as well as the set and the quality of the underpinning. Photograph by Haas, courtesy Mrs. Sexton.

weight, must be able to endure long, hard runs; jump safely— preferably in their stride—all common obstacles in the field such as fences, walls, and ditches; and gallop fast enough to keep pace with the pack. They must also be intelligent and tractable and of such temperament that they do not become too hot in company.

A good hunter should have all the features of a weight carrier. He should have long, sloping shoulders, high withers, a short, strong back and loins, muscular hindquarters with thickness through the stifles, correct leg position, and ample bone. Quality in the make-up of a hunter that actually follows the hounds may be sacrificed to substance, but at the same time a hunter should show good breeding.

The Hunter Division in American horse shows may be subdivided into the following: Breeding (shown in hand), Conformation (Green and Regular), Working (Green and Regular), and Miscellaneous Hunter Classes.

Most of the horses shown in Conformation Hunter classes are Thoroughbreds. Such classes are judged on the basis of the horse's performance over the show-ring hunt course and his conformation. Working Hunters must be serviceably sound but need not be

Thoroughbred. They are judged on their performance and soundness. In both Conformation and Working Hunter classes the horses should maintain an even hunting pace on the course and show good manners. Their jumping style together with faults and their way of moving over the course are also considered in the judging.

A Green Hunter is a horse of any age in his first or second year of showing in any class that requires horses to jump 3'6" or higher. Obstacles usually range from 3'6" to 4' in height.

A Regular Hunter is a horse of any age that is not restricted by previous showing in any division. Fences in Regular Hunter classes usually range from 4' to 4'6" in height. The fences on a hunter course simulate obstacles found in the hunting field, such as natural post and rail, brush, stone wall, white board fence or gate, chicken coop, aiken, hedge, and oxer.

The Green and Regular Hunter sections in very large horse shows may be further subdivided into the following classifications:
(a) Small—not exceeding 15.2½ hands
(b) Lightweight—up to carrying 165 pounds
(c) Middleweight—up to carrying 185 pounds
(d) Heavyweight—up to carrying 205 pounds
(e) Thoroughbred—registered in any stud book recognized by the Jockey Club
(f) Non-Thoroughbred—not registered as in (e)
(g) Qualified—a Qualified Hunter is a horse that has been hunted regularly and satisfactorily for one or more seasons with a pack of hounds recognized or registered by the Masters of Foxhounds Association of America or England.
(h) Corinthian, Appointment, and Formal Hunting Attire classes—a Corinthian Hunter is a horse ridden by an amateur who is a member of (or in case of subscription pack, fully accredited subscriber to) a Recognized or Registered Hunt in hunting attire. The rider in an Appointment or a Formal Hunting Attire class is neither required to be an amateur nor a member of a Recognized Hunt. Brilliance of performance is emphasized in the judging of these classes.

Miscellaneous Hunter Classes may include:
(a) Hunter Hacks
(b) Bridle Path Hacks (hunter type)
(c) Pairs of Hunters, abreast (or) tandem
(d) Hunt Teams—to be ridden in hunting attire
(e) Amateur Owners—horses to be ridden by amateur owners. The horses' manners are emphasized in the judging.

Hunters are ridden with a hunt seat saddle. Some are ridden with a hunting snaffle bit, some with a Pelham bit, and others with a full bridle.

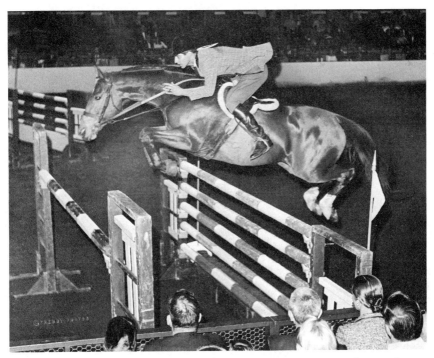

Australis, a star of the Jumper division in United States horse shows. American Horse Shows Association high point winner as a Green Jumper in 1963 and 1964 and as an Open Jumper in 1965 and 1966. This Thoroughbred mare was sired by Borealis and was out of Simplicity 2d by Nearco. Australis was owned and shown by Danny Lopez, Old Brookville, Long Island, N.Y. Note the light touch on the reins as the horse clears the obstacle. Photo by Freudy.

B. American Saddlebred Horses

The Saddle Horse Division in American horse shows is for horses of the American Saddlebred breed shown in the following subdivisions:

1. Breeding.   To be shown in hand.
2. Three-gaited Saddle Horses.   Entries in this division are shown today with a roached mane and tail. They are ridden with a full Weymouth bridle and flat English saddle. They are shown at the walk, trot, and canter. Some classes may be limited to horses of a specific height, such as 14.2 hands and not exceeding 15 hands, 15 hands and not exceeding 15.2 hands, and over 15.2 hands.

    Three-gaited horses should trot in form at a moderate

Roses Are Red, owned and shown by Miss Susan Lenahan, Greenwich, Conn. This chestnut mare sired by Battle Royal and out of Ashes of Roses was shown from Florida to Massachusetts. She won the American Horse Shows Assn. Horse of the Year award for Junior Hunters in 1966. She won championships at such shows as Devon, North Shore, Piping Rock, and the National Horse Show at Madison Square Garden. Photo by Budd.

speed. A balanced stride that shows considerable height, flexion, and impulsion is desired. The horses should go straight in front and work their hocks close together as viewed from the rear. Winging in or out with the front feet, landing on the heels, hitching or dwelling behind, spraddling behind, and trailing the hind legs are serious defects. The old Kentucky saying about cantering all day in the shade of an apple tree expresses the ideal for the canter. The horse should be on the correct lead, move slowly and collectedly, look animated enough to run, but restrain himself at the will of the rider. Three-gaited horses should perform at a walk when it is called for, but too often are permitted to prance, dance, and jig.

In three-gaited combination classes, the horses are first

William C. Steinkraus, Noroton, Conn., Captain of the United States Equestrian Team and individual Gold Medal winner in the jumping competition at the 1968 Olympic Games in Mexico City. In this photo, Mr. Steinkraus is riding Bold Minstrel and winning the Puissance at 7' 3" at the 1967 National Horse Show at Madison Square Garden. Bold Minstrel was loaned to the U.S.E.T. by William D. Haggard III. This superior jumper was sired by a Thoroughbred stallion and was out of a cross-bred mare that was sired by a Thoroughbred. Photo by Budd.

The grand champion hunt team, Gold Lode, Times Square, and Maple Leaf, owned by Mr. V. G. Cardy of Montreal, Canada. Photograph by ABC News Pictures, courtesy Mr. Cardy.

driven in light harness (but with a Liverpool bit), hitched to a four-wheeled show buggy. After performing at the trot and the walk, the horses are unhitched, unharnessed, saddled, and bridled, and then shown under saddle at the walk, trot, and canter. Judging is based 50 per cent on the performance in harness and 50 per cent on that under saddle.

3. Five-gaited Saddle Horses. Gaited horses customarily are shown with a full mane and tail. They are ridden with a full Weymouth bridle and a flat English saddle at the walk, trot, canter, slow gait, and rack. Since they are expected to go quite fast at the trot and at the rack, gaited horses are brought out wearing quarter boots on their front feet. The quarter boots protect the heels of the front feet in case a horse over-strides.

Gaited horses should trot faster than three-gaited horses,

Peggy Grey, sired by The Second Whip, a Welsh pony stallion, and out of a Shetland pony mare. Miss Marjorie Kays is in the saddle. Photograph courtesy Cook and Gormley.

but still maintain their form. They should go with their heads set and work their legs beneath them. The slow gait should be a slow, high, animated, syncopated motion, not just a slow rack. The rack should be a distinct, smooth, four-beat gait done at speed and in form. Horses should not swing into a pace on the turns.

Occasionally five-gaited combination classes are offered. The horses are driven at a walk and trot in light harness with a snaffle bit and overdraw check. Then they are shown under saddle at all five gaits.

4. Fine Harness Horses. Fine Harness horses are American Saddlebred horses driven in light harness with a snaffle bit and overdraw check rein, hitched to a small buggy with four wire wheels but without a top. They are presented in the style of a five-gaited horse: with full mane and tail and wearing quarter boots. They are driven at an animated park trot and an animated walk. Extreme speed at the trot is penalized. The best Fine Harness horses have excellent conformation and quality. They have a free, airy, balanced trot and show great style, brilliance, and presence both when in motion and when posed for the judges' inspection.

5. American Saddlebred Pleasure Horses. Classes in this section are for three- or five-gaited horses shown in a more

A tandem hitch of Clydesdale geldings owned by Anheuser-Busch, St. Louis, Mo. Photo by Abernathy.

natural style, with a more moderate way of going and without the brilliance expected in the other sections of the Saddle Horse Division. Classes are offered for both English and Western styles under saddle, as well as classes for pleasure driving. In the judging of all of these classes, manners and performance are paramount considerations.

C. *Appaloosas.* Used and shown principally under Western tack, but occasionally with English tack. Some Appaloosas are used as working stock horses, some as pleasure mounts, and a few are raced at short distances.

D. *Arabians.* Used and shown under either English or Western tack at the walk, trot, and canter (walk, jog, and lope). They are driven in light harness at the walk and trot. A few Arabians are trained for long distance racing. Many have excelled in long distance competitive trail rides.

E. *Jumpers.* Horses of any breed or cross shown in jumping classes where only their performance over the jumping course is considered.

F. *Morgans.* Used and shown under either English or Western tack at the walk, trot, and canter (walk, jog, and lope). Driven in light harness at the walk and trot.

G. *Paint Horses.* Paint horses are of the stock horse type and

A pair of farm chunks hitched to a walking plow. Such scenes are seldom encountered in this day of mechanized farm operations.

The walking plow was replaced by the gang plow. This picture shows a multiple hitch of five Percheron mares pulling a gang plow on a central Ohio farm in the 1920s.

have variable broken color patterns: white and black, brown, bay, or chestnut. They are shown most often under Western tack and in Western-style classes such as reining, trail, and working cow horse classes.

H. *Palominos.* Horses of a golden color with white or ivory mane and tail. May be of American Saddlebred, Quarter horse, Walking horses, Morgan, or other blood lines; they are used and shown accordingly.

I. *Parade Horses.* Horses of any breed, cross, or color used under elaborate silver-mounted Western, Mexican, or Spanish equipment in Parade horse classes, at an animated walk and a parade gait. The parade gait is a rather high, prancing, cadenced trot at about 5 miles per hour. Good parade horses have great style, beauty, quality, and presence. Riders wear colorful attire of Western, Mexican, or Spanish origin typical of the Old West.

Michael Matz, on Jet Run, won the first U.S.E.T. Open Jumping Champion-ship in 1981. Among the many successes of this pair were first place in the 1981 F.E.I. World Cup competition at Birmingham, England, the Individual Gold Medal at the 1979 Pan-American Games in Puerto Rico, and leading international rider at the 1979 National Horse Show, Madison Square Gar-den. Jet Run was loaned to the U.S. Equestrian Team by F. Eugene Dixon, Erdenheim Farm, Lafayette Hill, Pa. Photo by Alix Coleman, courtesy of the U.S.E.T.

J. *Pintos.*   Horses of variable broken color patterns ranging from predominantly white with black, bay, brown, or chestnut to predominantly dark colors with white. Pintos may be of Quarter horse, American Saddlebred, Arabian, Morgan or other extraction. Hence, Pintos may appear under Western, English, or Parade tack according to their type and the show classification.

K. *Quarter Horses*
   1. Short distance race horses on the flat
   2. Working stock horses on cattle ranches
   3. Polo ponies
   4. Rodeo competition horses
   5. Pleasure riding horses, usually with Western tack
   6. Working hunters

L. *Tennessee Walking Horses.*   Used and shown at the walk, running walk, and canter. Ridden with a flat saddle and a single curb bit, frequently one with rather long, S-shaped cheek pieces.

M. *Western Horses.*   In horse shows in the United States, horses shown in the Western Division may be of any breed or cross 14.1 hands and over, serviceably sound, and of stock horse type. Most horses in Western classes are of the Quarter horse, Appaloosa, Arabian, Morgan, Paint, or Pinto breeds or their crosses. The appointments of both the horses and the riders are of practical Western type. The horses are ridden at the walk, jog trot, and lope; they compete in stock horse, trail, and pleasure horse classes.

V.   Ponies

In American horse shows the term *horse* designates animals over 14.2 hands except Appaloosas, Arabians, Morgans, Paints, Palominos, Pintos, Quarter horses, and Western horses, some of which may be smaller. With the exceptions noted above, the term *pony* designates animals of any height up to and including 14.2 hands. The most common breeds of ponies in American horse shows are:

A. Connemaras
B. Hackneys
C. Harness Ponies
D. Shetlands
E. Welsh Ponies

For a more detailed discussion of types and breeds see Chapter 7, The Hackney; Chapter 8, The Standardbred; and Chapter 9, The Breeds of Saddle Horses and Ponies.

7

The Hackney

HEAVY HARNESS HORSES

The Hackney is the breed which has furnished the great majority of our best heavy harness horses. Hard roads in England antedated hard roads in America. For years, heavy English vehicles rolled along on top of hard stone roads easily, while American vehicles much lighter in weight were drawn laboriously and oftentimes hub-deep through the mud. Therefore, England and America developed different types of harness horses because these horses had different jobs to do. The horses, the tack, and the vehicles pulled were fashioned to suit the circumstances under which they had to be used.

Since the English have had hard roads for many years, the heavy harness horse hitched to a heavy vehicle has been their choice.

When heavy vehicles such as a phaeton, a coach, or a heavy gig appear in a horse show arena, they have to be pulled over soft tanbark footing that in many instances is altogether too deep. The soft footing of itself is a great handicap to the horse and, of course, when he is hitched to a heavy vehicle he is asked to operate under a severe disadvantage. Therefore it is necessary that the harness by which the horses are put to these vehicles be correspondingly heavy.

Hackney History
The name of this breed immediately distinguishes it. The word "hackney" is a very old one, and has come to denote both a general purpose horse and the vehicles which he draws. In England the word was specifically applied to a type of harness horse midway between the light and the heavy sorts.

Spartan King, grand champion Heavy Harness Gelding at such leading shows as the Canadian Royal at Toronto, Canada, and Devon, Pennsylvania. This famous gelding has been driven by his owner, Mr. James Franceschini, Dufferin Stock Farm, Toronto, Canada. Note that he can fold his knees, flex his hocks, set his chin and go collectedly. Photograph courtesy J. A. McClasky.

The word "hack" was much used in referring to riding horses in early days and is still in common use by horsemen. In the show classifications at the present time there are classes for road hacks, three-gaited park hacks, hunter hacks, bridle path hacks, the qualifying term in each instance suggesting the job which the entries in each class are supposed to do. During the formative days of the breed's development, the Hackney might have been described as a heavier strain of the old-time Norfolk trotter, so-called as a result of having originated in the county of Norfolk in England.

The two adjoining counties of Norfolk and Suffolk are the most easterly counties of England and are located directly opposite Belgium and Holland, which were the regions where the "great" and other heavy draft breeds of Europe were evolved in the Middle Ages. In Norfolk, which is the more northern county, the breeders made liberal use of Thoroughbred stallions crossed on the native mares. By means of a selective and refining process, these matings resulted in the Norfolk trotter and his derivative, the Hackney. In Suffolk, however, the emphasis of breeders was quite different for they made liberal use of seed stock from Belgium and Holland; the result was the Suffolk punch, a horse whose type was drafty in the extreme.

Foundation stock. The Hackney as a distinct type emerged in the mid-18th century largely from the crosses of Thoroughbred stallions on the native mares of Norfolk. The most important foundation sire was the Shales Horse, foaled in 1755. He was sired by the Thoroughbred stallion Blaze, a grandson of the Darley Arabian. Blaze was the great-great grandsire of imported Messenger from whom the American Standardbred descends.

The Hackney became specialized for use in the British hackney coach service of the eighteenth century, and, hitched to vehicles of many kinds, was later used by members of the well-to-do classes in their road driving. Horses were needed in the road service, and Hackneys were bred with that object in view, the road-driving assignment calling for a horse that was full-made as compared with a horse designed for racing, yet featuring in make-up the characteristics of finish, quality, substance, and speed, all of which were stressed as important requirements of horses whose job it was to pull a coach over the highways.

The Breeders' Goal. The aim of the breeders was to produce a horse of medium size and weight, 15 to 15-2 hands in height and weighing 900 to 1,100 pounds. Of course, the round-ribbed, full-bodied horses, the easy-keeping kind that stood correctly on their legs and could swing off at a smart trot were the horses most in demand as power units hitched to a coach. The preferred colors for horses in the coaching service were bay, brown, and chestnut with white trimmings. Before the advent of the carriage, these horses were occasionally used under saddle as well as for some light agricultural work.

The Place of the Hackney in America

Before the great tidal wave of motor development, the Hackney was a very popular horse in both England and America. In the former country the breed was very actively promoted and publicized, and had a stud book of its own. Many choice Hackneys were imported to America and used for park driving, for exhibition at the shows, and for breeding. In this country, however, they encountered strong competition from the Standardbreds and their derivatives.

Today, the Hackney in this country is used for purposes of show only. City planning boards are still including bridle paths in our parks and bridle trails in suburban territory on the outskirts of our large cities where saddle horses can be ridden in safety. That is to say, provision is still being made for those horse owners who seek pleasure and recreation on horseback. But motor cars and motor trucks have driven harness horses off the public highways.

HEAVY HARNESS HORSES AT THE SHOWS

There is no question about the pleasure which the spectator experiences in watching heavy harness classes at the shows. Such classes contribute interest because they diversify a show program. Furthermore, a bold, highstepping, heavy harness horse, going with his chin set and in form, rigged in harness that glistens and shines, and drawing a vehicle such as a phaeton, whose design suggests dignity and elegance, appeals to most show audiences.

In show competition, there are maiden, novice, limit, and amateur classes for both single and pairs of heavy harness horses.

A pair of Hackney ponies hitched tandem to a gig. Glenavon Filmstar and King's Melody were owned and shown by the Dodge Stables, trained and driven by Reed Bridgford, a master of the difficult art of driving a tandem hitch. Photo by McClasky.

A team of four high-stepping Hackney horses with postilions, drawing a George IV phaeton. This most festive method of conveying a bride was used by Chauncey D. Stillman, Commodore of the New York Yacht Club, as he accompanied his daughter to her wedding at Lithgow, N.Y. Photo by Brookfield, courtesy Chauncey Stillman.

Brig o' Doon and Ensor Doon, the pair of Hackney horses that won the Ladies' Phaeton class at the Royal Winter Fair, Toronto, in 1966. The horses are owned by Chauncey Stillman of New York. Mrs. Helen Southgate, Kitchener, Ontario, drove the pair to victory. Photo by Budd.

The brilliant high-stepping trot of a top Hackney pony is shown in this photograph of Cadet Commander. Champion at the American Royal, the International Livestock Exposition, the National Horse Show in New York, and at many state fairs, Cadet Commander won 105 blues. Upon retirement to stud he became one of the best Hackney sires. He was owned by Virginia Penfield Seybold, Columbus, Ohio, and was trained and driven by R. C. ("Doc") Flanery, St. Charles, Ill. Unretouched photo by McClasky.

There are gig classes, tandem classes, and four-in-hand classes, where four matched horses in park harness are hitched to a park drag or where the four horses are hitched to a road coach, in which latter instance the horses are rigged with road harness and need not be matched in color but they should have substance and be able to go at a brisk trot.

Most shows include a class for a lady's single harness horse, mare, or gelding hitched to a phaeton. In all classes, ladies to drive, a horse's manners are paramount. All-round, animated action at a park pace is very important, but speed is not required. Horses must stand and back quietly and must not take a hard hold of the bit when in motion. The entries in such classes are to be judged on manners, conformation, quality, and performance. Appointments in these classes usually count 40 per cent.

Quality and refinement, balanced conformation, and ideal set to the underpinning are evident in this picture of Cadet Commander. This great show pony was sired by King of the Highlands and was out of an imported mare Penwortham Dream. Photo by McClasky

Eligibility of Entries to the Various Show Classes

A maiden class is open to horses which have not won a first ribbon at a recognized show in the particular performance division in which they are shown.

A novice class is open to horses which have not won three first ribbons at a recognized show in the particular performance division in which they are shown.

A limit class is open to horses which have not won six first ribbons at recognized shows in the particular performance division in which they are shown.

For horse show purposes, an amateur is one who rides or drives for pleasure and for the love of the sport and who draws no profit from the sport, either directly or indirectly.

8

The Standardbred

Harness race horses and harness racing in the United States date back to June 10, 1806 when official records were computed for the first time. Copies of the *New York Commercial Advertiser* of June 11, 1806 carried the following race account.

"*Fast trotting.*——Yesterday afternoon the Haerlem race course of *one mile's distance*, was trotted around in *two minutes* and *fifty-nine seconds*, by a horse called *Yankey*, from New-Haven, a rate of speed, it is believed, never before-excelled in this country, and fully equal to any thing recorded in the English Sporting Callenders."

Yankey's record was the first mile trotted under three minutes.

The contemporary spelling of Haerlem and Yankey was accepted as correct by newspapers and dictionaries of the time. The Harlem race track was located just south and east of the present intersection of 125th Street and Seventh Avenue in New York City.

It is also accepted that Yankey's record was made to saddle and not hitched to a sulky, as the trotters of the period raced with riders on their backs in the manner of running horses. It was not until about 40 years later that high, two-wheeled sulkies came into general use in harness races.

The grey-trotting mare, Lady Suffolk, was the first world champion to race regularly with a sulky in the 1840s. As a twelve-year-old she took a mark of 2:29½ at Hoboken, New Jersey, in 1845. This was the first mile trotted in harness under 2:30. Horses could trot faster with sulkies than with riders astride, but almost a century elapsed from the time of Yankey's record until the first two-minute mile was trotted. Lou Dillon, a five-year-old chestnut mare took a 2:00 mark at Readville, Massachusetts, in 1903. However, the bay-pacing stallion Star Pointer had set a record of 1:59¼ in 1897, also at Readville, Massachusetts.

The present world record for the trot is 1:54⅕, a mark taken

A large field of trotters getting off to a good start behind a mobile start-ing gate. Photo courtesy U.S. Trotting Assn.

Greyhound TT 1:55¼, World's Champion Trotter, shown with his trainer and driver S. F. ("Sep") Palin. The grey gelding set the record in a time trial at Lexington, Ky., on September 29, 1938. Greyhound won 71 of 82 starts in an incomparable career that ran from 1934 through 1940. He trotted a mile in 2:00 or faster 9 times in races and 15 times in exhibitions. Photo courtesy U.S. Trotting Assn.

in a time trial by Nevele Pride, a four-year-old stallion, on August 31, 1969 at Indianapolis, Indiana. He was driven by Stanley Dancer.

The current world record for the pace, 1:49$\frac{1}{5}$, was set in a time trial by Niatross, a three-year-old stallion, on October 1, 1980, at Lexington, Kentucky. He was driven by Clint Galbraith, his trainer and part owner.

ORIGIN OF THE STANDARDBRED

The Standardbred breed was developed during the 19th century in the northeastern United States. People in this region needed driving horses to provide rapid road transportation to light vehicles. In the Southern and Border States with a rural, argicultural economy and few improved roads, horsemen developed breeds of riding horses.

Standardbreds came from a blending of the blood of Thoroughbreds that had a good trotting gait, Norfolk Trotters or Hackneys, Morgans, and the so-called Canadian pacers.

During the formative period of the breed, four stallions were prominent. The most noteworthy of these early sires was Messenger, a grey Thoroughbred imported from England in 1788 at eight years of age. Messenger was a great-great-great-great-grandson of the Darley Arabian. He also traced to the Byerly Turk and the Godolphin Arabian. Therefore he was descended from all three of the principal foundation sires of the Thoroughbred breed. Although he was a Thoroughbred and got some good runners, Messenger, and many of his get, had a strong natural inclination to trot. He stood for service in the north where there were fewer Thoroughbreds than in Virginia, and was not always bred to the best of mares. He died on Long Island in 1808.

Messenger sired Mambrino. Mambrino sired Abdallah. Abdallah sired Hambletonian 10, a foal of 1849. Hambletonian 10 became the foundation sire of the Standardbred breed as we know it today. (Mambrino also was the sire of Mambrino Paymaster that sired Mambrino Chief, the founder of the "Chief" family of the American saddle-horse breed.)

A second important early day sire was Bellfounder. He was a Norfolk Trotter or Hackney imported to Boston in 1822 at seven years of age. Bellfounder is important mainly because he sired the dam of Hambletonian 10.

A third influential stallion was Justin Morgan, foaled in Massachusetts in 1789. He founded the Morgan breed. Many Morgan mares became the dams of trotters when mated with Hambeltonian stallions.

Greyhound TT 1:55¼, the World's Champion Trotter, hitched with Rosalind TT 1:56¾, the champion trotting mare. This speedy pair driven by S. F. ("Sep") Palin in a time trial at Indianapolis, Ind., in 1939 set the world record of 1:58¼ for a trotting team to pole. Photo by Horseman & Fair World.

In 1940, Greyhound set the world record for a trotter under saddle by trotting a mile in 2:01¾. He was ridden by Frances Dodge, later Mrs. Frederick Van Lennep, owner of Castleton Farm, Lexington, Ky. Photo by Horseman & Fair World.

After his retirement from racing, Greyhound was exhibited for a number of years at race meetings. This photo shows the World's Champion Trotter on the occasion of his last public appearance during the Grand Circuit meeting at Delaware, Ohio, September 17, 1947. He was driven by R. C. ("Doc") Flanery who drove him in most of his exhibitions. Greyhound's owner Col. E. J. Baker then sent him to live permanently at Mr. Flanery's farm at St. Charles, Ill., where an over-sized box stall adjoining a paneled lounge filled with racing memorabilia had been prepared to house him in style. Greyhound lived for almost 18 more years and died February 4, 1965, just one month short of his 33d birthday.
Photo courtesy R. C. Flanery.

A fourth stallion, Tom Hal, a pacer perhaps of Canadian ancestry but used in the stud in Tennessee, became the progenitor of a famous pacing family among Standardbreds. This horse was known as Kittrel's Tom Hal after his owner, a Major Kittrel of Taylorville, Tennessee. A mating of Kittrel's Tom Hal to a mare believed to be fully one-half Thoroughbred produced a stallion called Tom Hal Jr. He in turn sired the noted pacer, Little Brown Jug, after whom the present day classic pacing race for three-year-olds was named.

FOUNDATION SIRE

Hambletonian 10 is considered to be the foundation sire of the

The Standardbred as a road horse. Leader of the Band by Long Key was retired from racing to a successful career as a competitor in roadster classes at horse shows. He was owned and driven by R. C. ("Doc") Flanery, St. Charles, Ill. Photo by McClasky.

Standardbred breed of horses. He was sired by Abdallah, by Mambrino, by imported Messenger. His dam was the Charles Kent mare, a daughter of imported Bellfounder. His second dam was One Eye a double granddaughter of imported Messenger. Hambletonian 10 was foaled May 5, 1949, in Orange County, New York, the property of Jonas Seeley.

Mr. Seeley sold Hambletonian 10 as a suckling colt along with his dam, then 17 year old and crippled, to William Rysdyk, the Seeleys' hired man, for $125.

Hambletonian 10 was a bay horse with both hind ankles white. He matured to a height of 15.1¼ and stood 2 inches higher at his hips. He weighed in stud condition from 1250 to 1300 pounds.

As a three-year-old, Hambletonian 10 was trained for a few weeks. He went in 2:48. Thereafter he was used in the stud. His service fee at first was only $25. However, as he got good horses from ordinary mares, owners of higher class mares began to patronize him, and the fee was gradually increased until it reached $500 in 1866 and remained at this level for the rest of his life.

Hambletonian 10 was in the stud for 24 seasons, 1851 to 1875.

(He was not bred to any mares in 1868.) During this time he bred 1,908 mares and got 1,331 foals (69 per cent). His stud career stands as the great classical example of a stallion being widely and heavily used in the days before artificial breeding was practiced. William Rysdyk, the former hired man, presumably finding it easier to collect stallion service fees than to work hard, mated his stallion in 1862 to 158 mares, in 1863 to 150, in 1864 to 217, in 1865 to 193 mares. After 1867 Hambletonian 10, partly from necessity, was limited to about 30 mares per year at a $500 fee. He must have been an extremely healthy, sound, virile, potent stallion to remain so highly fertile over so many years of heavy breeding service. He was truly the father of the breed.

Hambletonian 10 sired 40 trotters that took records of 2:30 or faster. Since 1867 the trotting champion has been a direct descendant except for the period 1894 to 1900. (During that hiatus the champion was Alix 2:03¾, a mare with three close crosses to Hambletonian 10) Of his sons, 150 became the sires of horses of standard speed, and 80 of his daughters were successful dams.

The classic trotting race for three-year-olds, the Hambletonian Stake, was begun in 1926. Each winner has traced to Hambletonian 10 in the direct male line.

Worthy Forbes and Worthy Matron, a perfectly matched pair of black Standardbred roadsters owned and shown by R. C. ("Doc") Flanery, St. Charles, Ill. Photo by Haas, courtesy R. C. Flanery.

Star's Pride, 3, 1:57⅕, leading trotting sire of modern times. He raced 4 years and won 36 of 77 starts and $140,969. Star's Pride headed the stud at the Hanover Shoe Farm, Hanover, Pa. He sired 41 trotters and 7 pacers with records of 2:00 or faster and 8 winners of the Hambletonian Stake. He died in 1977, aged 30. Photo courtesy U.S. Trotting Assn.

DEVELOPMENT OF THE BREED

One hundred years ago Standardbreds were widely used as driving horses. Many Standardbred stallions were mated to draft mares to produce active, light-weight farm work horses. And, of course, Standardbreds with speed have always been raced on the harness tracks. This testing in competition has been the chief element in the development and improvement of the breed.

Compared to Thoroughbreds, there is much more opportunity for Standardbred fillies and mares to be raced and thus be proved as to speed. Standardbred records are one-mile records, whereas Thoroughbreds run at many distances and with various weight handicaps. The Standardbred breeder, therefore, has a definite record of performance for both stallions and mares upon which to base his judgment when determining what matings to make.

Niatross, the World Champion Harness horse. He set his record by pacing a mile in 1:49⅕ in a time trial at Lexington, Ky., on October 1, 1980. He was driven by his trainer and part-owner, Clint Galbraith. Syndicated and retired after racing for two years and winning 38 of his 40 starts and $2,019,212, Niatross entered stud at Castleton Farm, Lexington, Ky., in 1981. Photo courtesy U.S. Trotting Assn.

Trotters went faster when high-wheeled sulkies replaced jockeys in the 1840s. The speed increased again when the bicycle-wheel sulky replaced the high-wheeled model around 1892. Track surfaces are faster today and mobile starting gates are used. But above and beyond the improvement wrought by various mechanical means, there has been much more progress made in increasing the speed of the Standardbred horse and the certainty of reproducing that speed than there has been in the Thoroughbred world.

THE BREEDERS' GOAL

Most Standardbred breeders want their young trotters and pacers to have the qualities listed below.
1. Early natural speed
2. Early physical development
3. Gameness, courage, competitive spirit, the desire to win
4. Mental balance and determination to stick to their gait
5. Soundness

In order to get these qualities in their stock, breeders try to patronize stallions that had the same qualities and were fast race horses themselves. Breeders also look for purity of gait in the stal-

Volomite, 3, 2:03¼, sire of 33 horses with 2:00 records, was for many years in stud at the Walnut Hall Farm, Donerail, Ky. Photo courtesy U.S. Trotting Assn.

lion. They like a bold, round, rapid stride in front and a frictionless, powerful, propelling power behind. And they seek a horse with underpinning of such conformation that at all degrees of speed there is proper clearance and no chance for interference.

REGISTRATION

In the United States, all Standardbreds, both trotters and pacers, are registered through the facilities of the United States Trotting Association. To be eligible to race, all horses must be registered either Standard or Non-Standard. They can be registered Standard if purebred or if they have sufficient speed plus a sufficient basis of Standard breeding. (A standard record is a time of 2:20 or faster for two-year-olds; 2:15 or faster for three-year-olds.) A Non-Standard horse is a trotter or pacer whose bloodlines are not clear or whose proof of ancestry has been lost.

For many years Ohio has ranked as the leading state in the registration of Standardbreds. Other important breeding states are New York, Illinois, Pennsylvania, Indiana, Michigan, and Kentucky. The U.S.T.A. registered 14,691 horses in 1980.

The United States Trotting Association, in addition to maintaining the stud book registrations, acts as the governing body of the sport of harness racing. Racing drivers and race officials such as judges and starters are licensed by the association. District boards of the association serve as hearing panels for cases involving any infractions of the rules of racing. The U.S.T.A. also regulates track membership and maintains an active promotional department.

SOME PROMINENT MODERN DAY BREEDERS

Standardbreds are produced all over America by thousands of breeders. The few discussed briefly in the following paragraphs have in their own ways made significant contributions to the development and improvement of this distinctive American breed of light harness horses.

Hanover Shoe Farm. The Hanover Shoe Farm, located at Hanover, Pennsylvania, is the largest Standardbred breeding establishment in the world. It is probably the most successful large scale stud in the history of the horse business anywhere in the world. Headed for many years by the late Lawrence B. Sheppard, a former president of the U.S.T.A., the Hanover Shoe Farm, for over five decades, has continued to produce Standardbreds that developed first into fast race horses and later into important sires and brood mares.

Standardbred brood mares and foals on pasture at the Castleton Farm, Lexington, Ky. Photo by the author.

The scope of the farm operations can be seen in the report of the sale of Hanover yearlings at the Standardbred Horse Sale conducted at Harrisburg, Pennsylvania, in the fall of 1979. The Hanover Shoe Farm sold 180 yearlings for $6,256,400, or for an average price of $34,758.

However, the Hanover business is not simply large. It is a high quality stud. The large band of brood mares includes a great many that not only were powerful race mares in their day but also are representatives of successful blood lines.

About 20 stallions stand for service at Hanover. The farm had a one-third interest in the great sire Adios for several years before his death in 1965. Other important sires at the farm have included Tar Heel, Albatross, Best of All, Star's Pride, Hickory Smoke, and Steady Star.

Walnut Hall Farm. For over 70 years Walnut Hall Farm, at Donerail, Kentucky has exerted a tremendous influence on the Standardbred breed. The farm has always used excellent stallions, and has crossed them with mares of the great brood-mare families. As a result, every major Standardbred breeder in this country has used at least one stallion of Walnut Hall ancestry, and has valued brood mares of Walnut Hall blood lines.

Good Time, p, 3, TT 1:57⅘, sire of 93 horses with 2:00 records, shown during his racing days when he was trained and driven by Frank Ervin. Good Time was sired by Hal Dale and was out of On Time by Volomite. Good Time was in stud at Castleton Farm, Lexington, Ky. He died in 1977, aged 31. Photo courtesy U.S. Trotting Assn.

The noted stallion Volomite, 3, 2:03¼ was bred by Walnut Hall and was foaled there in 1926. He was sired by Peter Volo, 4, 2:02 and was out of Cita Frisco by San Francisco 2:07¾. Volomite was sold as a yearling for $5,000. After his racing career he was purchased at an auction for $13,500 by Walnut Hall, and was returned to the farm for stud duty. He entered the stud in 1930, and was used through the 1950 season when a hip trouble stopped his service career. His get proved to be brilliant race horses. His service fee rose from $100 to $5,000 with such constant over-subscription that his book was filled two years in advance. Volomite sired 33 horses with marks of 2:00 or faster, 22 pacers and 11 trotters. He sired four winners of the Hambletonian Stake. Volomite had over 50 sons in the stud and his daughters' production of fast race horses made him the leading brood-mare sire of his era. In 1966, 321 horses, all the produce of the daughters of Volomite, won more dashes (1,149) and more money ($1,755,062) than the offspring produced by the daughters of any other sire.

The former Champion Harness Horse, Bret Hanover, p, 4, TT 1:53⅗ shown with his trainer and driver Frank Ervin. Bret Hanover entered stud at Castleton Farm, Lexington, Ky., in the spring of 1967. Photo courtesy U.S. Trotting Assn.

Gene Abbe, p, TT 2:00⅖, for many years premier sire at Pickwick Farms, Bucyrus, Ohio. He sired 38 horses with 2:00 records. He died in 1978, aged 34. Photo courtesy U.S. Trotting Assn.

Volomite died January 6, 1954 at 28 years of age. He was buried at Walnut Hall near his sire and other famous stallions. Volomite's service fees and the sales of his yearlings at public auction brought Walnut Hall over $1,500,000.

Castleton Farm. The Standardbreds at Castleton Farm, Lexington, Kentucky, comprise a substantial part of the wide-ranging horse interests of Mr. Frederick Van Lennep. Separate divisions of the stud are maintained at Trenton, Florida, Goshen, N.Y., and Wilmington, Ohio. A large racing stable represents Castleton at the major harness race meetings.

The world champion harness horse, Bret Hanover, p, 4,

Widower Creed, p, 1:56¼, one of the world's fastest pacing stallions, displayed extreme speed race after race, winning 13 races in 2:00 or faster with three of them on half-mile tracks. He was in stud at the Bonnie Brae Farms, Wellington, Ohio. Photo courtesy U.S. Trotting Assn.

Delmonica Hanover, 1:59⅖, one of the greatest trotting mares in history. In five seasons she won 52 of 124 starts, including the Roosevelt International in 1973 and 1974 and the Prix d'Amèrique in France in 1974, and a total of $843,823. She was bred by the Hanover Shoe Farms and sold as a yearling for $5,000 to Delvin Miller, her trainer and driver. She was sired by Speedy Count, 3, 1:58⅘, and out of Delicious, 3, 2:04 by Kimberly Kid, 4, 1:59. Photo courtesy U.S. Trotting Assn.

TT1:53⅗, entered the stud at Castleton in the spring of 1967. A $2,000,000 transaction brought this great pacer to the farm following his retirement from racing.

Bret Hanover, sired by Adios and out of Brenna Hanover by Tar Heel, was bred by the Hanover Shoe Farm and foaled in 1962. Sold for $50,000 as a yearling, he was owned during his racing career by Richard Downing of Shaker Heights, Ohio, and was trained and driven by Frank Ervin. He was named Harness Horse of the Year in 1964, 1965, and 1966. During those three years Bret Hanover made 68 starts. He won 62 of them, was 5 times second, and once third. He paced a mile in 2:00 or faster on 31 occasions. This beat the record of 30 set by Dan Patch over 50 years before. In addition to setting the world's speed record, Bret Hanover won a total of $922,616, a money-winning record for the sport until 1968.

Castleton Farm stands about 16 stallions in Kentucky and 3 stallions at their Florida division. The noted race horse Good Time, p, 1:57⅘ has been a successful sire at the Kentucky farm. Through 1980 he had sired 93 pacers that took records of 2:00 or faster. Other fast stallions at Castleton have included Florican, 1:57⅖; Worthy Boy, 3, 2:02¼; Speedy Scot, 3, 1:56⅘; Bret Hanover, p, 4, TT 1:53⅗; Race Time, p, 3, 1:57; and Niatross, p, 3, TT 1:49⅕.

Castleton yearlings sold at Tattersall's in the fall of 1966 brought a record average of $11,125. The total for the 77 yearlings from the farm was $856,700.

Pickwick Farms. Pickwick Farms, owned by Walter R. Michael of Bucyrus, Ohio, was the home of Gene Abbe, p, TT2:00⅗, probably the most prolific Standardbred stallion in modern history. In 1968, 354 sons and daughters of Gene Abbe went to the races. They won $1,739,580. This was the seventh successive year that the get of Gene Abbe won over one million dollars. Of the 354 starters, 268 won a total of 1,041 dashes. This was more winners and more dashes won than were accounted for by the get of any other stallion.

Bonnie Brae Farms. Unlike the breeding establishments previously discussed, the operation of the Bonnie Brae Farms at Wellington, Ohio was not backed by fortunes made in oil or motor cars or other large industrial enterprises. This stud stands as a splendid example of how much can be accomplished in the horse business by highly competent, knowledgeable horsemen pursuing a goal of improving their stock over two generations in the life of a hardworking family.

The late William Murray was an expert horseman. As a young man he trained and drove Standardbreds. He accompanied some horses sold for export to Russia and spent a few years in that country as a race horse driver around the turn of the century. Upon

The Widower, p, 3, TT 1:59½, sire of 8 horses in 2:00 and 71 in 2:05, for many years was the premier stallion at the Bonnie Brae Farms, Wellington, Ohio. Photo courtesy William B. Murray.

his return to America he started farming a relatively small family-sized general farm. He did his farm work with Percherons, but he always kept a few Standardbreds. These were trained on a half-mile track at the farm and were raced occasionally at some county fairs in Ohio.

His son, William B. Murray, grew up with a great love for horses, and learned much from his father's experience and precepts. Following his graduation from the Ohio State University, William B. Murray developed the band of Percherons at Bonnie Brae. During the 1930s he campaigned one of the most successful show strings of draft horses on the Middle West state fair show circuit. He sold champion Percherons at high prices during the Depression years.

When the Murrays saw the draft horse business fading as American agriculture became increasingly mechanized, they decided to concentrate their horse interests in Standardbreds. One of the last Percherons they sold was a stallion exported to South Africa. William B. Murray trucked the horse to New York to be put aboard ship. On his return trip to Ohio he purchased two Standardbred mares with good breeding and respectable race records. These mares cost less than $200 each. The Murrays bred them to Billy Direct, p, TT1:55, then the world champion harness horse that was standing for service in Ohio.

Adios, one of the greatest sires of extreme speed in the history of Standardbred horses. He sired 79 horses with records of 2:00 or faster. Photo courtesy of U.S. Trotting Assn.

From such comparatively humble beginnings the Bonnie Brae Farms developed. The growth of their breeding operations paralleled that of harness racing following World War II. In 1949 the Murrays purchased the stallion The Widower, p, 3, TT1:59½. Three or four stallions have usually been in service at the farm. The brood-mare band is small, but many outside mares are sent to the stallions. Consequently, in most years over 150 mares are bred at Bonnie Brae and a like number of foals are born there.

The Murrays, father and son, not only have been good judges of horses but also have been keen students of blood lines. Thus they have selected good breeding stock and have made advantageous matings. The Murrays have been good feeders. Their horses have always shown bloom. The fine farming practices at Bonnie Brae contribute to the well-being of the stock. The top prize for clover hay at the Ohio State Fair has gone on more than one occasion to hay produced at Bonnie Brae Farms. The Murray family have always excelled in caring for horses. And for years they have sold their Standardbred yearlings profitably. Thus, all aspects

Tar Heel, p, 4, TT 1:57. This black Standardbred stallion was two-year-old pacer of 1950 and three-year-old pacer of 1951. He was sired by Billy Direct, p, 4, TT 1:55, out of Leta Long by Volomite. In stud at the Hanover Shoe Farms, Tar Heel sired 156 horses with 2:00 records and winners of over $26,000,000. Photo courtesy U.S. Trotting Assn.

of the business—selecting, breeding, feeding, managing, and selling —have been well handled, and the Bonnie Brae Farms have a sound, established reputation in the Standardbred world.

For 18 years the good pacing sire The Widower, p, 3, TT1:59½ headed the stud. This horse sired 8 horses that took records of 2:00 or faster and 71 in 2:05. After his death in 1967 at 32 years of age, the main stud horse was Widower Creed, a son of Jimmy Creed from Bertha Dale by The Widower. During his racing career Widower Creed made the following records, all in pacing races: at 4, 1:58⅗; at 5, 1:57⅕; at 7, 1:56⅘. Also at 7 years he took a mark of 1:59⅘ in winning a race on a half-mile track. He won 13 races in 2:00 or faster.

William B. Murray is a director of the United States Trotting Association. In the fall of 1979, he leased Bonnie Brae to another

Nevele Pride, 4, TT 1:54⅘, successor to Greyhound as World Champion Trotter. Trained and driven by Stanley Dancer, Nevele Pride was named Harness Horse of the Year in 1967-68-69. As a 3-year-old he won the Hambletonian Stake, Kentucky Futurity, Yonkers Trot, the Dexter Cup, and the Colonial. In his career he had 57 wins, 4 seconds, and 3 thirds from 67 starts, and won $873,238. He was sired by Star's Pride and was out of Thankful by Hoot Mon. He was syndicated and stood for service at the Stoner Creek Stud, Paris, Ky. Photo courtesy U.S. Trotting Assn.

Standardbred breeder, Thurman Downing of Cleveland, Ohio, but continued to keep a small band of his own brood mares on the farm.

ADIOS, AN INFLUENTIAL SIRE

During his lifetime, the Standardbred stallion Adios was the most influential sire of any breed of livestock in America. No other sire so dominated his breed by consistently siring offspring that could truly excel at their job. Adios had the ability to sire early and at extreme speed. The influence of his sons and daughters in the stud will go on for many years.

Adios was foaled January 3, 1940, at the Two Gaits Farm of his breeder, Leo C. McNamara, at Carmel, Indiana.

Adios was sold as a yearling for $2,000 to Thomas Thomas of Cleveland. He was trained and driven by Rupe Parker at two and three. After Mr. Parker's death, the noted driver Frank Ervin took over the training chores and drove Adios during the racing seasons of 1944-45-46.

Altogether Adios made 87 heat starts. He won 43, was 30 times second, and 10 times third. Thus he was only four times back of third. He won a total of $33,329.10 during those years of comparatively low purses.

Early in 1946 Adios was sold to L. K. Shapiro and Harry Warner of California. He entered the stud in California in 1947 and was bred to the small band of mares assembled by his owners. Five Adios foals were born in 1948, six in 1949.

Adios was sold again in the dispersal of his owners's breeding stock on October 7, 1948 at Lexington, Kentucky. He was purchased for $21,000 by Delvin Miller, a leading trainer and driver who maintains a breeding farm at Meadow Lands, Pennsylvania. Mated to Mr. Miller's mares and other good mares available in the East, Adios soon proved to be an exceptional sire. The crop of foals born in 1951 really established his reputation. The foals included two 2:00 two-year-olds, Adios Boy and Adios Betty, and also Adios Harry, for a time world champion pacer.

In August, 1955 Delvin Miller sold Adios to the Hanover Shoe Farm for $500,000. Mr. Lawrence B. Sheppard of Hanover later re-sold one-third interests in the stallion to Delvin Miller and to Max Hempt. From that time on a number of other good sires have been syndicated.

Seventy-nine sons and daughters of Adios took records of 2:00 or faster. All but one were pacers. This was almost twice the number of 2:00 horses sired by any other contemporary stallion. (During the 1970s several sires surpassed the record set by Adios.) Adios sired three successive world champions: Adios Harry 1:55, Adios Butler 1:54¾, and Bret Hanover 1:53¾.

Through 1966 Adios had sired more than half of the winners of the Cane Futurity, more than half the winners of the Messenger Stake, and more than half the winners of the past 13 Little Brown Jug Stake. Thus his colts had dominated the Triple Crown classics for three-year-old pacers.

Adios was the first harness horse stallion to sire the winners of $1,000,000 in a season (1956) and he did it for the next 10 years in succession.

At the time of his death, his get had won $14,567,130. Not only was this figure a record for a harness horse sire, but also it exceeded the total earnings credited to the get of any Thoroughbred stallion.

Meadow Skipper, p, 3, 1:55⅕, leading sire of speed in the Standardbred breed. He was sired by Dale Frost, p, 1:58 and out of Countess Vivian, p, 3, 1:59 by King's Counsel, p, 1:58. After his racing career Meadow Skipper was syndicated and in service at the Stoner Creek Stud, Paris, Ky. He sired over 250 horses with 2:00 records. Action Photo courtesy U.S. Trotting Assn.; conformation photo courtesy Horseman & Fair World.

STANDARD SIRE FAMILIES

(Foaling dates and, in some cases, the breeding farm at which the stallion served are given in parentheses.)

Peter the Great Family (basically a trotting family with a pacing branch)

Hambletonian 10 (1849)
  Happy Medium (1863)
    Pilot Medium (1879)
      Peter the Great (1895)
        Peter Volo (1911)
          Volomite (1926, Walnut Hall)
            Worthy Boy (1940, Castleton)
              Star's Pride (1947, Hanover)
                Ayres (1961, Hanover)
                Nevele Pride (1965, Stoner Creek)
                Super Bowl (1969, Hanover)
            Sampson Hanover
              Sampson Direct (1957, Walnut Hall)
            Victory Song (1943, Castleton)
              Noble Victory (1962)
          Poplar Byrd (1944)
            Bye Bye Byrd (1955)
        Peter Scott (1909)
          Scotland (1925, Walnut Hall)
            Spencer Scott (1937)
              Rodney (1944, Walnut Hall)
                Speedster (1954, Castleton)
                  Speedy Scot (1960, Castleton)
                  Speedy Count (1961, Hanover)
          Hoot Mon (1944, Hanover)

Axworthy Family (basically a trotting family with a pacing branch)

Hambletonian 10 (1849)
  George Wilkes (1856)
    William L. (1882)
      Axtell (1886)
        Axworthy (1892)
          Guy Axworthy (1902)
            Truax (1921)
              Calumet Chuck (1929)
                Nibble Hanover (1936)
                  Knight Dream (1945, Hanover)
                Titan Hanover (1942)
                  Hickory Smoke (1954, Hanover)
            Guy McKinney (1923)
              Spud Hanover (1936)
                Florican (1947, Castleton)
                  Songflori (1972, Hanover)

Direct Family (a pacing family)

Hambletonian 10 (1849)
  Dictator (1863)
    Director (1877)
      Direct (1885)
        Walter Direct (1900)
          Napoleon Direct (1909)
            Billy Direct (1934)
              Tar Heel (1948, Hanover)
                Steady Beau
                  Steady Star (1967, Hanover)

The Abbe Family (a pacing family)

Hambletonian 10 (1849)
  Electioneer (1866)
    Chimes (1884)
      The Abbe (1903)
        Abbedale (1917)
          Hal Dale (1926)
            Adios (1940, Meadowlands)
              Bret Hanover (1962, Castleton)
            Good Time (1946, Castleton)
              Best of All (1964, Hanover)
              Race Time (1964, Castleton)
              Columbia George (1967, Hanover)
            Dale Frost (1951)
              Meadow Skipper (1960, Stoner Creek)
                Most Happy Fella (1967, Blue Chip)
                Albatross (1968, Hanover)
                  Niatross (1977)
        Bert Abbe (1922)
          Gene Abbe (1944, Pickwick)

A total of 365 yearlings sired by Adios were sold at auction. They brought $6,756,800, an average of $18,512.

Adios died June 22, 1965, at 25 years of age at Delvin Miller's Meadowlands Farm. His last foals were born in 1966.

MEADOW SKIPPER, SIRE OF EXTREME SPEED

During the 1970s there was an unparalleled rapid increase in the number of Standardbred horses taking 2:00 records. Many horses even beat 1:55. The stallion most responsible for the rewriting of the record books was the great pacing sire Meadow Skipper, p, 3, 1:55$\frac{1}{5}$. He was a syndicated stallion in service at the Stoner Creed Stud owned by Norman S. Woolworth and David R. Johnston at Paris, Kentucky.

A foal of 1960, Meadow Skipper was sired by Dale Frost, p, 1:58 and was out of Countess Vivian, p, 3, 1:59 by King's Counsel, p, 1:58. He was bred by Christy S. Hayes of Columbus, Ohio. Sold to Hugh Grant, he was campaigned at first by Delvin Miller. Later the property of Clearview Stables, Meadow Skipper was handled by Earle Avery until retired to stud duty at Stoner Creek.

Meadow Skipper was a world's or season's champion pacer every year he raced. At age 2 he had 15 wins and a record of 1:59$\frac{4}{5}$. In 1963 he became the fastest 3-year-old with a mark of 1:55$\frac{1}{5}$, won the Cane Futurity, and set two track records. At 4 he won the $50,000 American Pacing Classic. He paced 10 winning miles in 2:00 or faster.

A fast, courageous race horse himself, and the product of a fast sire and dam, Meadow Skipper soon became even more noted as a sire. He seemed to cross well with mares of almost any family. His sons and daughters when put into training proved to be extremely speedy. The number taking 2:00 records soon passed the get of Adios. By mid-1981 Meadow Skipper had sired 251 performers with records of 2:00 or faster. Along with two of his sons, Albatross, p, 4, 1:54$\frac{3}{5}$F and Most Happy Fella, p, 3, TT 1:55, Meadow Skipper made up a trio of stallions that were the leading sires of the decade 1970–1980. Albatross, in turn, sired the world champion harness horse Niatross, p, 3, TT 1:49$\frac{1}{5}$.

HARNESS RACING IN THE UNITED STATES

Harness racing for many years was a country fair sport in America. The fair circuits still make up the major share of the meetings conducted in the sport. Harness racing is a popular rural attraction and has its roots in the rural areas. The fair circuits of race meetings attract the small stable owner and the man who loves to drive his horse himself. Really the life blood of the sport of harness racing is found in the fair meetings, more than 360 of which are sponsored by county fair boards all over the country. These fair meetings offer over 1,000 days of racing and more than 5,400 races.

The Pari-Mutuel Tracks. Harness racing on the modern pari-mutuel basis was first conducted at Roosevelt Raceway, Westbury, Long Island, in 1940. The track was lighted, racing was at night, and pari-mutuel betting was part of the attraction. Since that time major raceways have been established near practically every large city in the north from Portland, Maine to Boston, New York, Philadelphia, Washington, Baltimore, Albany, Rochester, Saratoga, Buffalo, Pittsburgh, Cleveland, Columbus, Dayton, Cincinnati, Lexington, Toledo, Detroit, Chicago, San Francisco, and Los Angeles.

About 90 large pari-mutuel meetings are now held each year in the United States.

The mobile starting gate was introduced at Roosevelt Raceway in 1946. Its widespread adoption even at small fairs made harness racing more attractive to the racing public.

Attendance at the pari-mutuel tracks increased rapidly, the tracks prospered, and purses became larger. The growth in harness horse breeding and racing can be seen in the following figures compiled by the U.S.T.A. In 1956, 4,660 horses were registered and 14,622 horses raced in harness in America. In 1980, 14,691 Standardbreds were registered and 49,723 raced. Purses increased from $21,862,611 in 1956 to $233,421,503 in 1980.

The Grand Circuit. The Grand Circuit is regarded as the "big league" of harness racing. Founded in 1873 with 4 member tracks for the purpose of setting up a definite itinerary for harness horse owners, the organization has grown to a large circuit that attracts the best trotters and pacers in training. In 1981 the Grand Circuit had 19 member tracks. The season opened in March at Pompano Park, Pompano Beach, Florida; it closed in December, also at Pompano Park.

Trotting's Triple Crown. The most important race for three-year-old trotters is the Hambletonian Stake, raced in recent years at DuQuoin, Illinois during the Grand Circuit meeting at the DuQuoin State Fair. The Hambletonian, first conducted in 1926, is raced on the two-in-three heat plan at the distance of one mile.

The oldest of the Triple Crown races is the Kentucky Futurity,

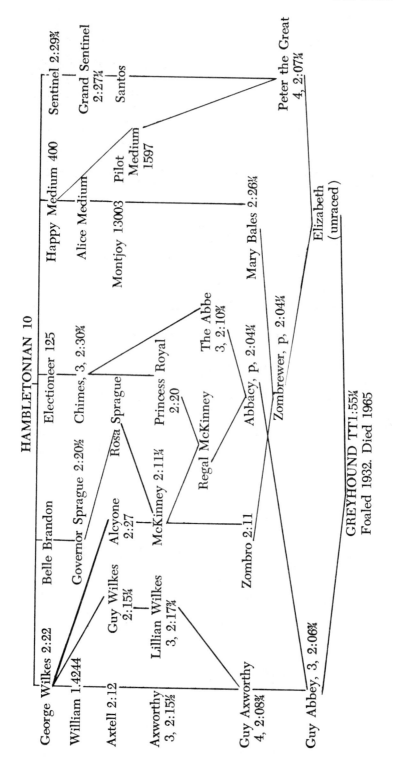

HAMBLETONIAN 10

George Wilkes 2:22
William 1.4244
Axtell 2:12
Axworthy 3, 2:15½
Guy Axworthy 4, 2:08¾
Guy Abbey, 3, 2:06¾

Belle Brandon
Guy Wilkes 2:15¾
Lillian Wilkes 3, 2:17½

Electioneer 125
Governor Sprague 2:20½
Alcyone 2:27
McKinney 2:11¼
Zombro 2:11

Chimes, 3, 2:30¾
Rosa Sprague
Princess Royal 2:20
Regal McKinney
Abbacy, p, 2:04¼

Happy Medium 400
Alice Medium
Montjoy 13003
The Abbe 3, 2:10¼
Zombrewer, p, 2:04¼
Mary Bales 2:26¾
Elizabeth (unraced)

Sentinel 2:29¾
Grand Sentinel 2:27¾
Santos
Pilot Medium 1597
Peter the Great 4, 2:07¾

GREYHOUND TT1:55¼
Foaled 1932. Died 1965

This chart shows the lines through which GREYHOUND traced to HAMBLETONIAN 10, the Foundation Sire of the Standardbred breed.

PEDIGREE OF THE STANDARDBRED STALLION
MEADOW SKIPPER, *the leading sire of modern times*
p, 3, 1:55⅕

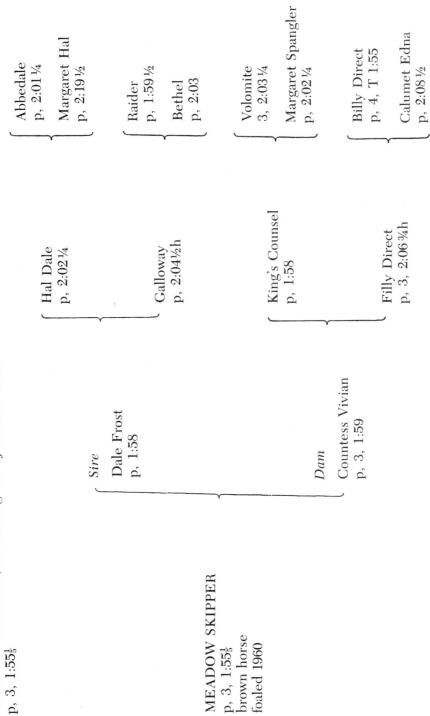

MEADOW SKIPPER
p, 3, 1:55⅕
brown horse
foaled 1960

Sire
Dale Frost
p, 1:58

Hal Dale
p, 2:02¼

Abbedale
p, 2:01¼

Margaret Hal
p, 2:19½

Galloway
p, 2:04½h

Raider
p, 1:59½

Bethel
p, 2:03

Dam
Countess Vivian
p, 3, 1:59

King's Counsel
p, 1:58

Volomite
3, 2:03¼

Margaret Spangler
p, 2:02¼

Filly Direct
p, 3, 2:06¾h

Billy Direct
p, 4, T 1:55

Calumet Edna
p, 2:08½

started in 1893, and for many years a feature of the Lexington Trots meeting of the Grand Circuit each fall.

The newest of the three big races for three-year-old trotters is the Yonkers Futurity, first held in 1955. It is raced on the half-mile Yonkers Raceway, Yonkers, New York, as a single dash at a mile and one-sixteenth.

Pacing's Triple Crown. The first major purse for three-year-old pacers was the Little Brown Jug, established in 1946. It is held on the heat plan at the half-mile track at Delaware, Ohio during the Grand Circuit meeting each fall at the Delaware County Fair.

The William H. Cane Futurity (1955) and the Messenger Stake (1956) comprise the rest of the pacing Triple Crown. Both are conducted as single dashes at a mile, the Cane over the half-mile track at Yonkers, the Messenger over the half-mile track at Roosevelt Raceway, Old Westbury, Long Island.

Some Harness Racing Terms. Every sport has its own terminology. Some common harness racing expressions are listed below.

Trot. Diagonal two-beat gait.

Pace. Lateral two-beat gait.

Free-legged pacer. A pacer that races without hopples.

Record. The fastest time made by a horse in a heat or a dash that he wins, or in a performance against time.

Winner. The horse whose nose reaches the wire first. If there is a dead heat for first, both horses are considered winners.

Dash. A race decided in a single trial.

Heat. A single trial in a race that will be decided by winning two or more trials.

Blowout. A workout prior to the race, usually the day before.

Jogging. A slow warm up or exercise for several miles with the horse going the "wrong way" of the track.

Scoring. Preliminary warming up of horses before the start. The horses are turned near the starting point and hustled away as if in a race.

Breaking. A horse leaving his gait and "breaking" into a gallop. A trotter or pacer must remain on his gait in a race. If he makes a break, the driver must immediately pull him back to his gait.

Parked out. Lapped on horses at the pole or rail so there is no chance to get in. A horse parked out has farther to go and often tires and falls back unless he is far superior to other horses in the race.

Rating. Maintaining an even rate of speed and timing the

On October 9, 1889, at Terre Haute, Indiana, the famous Axtell, hitched to a high-wheeled sulky, trotted a mile in 2:12, lowering the world's record for three-year-old trotters. On the evening of that day a syndicate of breeders bought Axtell from his owner, Mr. Charles Williams, for $105,000, a record price up to that time for a trotter or a pacer. Currier & Ives.

In a time trial at Lexington, Kentucky, on September 29, 1938, the six-year-old gelding named Greyhound trotted the mile in 1:55¼—a new world record for the distance. This record lasted for 31 years.

finishing rush. Racing drivers carry stop watches, and rate their horses to a fraction of a second. Unlike running horses which often run the first quarter fastest and slow up in each succeeding quarter, trotters and pacers usually negotiate the final quarter fastest.

9

The Breeds of Saddle Horses and Ponies

Many years ago the officials of the American Saddle Horse Breeders Association agreed upon the following list of saddle horse qualifications. In preparing this list, these gentlemen of the early days not only aimed to include the most important qualifications of a saddle horse, but also attempted to list these qualifications in the order of their importance as follows:

1. Sure-footedness
2. A kind disposition coupled with a good mouth
3. Courage and ambition
4. Conformation of a weight carrier
5. Gaits and manners

The characteristics in this list really are basic requirements for all of the breeds discussed in this chapter and for any horse of any background that is used under saddle.

THE ARABIAN

The Arabian horse apparently has existed as a distinct type in the deserts of Arabia since long before the Christian era. As such it is our oldest breed. Knowledge of Arabian blood lines was passed from generation to generation by word of mouth. It was not recorded. Thus the stud books for a number of our other breeds of horses antedate those established for Arabian horses in various countries.

The Bedouin tribes became very skillful horsemen. They depended on their horses in caring for and protecting their stock as they moved from oasis to oasis. They used their horses in the fre-

quent forays and raids of inter-tribal warfare. The best horses sup-
posedly were those bred by the tribes in the inner desert. These
were rarely sold. Other Arabian horses were sold into Egypt, Spain,
Poland, and England. In all of these countries there is a long tradi-
tion of Arabian breeding. In England, of course, Arabian blood was
instrumental in the development of the Thoroughbred and the
Norfolk Trotter or Hackney.

Abbas Pasha I who ruled Egypt from 1848 to 1854 assembled
a large stud of the classic type of Arabians from the inner desert.
The excellence of his horses became widely known, and they brought
high prices at the dispersal sale held in 1860, six years after his
death. Ali Pasha Sherif bought many of the best of these horses
and continued the breeding program until his death in 1897. At
the sale which followed, some of the good horses went to Lady
Anne Blunt.

Lady Anne Blunt and her husband, Wilfrid Scawen Blunt,
the poet, had made several journeys to Egypt and to the deserts
from 1879 to 1881. They bought some horses from Ali Pasha Sherif
and some from the desert, and devoted their lives to breeding
classic Arabians at their English estate Crabbet Park in Sussex and
at their Sheykh Obeyd Stud near Cairo. Lady Anne Blunt, through
her mother, was a granddaughter of the poet George Gordon, Lord
Byron.

The Blunt's daughter succeeded her mother as 16th Baroness
Wentworth in 1917 and inherited Crabbet Park. She continued the
Arabian stud for the next 40 years until her death at 84 on August 8,
1957. Crabbet Park was the source of a large percentage of the best
Arabians imported over the years into the United States. Lady
Wentworth was regarded as the leading authority on Arabian
breeding during her lifetime, and her books on the subject are
classics of their type.

Of the many stallions used at the Crabbet Park Stud, one of
the most noted was Skowronek. This stallion had been bred at one
of the famous old Polish breeding farms, the Antoniny Stud of
Count Joseph Potocki. Skowronek was sired by Ibrahim, a horse
bred in the desert, that was imported to Poland by Count Potocki
in 1907. Skowronek was out of Jaskoulka, the leading mare of the
Antoniny Stud. (In Polish Jaskoulka means Swallow, Skowronek
means Lark.) Skowronek was purchased by an American, Walter
Winans, and imported into England in 1913. He was owned briefly
by H. V. M. Clark, then passed into Lady Wentworth's possession.
He stood at Crabbet Park the rest of his life. Mated to his own
daughter, °Rifala, Skowronek got the stallion °Raffles. Both °Raffles,
foaled in 1926, and his dam were imported to the Selby Arabian
Stud at Portsmouth, Ohio. In the 1930s and 1940s Mr. Roger Selby's

Serafix, a champion Arabian stallion and consistent sire of high-quality Arabian horses. Bred by Lady Wentworth, Crabbet Park, imported by John M. Rogers, Alamo, Calif. Premier stallion of the Rogers Arabian Stud. This photo shows him aged 17 in July, 1966. Photo by Johnny Johnston, courtesy John M. Rogers.

stud was one of the largest Arabian breeding establishments in America. A closely inbred horse, *Raffles proved to be an excellent sire and his blood is found in almost every major Arabian stud in the United States. He died in 1953 the property of Mrs. Alice Payne's Asil Arabian Ranch in California.

Arabians in the United States

Although there had been occasional small importations ever since Colonial times, Arabians as a breed became better known in America at the World's Columbian Exposition at Chicago in 1893. Some Syrian rug merchants brought from the desert 28 horses, some camels, and Bedouin attendants. The show put on by this troupe interested a number of horsemen, and after the fair some of the horses were acquired by men who began to breed pure Arabians. One of the mares, *Nejdme, was given the first registration number in the American stud book when it was founded.

Homer Davenport of Morris Plains, New Jersey saw the horses in Chicago, and decided to become an Arabian breeder. From

Bennfield's Ace, a Morgan stallion of excellent type. During the 1970s he was many times champion at the largest Morgan horse shows. He was owned by Mrs. Edna Avery, Ledyard, Conn., and was shown in hand and under saddle by Billy Parker and in harness by Joe Parker, Amenia, N.Y. Conformation photo by Judith Livingston, action photo by Warren Patriquin, courtesy of Mrs. Avery.

Pine Pep, winner of the Maryland Hunt Cup in 1949 and 1950, shown here over the next-to-last fence in the 1952 running of this classic steeplechase, which he also won. Owned by Mrs. William J. Clothier, Pine Pep was ridden by Mike Smithwick, later a leading trainer of steeplechasers. Photo by Bert Morgan.

1906 to 1907 he went to the desert and selected 25 head that he brought to the United States. He got other Arabians in England.

Arabian breeders in America founded the Arabian Horse Club Registry in 1908. The Davenport importation provided a broad foundation to the breed of great importance to future generations.

Arabian breeding in this country increased very slowly until comparatively recent times. The breed is fairly well distributed all over the United States, but the chief interest has been on the West Coast and in the Southwest.

Some Prominent Breeders

Ben Hur Farm. Founded in the early 1920s, the Ben Hur Farm of Herbert Tormohlen, Portland, Indiana, was an influential Arabian stud for half a century. The foundation mare was Dahura, foaled in 1909 and number 90 in the Registry. An early sire used by Mr. Tormohlen was Hanad, the most potent progenitor of the stock from the Davenport importation. Hanad and two of his get from Dahura, Valencia and Ameer Ali, were purchased by H. H. Reese for the Kellogg

Ranch in California. Under Mr. Reese's care, Hanad and Valencia became the first Arabian champion stallion and champion mare in the United States.

The Ben Hur Farm breeding program featured a persistent line breeding pattern for over four decades to produce the classic type of Arabian. Several sons of *Raffles were used. Ben Hur had horses that represented seven generations of breeding at the farm at the time of Mr. Tormohlen's death. His Ben Hur Arabians made impressive show records at the largest horse shows in America.

Al-Marah Arabian Farm. The largest collection of Arabian horses in the United States was maintained for many years by Mrs. Garvin E. Tankersley at Al-Marah Arabian Farm, Barnesville, Maryland. Many stallions of the best breeding stood at Al-Marah. One of the most noted was Indraff, a son of *Raffles from the mare *Indaia. Both sire and dam were bred at Crabbet Park and imported to the Selby Stud.

Following Lady Wentworth's death in 1957, Mrs. Tankersley bought a number of the Crabbet Park horses. These, together with some other English purchases, constituted the largest single importation of Arabians ever brought to the United States, some 30 head. Al-Marah retained some of the imported stock and sold others at the 1958 Al-Marah auction.

In recent years the Al-Marah stud has been located at Tucson, Arizona, and Micanopy, Florida.

Rogers Arabian Stud. John M. Rogers of Alamo, California, compiled a brilliant record in producing high quality Arabian horses of the classic type. His most successful stallion was *Serafix, imported from Lady Wentworth's Crabbet Park Stud in 1954. All of Mr. Rogers's brood mares were very carefully selected. *Serafix, although never bred to a large number of mares, sired 54 champions at Class A shows. Mr. Rogers was the only breeder to have 4 mares selected for the Top Ten in the U.S. National Championship class in one year. All were sired by *Serafix. One year he had 4 stallions foaled on his ranch selected for the Top Ten in the U.S. National Championship class.

This stud was dispersed on August 14, 1971; Mr. Rogers died in the winter of 1979.

Recent Importations

The foregoing paragraphs show that many prominent Arabian horses in the United States are quite close to imported blood. In recent years Lasma Arabians at Scottsdale, Arizona; Mike Nichols, the theatrical director; Sir William Farm, Hillsdale, N.Y.; Gleannloch Farm, Spring, Texas; Double U Ranch, Ltd., Kelowna, British Columbia; and other breeders have imported Arabians of the finest quality. Importations have come from Egypt, Spain, England, Poland, and Russia. The Polish horses in particular have shown great elegance, style, and the classic beauty associated with Arabian breed character. Some have been a bit bigger than many American Arabians. Some have had longer necks, sharper withers, and more sloping shoulders. In motion, many of the Polish imports have shown great brilliance, with the impulsion, lift, and drive off of their hocks that is desired in all high class horses.

Arabian Characteristics

Arabian horses are noted for their style, spirit, substance, speed, stamina, and wearing qualities. The exigencies of their desert upbringing have fitted them ideally for endurance rides, trail rides, and work as cow ponies. Arabians make excellent all-purpose horses. Under English or Western tack, in harness, over jumps, or on the trails they perform most satisfactorily.

Most Arabians measure from 14 to 15.1 hands in height, and weigh between 850 and 1,100 pounds. Bay, grey, chestnut, and brown are common colors. There are a few black and a few pure white Arabians.

A good Arabian has a sharply defined head, prominent eyes, fine ears, somewhat dished face, large nostrils, prominent jaw, and fine muzzle. Typically the neck is arched and medium long, the shoulder and withers well laid back, the back quite short, and the ribs rounding. Arabians are to be commended for their dense, hard bone and tough feet of excellent shape. The best Arabians show a free, easy motion at all gaits and a high tail carriage.

Common Criticisms

When not of the best quality Arabians show several serious faults. Sickle hocks are far too common. Light muscling over the arms and forearms and particularly through the thighs and gaskins is another common shortcoming. Some owners who have emphasized the head above all else present Arabians whose ability in motion is at best indifferent.

Good Arabians breeders try to correct these deficiencies. An animal must first be a good horse before he can be truly a good Arabian.

SOME INFLUENTIAL SIRE LINES IN THE ARABIAN BREED

Skowronek (1909–1929) Bred in Poland. Sired by a stallion imported from the desert in 1907 by Count Potocki. Sold to England at 4, and to Lady Wentworth at Crabbet Park in 1920.

* Raffles (1926–1953)
  Indraff (1938–1963)
     Al-Marah Indraff
  Aaraf (1943)
  Aarief (1946)
     The Real McCoy (1960)
  Kubriya (1946)
  Rapture (1946)
  Rifraff (1947)
  Azraff (1949)
  Mraff (1952)
  Rafferty (1953)
  Sotep (1953)
* Raseyn (1923–1952)
  Ferseyn (1937–1962)
     Ferneyn
        Ferzon (1952)
           Gazon
              Raffon (1961)
           Gai Parada (1969)
     Amerigo (1962)
        Khemosabi (1967)
  Sureyn (1940)
     Saneyn (1956)
Naseem (1922–1953)
  Raktha (1934)
     Indian Magic (1944)
        * Electric Storm (1952)
     * Serafix (1949–1973)
        Meteor (1959)
  Negatiw (1945–1973)
     * Naborr (1950–1977)
        * Faraon (1958)
        * Gwalior (1961)
        * Aramus (1962–1976)
        Desert Sands (1965)
        Kaborr
     * Salon (1959)
        * Muscat (1971)
     * Tryneg (1968)
     * Buszman (1968)
     * Etiw (1969)

* Imported to the United States

Mesaoud (1887) *Bred in Egypt by Ali Pasha Sherif. Imported to Crabbet Park in 1891. Later sold to Poland.*
 *Astraled (1900–1923)
  Gulastra
  |Julep
  | Synbad (1955)
  |Rahas
  | Rabiyas
  | Abu Farwa (1940)
  | Ga'zi (1949)
  |Azkar
  | Aalzar

Mirage (1909) *Bred in the desert by the Anazeh. Selected for King Faisal of Iraq. Later sold to Crabbet Park, and then sold to the Selby Stud in the U.S.A.*
 |Rifage (1936–1967)
 | Gaysar (1942)
 | Skorage (1947–1975)
 |Image
     Arabi Kabir
     Errabi
       Bay-Abi (1957)
       Bey-El-Bay (1969)

Fadl (1930) *Bred in Egypt by Prince Mohammed Ali*
  Fadheilan (1942–1964)
    Fadjur (1952)
    Ibn Fadjur (1959–1966)

Ofir (1933) *Bred in Poland. Sired by an imported desert-bred horse. Captured by Russians in 1939 and sent to Tiersk.*
 | *Witez II (1939–1965) *Captured by the Germans. Later captured by General Patton and sent to U.S.A.*
 | |Natez (1951)
 | |Witezar (1955–1974)
 | |Kosciusko (1958)
 | Wielki Szlem (1938)
 | Czort (1949)
 | | * Sambor (1965)
 | | * El Paso
 | Witraz (1938)
      * Bask (1956–1979)
      Gdansk (1968)

Nazeer (1934–1960) *Bred at an Egyptian stud farm sponsored by the Royal Agricultural Society.*
 | * Morafic (1956–1974)
 | * Ibn Moniet El Nefous (1964)
 | * Ansata Ibn Halima (1958)
  Aswan
    * Marsianin

THE THOROUGHBRED

The history of the Thoroughbred horse begins in England over 300 years ago. The light horses of England were small, most of them under 14 hands. English horsemen wanted a horse as tall as their draft horses, but considerably lighter, a horse that combined speed and agility with stamina. From the time of the first crusades the reputation of the "desert horse" for speed and endurance had been well known. Therefore, the English began to import Arabian, Turk, and Barb stallions from the Near East and from North Africa to cross on their mares. Many such stallions, and some mares, were imported from the middle of the 17th century to the middle of the 18th century. These stallions, their sons, and grandsons were mated to English mares, and the English horsemen gradually developed a breed of horse that suited them better than anything they could import. So importations stopped, and the new breed, known today as the Thoroughbred, was kept pure.

Thoroughbred brood mares and foals on pasture at the Spendthrift Farm, Lexington, Ky. Photo by "Skeets" Meadors.

Tom Fool, stakes winner of 21 races, including the Handicap Triple Crown in 1953, sire of the classics winners Buckpasser and Tim Tam, and premier sire at the Greentree Stud, Lexington, Ky. Photo by "Skeets" Meadors.

Sword Dancer, stakes winner of 15 races and $829,610, and Horse-of-the-Year in 1959. Sire of Lady Pitt, best three-year-old filly of 1966, and of Damascus, the best three-year-old colt of 1967.

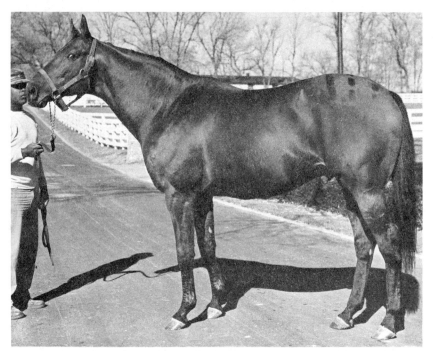

*Ribot, greatest European race horse of the 20th century and sire of classics winners in five countries. He was in stud at John W. Galbreath's Darby Dan Farm, Lexington, Ky., and died April 28, 1972, aged 20. Photo by "Skeets" Meadors.

*Nasrullah, sire of more high-class race horses than any stallion of the 20th century—53 stakes winners in the United States and 46 principal race winners in Europe. He was in stud in England, Ireland, and for many years at the Claiborne Farm, Paris, Ky. He was sired by Nearco and was out of Mumtaz Begum by *Blenheim II. Photo by "Skeets" Meadors.

*Round Table, one of the prominent stallions at the Claiborne Farm, Paris, Ky. Sired by *Princequillo, Round Table won 43 races and $1,749,869. He has sired 82 stakes winners.* Photo by "Skeets" Meadors.

Early Racing

The years of the Restoration—1660 to 1688—are thought of as the beginning of modern racing. King Charles II was an avid horseman, and the patronage of the Court lent prestige to racing. The racing of the 17th and 18th centuries differed in many respects from that of today. Horses were not raced until four years of age. Most races were match races at long distances and on the heat plan. Horses carried very high weights, often 12 stone (168 pounds) or more. Prize money was comparatively low.

Early Records

As more speed horses were bred, racing increased in volume. However, neither racing nor breeding became a matter of public record until late in the 18th century. Some of the larger studs, of course, did keep private records.

The Sporting Calendar, which carried reports of races, was begun about 1769. It was published by the Weatherby family until 1902 when it was purchased by the Jockey Club for whom the Weatherbys continued publication.

Thoroughbred mares and foals grazing on pasture at the Claiborne Farm, Paris, Ky. Photo by "Skeets" Meadors.

James Weatherby, Jr. put out *An Introduction to a General Stud Book* in 1791 and Volume I of the *General Stud Book* in 1793. This stud book for Thoroughbred horses is the oldest pedigree record of any breed of livestock anywhere in the world.

Important Early Sires

The three strains that made up the great bulk of the ancestry of the Thoroughbred were the Arabian, the Barb, and the Turk. The Arabian of the time stood about 14.2 hands, weighed about 900 pounds, and could carry weight long distances. The Barb known for speed and endurance, was brought into Spain by the Moors from the Barbary Coast of Africa. The Turk was a mixture of Arabian, Persian, and other strains, and was often 15 to 16 hands high.

Of the many stallions imported to England only three have male lines in existence today. The *Byerly Turk* that served as Captain Byerly's charging horse in the Irish wars was foaled about 1679 and was still in the stud in 1698. The *Darley Arabian* was bought as a four-year-old in Aleppo, Syria by Thomas Darley and shipped

Bull Lea, five times leading American sire, was the foundation of the extraordinary racing and breeding success of the Calumet Farm. He sired 58 stakes winners. An important factor in his success as a sire was his ability to get horses of even temperament and good disposition as distinguished from the fire and eccentricities of some Thoroughbred families. Photo by "Skeets" Meadors.

to his father in England in 1704. The *Godolphin Arabian,* foaled about 1724, eventually got to England and to the stud of the Earl of Godolphin. A grey stallion called *Alcock's Arabian* seems to be responsible for the color of almost all of the grey Thoroughbreds.

Every Thoroughbred in the world today traces in the male line to the Darley Arabian, the Godolphin Arabian, or the Byerly Turk. However, the male line to each of these stallions goes through a single descendant.

The Darley Arabian was the great-great-grandsire of *Eclipse,* a horse foaled in 1764 and bred by the Duke of Cumberland. About 80 per cent of all Thoroughbreds today trace to Eclipse. Bold Ruler, the leading American sire of recent years is 17 generations removed from Eclipse.

The Godolphin Arabian was the grandsire of *Matchem,* foaled in 1748. Man o' War's male line traced to Matchem.

The Byerly Turk was the great-great-grandsire of *Herod,* foaled in 1758.

In 1980 there were 175 winners of 277 graded stakes races in North America. Of these, 165 traced in the male line to Eclipse, 9 to Matchem, and 1 to Herod.

Thoroughbred Characteristics

The race horse has grown in size in the last 200 years. The great majority of Thoroughbreds measure within a range of five inches in height—from 15.1 to 16.2 hands—and within a range of 250 pounds (when in racing condition) from 900 to 1,150 pounds. In breeding condition most horses are 200 pounds heavier. The modern Thoroughbred has increased in speed, too, being much faster than the modern Arabian.

Briefly, the modern Thoroughbred is the result of almost 300 years of selective breeding for speed and stamina, as these qualities are tested on the race track, and has improved greatly over the stock upon which the breed was built.

The Thoroughbred represents the speed type in the extreme, and, since it was the first breed improved, its distinctive characters are well marked and fixed. Quality and refinement in head, hair, and bone, a small, well-proportioned head, clearly defined facial features, a neat ear, a fine throttle, sloping shoulders, high, sharp withers, muscular thighs and quarters, correctly placed legs, often slightly bucked knees, oblique pasterns, and shapely feet of dense texture are typical Thoroughbred characteristics.

The way of going is usually low and pointy at the walk and trot, but perfection when in motion at the gallop.

Their temperament is naturally racy, and they are of such a highly nervous organization that they are likely to become "hot" and erratic. Bay, brown, and chestnut with more or less white markings are the common colors, although grey, roan, and black are also found.

The Thoroughbred as a breed has largely a rich man's patronage. But it is a breed of great historic importance because of its influence during the formative days of other breeds. Anyone familiar with the stamp of the Thoroughbred horse will recognize in the blood of the Thoroughbred an influence that when intelligently and judiciously used produces most desirable results.

"Blood" is a term frequently used to indicate Thoroughbred breeding. "Blood-horse," "of the blood," and "bloodlike" are expressions that refer to the Thoroughbred. This being "the blood" and this breed being altogether of it, horses carrying but a fractional percentage are designated as part-bred and the number of parts are specified. Half-bred is the designation of the get of a Thoroughbred sire out of a common-bred mare. Three-quarters, or three parts, is used to designate the get of a Thoroughbred out of a half-bred mare.

Distribution of the Breed

From England, Thoroughbreds have spread all over the world. Not only the English blood, but also the English pattern of racing have been used. Next to racing in the British Isles, racing in France is the most important in Europe. Germany and Italy have long traditions in racing and breeding. Japan, India, Ceylon, Burma, and China have many race tracks. Australia, New Zealand, and all South American countries breed and race Thoroughbreds. Mexico, the Central American countries, and several Caribbean islands have beautiful race courses. Canada has the oldest stakes race in North America.

The scope of Thoroughbred breeding and racing in the United States eclipses that in any other country. However, the sheer size and extent of racing in the United States probably maintains thousands of cheap horses that would be discarded in any other major Thoroughbred breeding country.

Although Thoroughbreds are raised in almost every state, Kentucky leads the nation in the production of high-class race horses. Breeding is carried on in considerable volume in California, Florida, Maryland, Virginia, New Jersey, Ohio, Illinois, Texas, and Washington. Such wide spread breeding operations indicate that the limestone soils of Kentucky are not the only thing necessary. Good horses may be bred in other sections of the country provided those areas have good breeding stock.

Man o' War, greatest American race horse of the first half of the 20th century, pictured as a mature stallion. Photo by McGaughey, courtesy *The Thoroughbred Record.*

War Admiral, the best racing and breeding son of Man o' War. He won the Triple Crown in 1937. He sired 40 stakes winners. Photo by *The Thoroughbred Record.*

Registration of Thoroughbreds
    The stud book for Thoroughbreds in the United States has been maintained by the Jockey Club since 1896. It had been started in 1873 as a private enterprise by Sanders D. Bruce from whom it was purchased by the Jockey Club.

Uses of Thoroughbreds
    The Thoroughbred is recognized throughout the world as the best race horse on the flat. He is also used in steeplechasing or racing over jumps. The best hunters are Thoroughbreds or part Thoroughbred. The leading polo players of the world are mounted on Thoroughbreds. Many of the best jumpers in international competition are Thoroughbreds. Thoroughbreds that are not too hot-blooded make excellent hacks. Throughout their history Thoroughbreds have been used in the formative stages of the development of many other breeds of light horses and in grading-up the common horses of many areas.

Thoroughbred racing is big business. In 1980 in North America, 64,499 Thoroughbreds started in 68,243 races. Of these races, 2,092 (3.07%) were stakes races. A stakes race is a top-quality race in terms of purse (the money to be won) and Thoroughbreds competing. Owners pay stipulated amounts (stakes) in nomination and starting fees. The purse is increased substantially by "added money" put up by the racing association conducting the race meeting. In 1980 the total added money for the 2,092 stakes races amounted to $70,480,825— an average of $33,691. The North American stakes races of 1980 were won by 1,404 horses, or 2.18% of all the horses that raced. Therefore, a stakes winner is in an elite class. A stallion that sires over 10% stakes winners is a very successful stallion.

Some stakes races, because of purse, distance, prestige, or historic importance, regularly attract superior quality horses. In recent years these stakes have been rated subjectively by a committee representing various racing interests, and have been designated as "graded stakes." The 277 graded stakes of 1980 were won by 175 horses, or 0.3% of all the Thoroughbreds that raced in America that year.

Steeplechase stakes races totaled 20 in 1980. These were won by 13 steeplechasers.

Some Prominent Present Day Breeders and Breeding Farms

Thoroughbred breeders in the United States have registered over 25,000 foals annually in recent years. Space permits mention of only a few breeders who have contributed for a long time to the improvement of the Thoroughbred horse and the maintenance of high standards on the American turf.

Calumet Farm. Calumet Farm, located on the Versailles Pike at Lexington, Kentucky, has long been an important breeding and racing establishment and one of the showplaces of the Bluegrass. Calumet had bred 148 stakes winners. These include two winners of the Triple Crown: Whirlaway in 1941 and Citation in 1948. Calumet bred Pensive and Tim Tam, both of which won the Kentucky Derby and the Preakness Stakes and were second in the Belmont Stakes. Calumet also bred three other winners of the Preakness and three other winners of the Kentucky Derby.

Since 1941 Calumet Farm has 12 times been the leading money-winning owner of race horses. During the same period Calumet has led the list of American breeders (money won by horses bred) 14 times. Calumet Farm has bred 24 Thoroughbreds that have won over $300,000. This is more big money winners than any other farm has bred.

The stallion responsible for much of this tremendous record was Bull Lea. He was a stakes-winning race horse for Calumet, and when retired to stud he sired 58 stakes winners.

Native Dancer, winner of 21 of his 22 races, sire of 45 stakes winners when in the stud at the Sagamore Farm of Alfred Gwynne Vanderbilt at Glyndon, Md. Photo by Winants Bros.

Kauai King, winner of the Kentucky Derby and the Preakness Stakes in 1966. Sired by Native Dancer. Don Brumfield is the jockey. Photo by "Skeets" Meadors.

The celebrated race horse Nashua, stakes winner of $1,288,565, in the paddock at the Keeneland race track Lexington, Ky., on his last public appearance October 18, 1956. His groom, Al Robertson, is on the lead strap. Also shown are his trainer, James (Sunny Jim) Fitzsimmons, and Leslie Combs II who formed the syndicate to buy Nashua for $1,251,250 at the dispersal of the horses of the Belair Stud after the death of William Woodward, Jr. Nashua was sired by °Nasrullah and was out of Segula by Johnstown. Retired to stud at Mr. Combs' Spendthrift Farm in 1957, Nashua has sired 74 stakes winners. He died February 3, 1982.
Photo by "Skeets" Meadors.

Calumet Farm was developed as a Thoroughbred stud by Warren Wright in the early 1930s. Both the stud and the racing stable were maintained by his widow, later Mrs. Gene Markey. Calumet enjoyed a renaissance during the late 1970s; the trainer, John Veitch, developed several racing stars. One of these was Alydar, a multiple stakes winner, and second to Affirmed in the Kentucky Derby, Preakness, and Belmont Stakes of 1978. Calumet also bred and raced Our Mims and Davona Dale, the best three-year-old fillies of 1977 and 1979, respectively, and Before Dawn, the champion two-year-old filly of 1981.

Claiborne Farm. For over 70 years Claiborne has been one of the great Thoroughbred nurseries of the world. The farm, covering some 4,700 acres near Paris, Kentucky, has been owned and managed by three generations of the Hancock family. The Hancocks have both bred and raced horses. However, Claiborne has long been known as the headquarters for some of the best stallions and brood mares in America, often owned by partnerships or syndicates that make use of the horse production skills and knowledge of the Hancocks and their staff.

Among the chief breeders patronizing Claiborne have been the late Mrs. Henry Carnegie Phipps, whose horses raced under the name of the Wheatley Stable; her son, Ogden Phipps, who served as President of the Jockey Club; and his son, Ogden Mills Phipps. Bold Ruler, eight times the leading Thoroughbred sire in America, was bred and raced by the Wheatley Stable; he spent his entire stud career at Claiborne. His greatest son, the Triple Crown winner Secretariat, was retired to stud at Claiborne.

Mr. Seth Hancock has managed Claiborne since the death of his father, A.B. Hancock, Jr., on September 14, 1972. There are usually about 25 stallions in service at the farm.

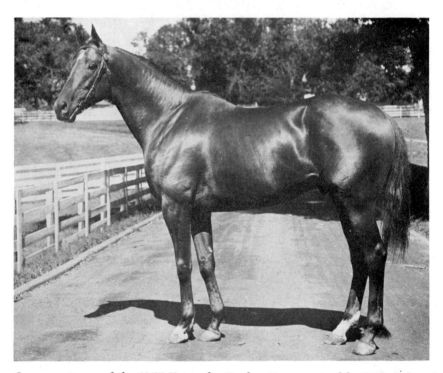

Swaps, winner of the 1955 Kentucky Derby. He was sired by *Khaled and was out of Iron Reward by *Beau Pere. His second dam, Iron Maiden, was by the Triple Crown winner War Admiral. Photo by "Skeets" Meadors.

John Henry (left), 1981 Horse-of-the-Year, Best Male Grass Horse of 1980 and 1981, and the first race horse to win $3 million. He is shown here coming on to win the first running (1981) of the Arlington Million under Jockey Bill Shoemaker at Arlington Park near Chicago. John Henry was bred by the Golden Chance Farm, Paris, Ky. He is a bay gelding, foaled in 1975. He was sired by Ole Bob Bowers and out of Once Double. His second dam was a great-granddaughter of Man o' War. John Henry was sold twice at public auction: for $1,100 as a yearling and for $2,200 as a two-year-old. Later he was sold privately for $25,000 to the Dotsam Stable of Sam and Dorothy Rubin, for whom he raced. He was trained by V.J. Nickerson and Ron McAnally. Known especially for his ability on the turf, John Henry also won several important stakes races on dirt tracks, including the 1981 Jockey Club Cup at Belmont Park. Photo courtesy Arlington Park.

Darby Dan Farm. Darby Dan Farm at Lexington, Kentucky, is owned by John W. Galbreath. Usually about a half-dozen stallions are in service there, most of them syndicated, but some owned by Galbreath family members.

Darby Dan for several years was the home of Swaps, the 1955 Kentucky Derby winner that Mr. Galbreath purchased from his breeder, Rex Ellsworth. Swaps sired Chateaugay, the horse that won the 1963 Kentucky Derby and Belmont Stakes for Darby Dan. In 1967 Swaps was syndicated and moved to the Spendthrift Farm.

The best racing Quarter Horse of 1981 was Special Effort, shown here winning the 440-yard All-American Futurity by 4 lengths in a time of :21.69. He was the first two-year-old to win the Tres Coronas (Kansas Futurity, Rainbow Futurity, All-American Futurity). He was sired by the Thoroughbred stallion Raise Your Glass. He was bred by Allen Moehrig, Seguin, Texas; owned by Dan and Jolene Urschel, Canadian, Texas; trained by Johnie Goodman; ridden by W.R. (Billy) Hunt. Photo courtesy The Quarter Horse Journal.

The great *Ribot, undefeated during his racing career, twice winner of the Prix de l'Arc de Triomphe, and regarded as the finest European race horse of the twentieth century, was on lease to Darby Dan for several years. *Ribot sired winners of classic races in 5 countries. His son Tom Rolfe won the Preakness; another son, Arts and Letters, took the Belmont Stakes in the United States. His daughter Long Look won the Oaks in England. His son Ragusa won the Irish Derby as well as the St. Leger Stakes, and the King George VI and Queen Elizabeth Stakes in England. His sons Molvedo and Prince Royal II both won the Prix de l'Arc de Triomphe in France. Molvedo won the Gran Premio de Jockey Club in Italy. Alice Frey won the Italian Oaks, and Ribocco the Irish Sweeps Derby. Ribero won the 1968 St. Leger and Irish Sweeps Derby. Two sons of *Ribot, the full brothers His Majesty and Graustark (the latter the sire of over 30 stakes winners), have stood for service at Darby Dan.

A second international stallion, *Sea-Bird, was on lease to Mr. Galbreath for several years. This horse had won the 1965 Epsom Derby and Grand Prix de Saint-Cloud. He sired Little Current, the winner of the 1974 Preakness Stakes and Belmont Stakes in Mr. Galbreath's colors before entering stud at Darby Dan.

Occasionally Mr. Galbreath raced a few horses abroad. The most successful of these was Roberto, winner of the Epsom Derby and the Benson and Hedges Gold Cup in 1972. This stallion, sired by Hail to Reason and named for the famous baseball player, Roberto Clemente, entered stud at Darby Dan in 1974.

Greentree Stud. Mrs. Payne Whitney, who had had a racing stable since 1910, established the Greentree Stud along the Paris Pike north of Lexington, Kentucky, in 1920. Both the racing stable and the breeding program were maintained and enlarged by Mrs. Whitney's son and daughter, John Hay Whitney, a member of the Jockey Club, and Mrs. Charles Shipman Payson. Five or six stallions usually are in service at Greentree, and there is a large band of well-bred brood mares. The chief stallion for several years was Tom Fool. This horse, bred by Duval A. Headly, won 21 races for Greentree and was named Horse-of-the-Year as a four-year-old in 1953 after he had won the Handicap Triple Crown. Tom Fool sired 36 stakes winners.

The top race horses Arts and Letters, Stage Door Johnny, Foolish Pleasure, and Key to the Mint stood at Greentree following syndication for stud duty, and proved to be good sires.

Spendthrift Farm. Named after an old time race horse, the Spendthrift Farm is owned by Leslie Combs II, a member of the Jockey Club. Located north of Lexington, Kentucky, Spendthrift is the home of nearly 40 stallions. Mr. Combs has been one of the most active breeders in forming syndicates for noted stallions. For example, the syndicated stallions Nashua, Gallant Man, Majestic Prince, and Raise a Native have spent their stud careers at Spendthrift. More recently the Triple Crown winners Affirmed and Seattle Slew went to Spendthrift for stud duty.

C.V. Whitney Farm. In 1930 Cornelius Vanderbilt Whitney purchased the Thoroughbreds owned by the estate of his father, Harry Payne Whitney. He then took over the breeding farm that had been started by his father in 1917 on the Paris Pike north of Lexington, Kentucky. Mr. Whitney's racing stable made him the country's leading owner in money earned in five different years. He also was the leading owner in races won in five seasons. The stable of his grandfather, W.C. Whitney, led the owners' list three times; that of his father led seven times; and his own stable, when topping the list in 1960 for the fifth time, became the second to earn more than a

The mighty Kelso in a familiar role being led to the winner's circle at Belmont Park by his owner Mrs. Richard C. duPont. Jockey Ismael Valenzuela up. Photo by Mike Sirico, N.Y.R.A.

Kelso in front of the stands at Aqueduct race track, New York, scene of many of his racing triumphs. Photo courtesy Mrs. Richard C. duPont.

Kelso after being paraded at Keeneland race track, Lexington, Ky., April 21, 1965. Ralph Via up. Larry Fitzpatrick, groom. A. B. Hancock, Jr. of Claiborne Farm and Kelso's owner Mrs. Richard C. duPont are at the right. Photo by "Skeets" Meadors.

million dollars in a single season.

Harry Payne Whitney bred 192 stakes winners from 1905 to 1930, inclusive. Cornelius Vanderbilt Whitney bred 169 stakes winners from 1931 to 1979, inclusive. His stud was headed for many years by the Epsom Derby winner *Mahmoud, imported from the Aga Khan. Mr. Whitney, a member of the Jockey Club, owns shares in several syndicated stallions. His colt State Dinner nearly won the Handicap Triple Crown in 1979 by taking the Metropolitan and the Suburban Handicaps and placing third in the Brooklyn Handicap. In 1980 State Dinner placed second in each of these Handicap events and won the Whitney Stakes at Saratoga.

Sagamore Farm. The Sagamore Farm of Alfred Gwynne Vanderbilt is located near Glyndon, Maryland. Mr. Vanderbilt, a member of the Jockey Club, has also had a racing stable for many years. One of its greatest stars was Native Dancer, bred by Mr. Vanderbilt and foaled in 1950. Native Dancer won 21 of his 22 races—all but the Kentucky Derby—and $785,240. Retired to stud duty at

Kelso in retirement being ridden by his owner Mrs. Richard C. duPont at her Woodstock Farm, Chesapeake City, Md. Photo by Paul Schafer, courtesy N.Y.R.A.

Jay Trump, the only American-bred, American-owned, American-ridden horse ever to win the English Grand National Steeplechase at Aintree, England. Bred by Jay Sensenich, owned by Mrs. Mary Stephenson, and ridden by Crompton ("Tommy") Smith. This photo shows Jay Trump cantering in front of the stands prior to the running of the 1965 Grand National which he won. Photo by Winants Bros.

Bold Ruler, eight times leading Thoroughbred sire in America. Bred, owned, and raced by the Wheatley Stable, he was in stud at the Claiborne Farm, Paris, Ky. This photo shows him at age 13 in the summer of 1967. Photo by "Skeets" Meadors.

Jay Trump, tired but in the lead after the last of 30 fences, being picked up by "Tommy" Smith for the 494-yard run-in to the finish of the English Grand National Steeplechase at Aintree. Photo by Winants Bros.

*Seattle Slew, winner of the Triple Crown in 1977, shown winning the 1978
Marlboro Cup Handicap at Belmont Park. In this race he was in the lead
from wire to wire, carried 128 pounds, and defeated the 1978 Triple Crown
winner, Affirmed. The time for 1⅛ miles was 1:45.4. The jockey was Angel
Cordero. NYRA photo by Bob Coglianese.*

Sagamore Farm in 1955, Native Dancer sired 45 stakes winners. He
died in November 1967. His sons and grandsons have proven to be
excellent sires.

Windfields Farm, Ltd. The Windfields Farm of E. P. Taylor at
Oshawa, Ontario, is the leading Thoroughbred breeding establishment in Canada. Mr. Taylor, a member of the Jockey Club, also
maintains a Windfields stud farm near Chesapeake City, Maryland.
The high-quality horses bred by Windfields made Mr. Taylor the
leading breeder in North America from 1974 to 1980, inclusive. He is
the world's leading breeder of stakes winners, having bred 238 stakes
winners through 1980.

About 20 stallions are distributed between the two farms as well
as a large band of brood mares. All of the foals produced are offered
for sale as yearlings at the big yearling auctions. Over the years
Windfields has compiled an unparalleled record. From 1954 through
1981 Mr. Taylor sold 1,135 home-bred yearlings at auction for
$50,724,200—an average of $44,691. He has also bought heavily in
the yearling market, usually getting well-bred fillies which have
served as replacements for the brood mare band after their racing
careers ended.

The top stallion at Windfields for many years was the home-bred Northern Dancer, a foal of 1961. Racing for Mr. Taylor, he won 14 races including the Kentucky Derby and the Preakness in the United States and the Queen's Plate in Canada (the oldest stakes race in North America).

Retired to stud, Northern Dancer became one of the leading sires of all time. He had sired 71 stakes winners from 369 foals (19.2% stakes winners) by the end of 1980. His get have won stakes in the United States, Canada, England, Ireland, France, and Germany. Among his most noted get were two winners of the Epsom Derby: Nijinsky II in 1970 and The Minstrel in 1977, both bred by E.P. Taylor.

Flight Time, American Saddlebred stallion bred by the Dodge Stables and chosen to succeed his sire, Wing Commander. His dam was The New Moon by Sparkling Waters; his second dam was by King's Genius. At the Dodge Stables dispersal sale Flight Time was purchased by the Earl Teater and Sons Farm, Lexington, Ky., for whom he proved to be a most successful sire.
Unretouched photo by Lois Rappaport, courtesy Louis D. Teater.

Northern Dancer, winner of the Kentucky Derby, Preakness Stakes, and Queen's Plate, and champion three-year-old of 1964. Bred and raced by E.P. Taylor's Windfields Farm, he was sired by Nearctic out of Natalma by Native Dancer. Northern Dancer sired 71 stakes winners by the end of 1980, including two winners of the Epsom Derby. Photo by The Drummer Boy, courtesy of Windfields Farm.

An informal picture of Secretariat as a three-year-old. Horse-of-the-Year in 1972 and again in 1973 when he won the Triple Crown, he is shown here with Eddie Sweat, his groom; Lucien Laurin, his trainer; Ron Turcotte, the jockey in most of his races; and Helen C. ("Penny") Tweedy of Meadow Stables, the owner. Photo by Paul Schafer, N.Y. Racing Assn.

Forego winning the 1976 Metropolitan Handicap by a head from Master Derby. Heliodoro Gustines was the jockey. Photo courtesy New York Racing Assn.

Forego, the great American champion, Horse-of-the-Year in 1974-75-76. He is shown here in the paddock at Belmont Park September 17, 1977, before the running of the Woodward Stakes, which won for the fourth time. Willie Shoemaker was the jockey. Photo by Dell Hancock.

TRIPLE CROWN RACES

The Kentucky Derby, the Preakness Stakes, and the Belmont Stakes are the most prestigious races for American three-year-olds. A horse that wins all three races is said to have won the Triple Crown. Through 1981 only 11 Thoroughbreds had accomplished this feat:

Year	Horse	Owner
1919	Sir Barton	J.K.L. Ross
1930	Gallant Fox	Belair Stud Stable (William Woodward)
1935	Omaha	Belair Stud Stable (William Woodward)
1937	War Admiral	Glen Riddle Farm (Samuel D. Riddle)
1941	Whirlaway	Calumet Farm
1943	Count Fleet	Mrs. John D. Hertz
1946	Assault	King Ranch
1948	Citation	Calumet Farm
1973	Secretariat	Meadows Stable
1977	Seattle Slew	Karen L. Taylor
1978	Affirmed	Harbor View Farm

The Kentucky Derby is run at 1¼ miles at Churchill Downs, Louisville, Kentucky. The Preakness Stakes is run at $1\frac{3}{16}$ miles at Pimlico Race Track, Baltimore, Maryland. The Belmont Stakes is run at 1½ miles at Belmont Park on Long Island.

For older horses, the Handicap Triple Crown consists of the Metropolitan Handicap at 1 mile, the Suburban Handicap at 1¼ miles, and the Brooklyn Handicap at 1½ miles, all run at Belmont Park. Through 1981 only three horses had won the Handicap Triple Crown:

Year	Horse	Owner
1913	Whisk Broom II	Harry Payne Whitney
1953	Tom Fool	Greentree Stable
1961	Kelso	Bohemia Stable (Mrs. Richard C. duPont)

FIVE NOTED AMERICAN THOROUGHBREDS
OF THE TWENTIETH CENTURY

From the thousands of Thoroughbreds that have appeared on American race tracks and breeding farms it is obviously impossible to objectively select only five. Purely on personal bias the author has chosen to discuss these five great horses. A few highlights from their careers are given.

Man o' War. Man o' War was the most famous American horse of the first half of the 20th century. He was foaled March 29, 1917 at the Nursery Stud, Lexington, Kentucky owned by August Belmont. He was sired by Fair Play and was out of Mahubah by *Rock Sand. Since Major Belmont was in the War he decided to sell all of his yearlings. On August 17, 1918 Man o' War was sold at Saratoga for $5,000 to Samuel D. Riddle, Glen Riddle Farm. The colt was trained throughout his career by Louis Feustel.

As a two-year-old in 1919 Man o' War won 9 of his 10 races, including the Keene Memorial, Youthful Stakes, Hudson Stakes, Tremont Stakes, United States Hotel Stakes, Grand Union Hotel Stakes, Hopeful Stakes, and the Futurity. He was second by a half length to Upset in the Sanford Memorial Stakes.

In six of his races as a two-year-old Man o' War carried 130 pounds. This is more weight than some handicap horses carry today. All during his race career he went to the post as odds-on favorite.

Mr. Riddle thought early May was too early for a three-year-old to run 1¼ miles, so Man o' War was not in the Kentucky Derby. He started his three-year-old season in 1920 by winning the Preakness, and continued by winning all of his races—the Withers Stakes, Belmont Stakes, Stuyvesant Handicap, Dwyer Stakes, Miller Stakes, Travers Stakes, Lawrence Realization, Jockey Club Stakes, Potomac Handicap, and the Kenilworth Park Gold Cup which was a match race with Sir Barton, the Triple Crown winner of 1919.

Man o' War's racing career showed that he had in abundance those qualities needed to make a great race horse—speed, stamina, courage, consistency, and ability to carry weight and still win. He won $249,465, a record at the time.

Physically Man o' War was a glowing red chestnut standing 16 hands 1⅝ inches. He girthed 71¾ inches and weighed in racing condition just over 1,100 pounds. As a breeding stallion his weight went to 1,370 pounds.

Man o' War entered the stud in 1921 as a private stallion. In 1922-23-24 he was in public service at a $2,500 fee. Thereafter his fee was $5,000. Actually not many services were available because the horse was always limited to no more than 25 mares and was used principally on Mr. Riddle's mares. When he was 26, Man o' War suffered a heart attack and was retired from breeding service. He lived to be 30 years old and died November 1, 1947. He was buried in his paddock and a larger than life sized statue by Herbert Heseltine was erected over his grave.

During all his years at Mr. Riddle's Faraway Farm near Lexington, Kentucky Man o' War became even more of a public institution than he had been when racing. A guest register was kept near his stall in the stallion barn. Many volumes were filled with signatures of visitors from all over the world.

Compared to leading sires of the present day whose mares are very carefully selected, Man o' War had relatively little help from his mares. Particularly in his later years he was seldom mated to truly outstanding mares. What he accomplished as a sire he did without the benefit of very many good mares. Hence his stud career is a tribute to his own greatness.

Man o' War was in the stud for 22 seasons. He sired 379 named foals. Of these 64 became stakes winners.

Man o' War's two best sons were War Admiral, the Triple Crown winner of 1937, and War Relic. Both of these stallions became very good sires.

For many years Man o' War's daughters gave him one of the highest ratings among brood mare sires. Of his daughters, 77 became the dams of 124 stakes winners.

Man o' War sired a number of good steeplechasers and hunters. His son Battleship won the Grand National Steeplechase at Aintree, and later sired good steeplechasers himself. A gelded son, Blockade, won the Maryland Hunt Cup three times. Another gelded son of Man o' War, named Holystone, raced for Mr. Riddle at two and three. Then he was converted to a hunter. He won hunter championships at Madison Square Garden and many big horse shows.

When one considers that Man o' War sired relatively few foals and lived so long ago, it is amazing to note how many of our top race horses trace to him in some line of their pedigree. Kelso, five times Horse-of-the-Year, was out of Maid of Flight. She in turn was out of Maidoduntreath by Man o' War. Buckpasser, 1966 Horse-of-the-Year, was out of Busanda, a daughter of War Admiral by Man o' War. Hail to All, winner of the 1965 Belmont Stakes, was out of Ellen's Best by War Relic by Man o' War. Sir Ivor, winner of the Epsom Derby and Washington, D. C. International in 1968 had as his third dam a daughter of Man o' War. Forego, Horse-of-the-Year in 1974-75-76, Triple Crown winners Seattle Slew and Affirmed, and John Henry, 1981 Horse-of-the-Year, also had Man o' War far back in their pedigrees.

Bold Ruler. Bold Ruler was one of our top race horses for three years and established a brilliant record in the stud. He was bred and raced by the Wheatley Stable of Mrs. Henry Carnegie Phipps. Bold Ruler was sired by *Nasrullah and was out of Miss Disco by Discovery; he was foaled in 1954. He was a dark bay horse about 16 hands 1½ inches in height.

Trained by James Fitzsimmons, Bold Ruler won the Youthful Stakes, Juvenile Stakes, and the Futurity as a two-year-old in 1956. The following season he won the Bahamas Stakes, Flamingo Stakes,

Wood Memorial, Preakness Stakes, Jerome Handicap, Benjamin Franklin Handicap (under 136 pounds), the Trenton Handicap, and was named Horse-of-the-Year for 1957. As a four-year-old in 1958, Bold Ruler won the Toboggan Handicap, Carter Handicap (with 135 pounds), Stymie Handicap (133), Suburban Handicap (134), and the Monmouth Handicap (134). Assigned 136 pounds for the Brooklyn Handicap, he went unplaced, came out of the race lame, and was retired from racing. He was one of the greatest weight carriers in American race history. In summary, Bold Ruler won 23 of his 33 races, was four times second, and two times third. He won $764,204.

Retired to stud, Bold Ruler proved to be a sensational sire. From 355 named foals he got 82 stakes winners (23.1%). Of these, 79 won stakes in North America. The most celebrated was the Triple Crown

*Bask, leading sire of champion Arabians at American horse shows during the 1970s. Bred by the Albigowa State Stud in Poland, *Bask was imported as a seven-year-old in 1963 by Lasma Arabians, Scottsdale, Arizona. He was National Champion in hand in 1964 and under saddle in 1965. He was in stud at Lasma until his death in 1979. Photo by Johnny Johnston, courtesy Lasma Arabians.

winner of 1973, Secretariat. Bold Ruler eight times was the leading sire in America based on money winnings of his get. He led the list of sires from 1963 to 1969 (inclusive) and again in 1973.

Bold Ruler stood for service at Claiborne Farm. He was bred to the best mares owned by the Wheatley Stable and the Phipps family and to very carefully selected outside mares. The breeding terms were unusual, but advantageous to both parties. A mare accepted for Bold Ruler would be bred for two successive seasons. One foal would go to the mare's owner, the other foal to the Phipps family. Thus owners of high-class mares were able to get a foal by Bold Ruler, and the Phipps family were able to get foals from mares of the best breeding and racing background.

In 1970 Bold Ruler developed a malignant tumor deep within his nasal passages just below the brain. He was given cobalt treatments for eight weeks at the Auburn University veterinary school. Following treatment, he was returned to Claiborne Farm; he bred 37 mares during the 1971 breeding season. However, the cancer spread during the summer and Bold Ruler had to be destroyed on July 12, 1971.

Kelso. The mighty Kelso was a racing machine that developed a personality, a style, and an ability that endeared him to millions of racing fans. His appearance on the New York tracks could draw spontaneous applause from the most blase race track crowds in the world.

A dark or brown foal of 1957, Kelso was bred by Mrs. Richard C. duPont, Woodstock Farm, Chesapeake City, Maryland. (Mrs. duPont's horses race under the name of Bohemia Stable.) Kelso was sired by Your Host, a stallion in which Mrs. duPont owned a few shares. Kelso's dam was Maid of Flight, a daughter of Count Fleet, the Triple Crown winner, and Maidoduntreath by Man o' War.

Kelso was trained as a two-year-old by Dr. John M. Lee. Dr. Lee gelded the colt, after which his action improved. Kelso raced only three times as a two-year-old in the fall of 1959. Thereafter he was trained by Carl Hanford. During his career Kelso was ridden by six different jockeys, but two of them were most closely associated with him. Eddie Arcaro rode the horse five times in 1960, and in all nine of his 1961 races. Ismael Valenzuela rode Kelso five times in 1962, in all of his races in 1963 and 1964, and all but one race in 1965.

Kelso compiled a brilliant record, and for five successive years (1960-64) was named Horse-of-the-Year. In 1961 he won the Handicap Triple Crown. He won the Jockey Club Gold Cup five times, the Woodward Stakes and the Whitney Stakes three times each. He set an American record of $3:19\frac{1}{5}$ for two miles in taking the Jockey Club Gold Cup of 1964. He set an American record of $2:23\frac{4}{5}$ for 1½ miles in winning the Washington D.C. International in 1964.

Kelso won races from six furlongs to two miles, on the dirt and on turf, on fast tracks and muddy tracks. He carried 130 pounds or more in 24 races, compared to nine times for Man o' War and only four times for Citation. Kelso won 12 races under 130 pounds or more, 2 races under 136 pounds. Therefore some people rank Kelso as the greatest American race horse of the 20th century.

On September 22, 1965 during the running of the Stymie Handicap which he won by eight lengths, Kelso was hit in the eye by a clod of dirt. The infection that developed forced him to miss the fall races. As a nine-year-old, Kelso was entered in the six-furlong Marlin Purse at Hialeah in March, 1966 and finished fourth. Shortly afterwards it was discovered that he had a hairline fracture of the inner sesamoid bone of his right fore ankle. He was then retired from racing, a legend in his own time.

The Blood-Horse of March 19, 1966, in commenting on Kelso's retirement, stated:

> Kelso demonstrated the durability of class.
> No horse in our time was so good, so long.
> His was mature greatness.

In summary, Kelso ran in 63 races in eight years. He won 39 races, was 12 times second, 2 times third, 5 times fourth. Thus he failed only five times to get even fourth place money. He retired as the leading money-winning race horse of history with earnings of $1,977,896.

Kelso was retired to Mrs. duPont's Woodstock Farm at Chesapeake City, Maryland where for some years he had had his own mail box for the mail addressed to him by racing fans. Mrs. duPont hunted Kelso for a few years with the Vicmead Hunt in Delaware and the Andrew's Bridge Hunt in Pennsylvania. She stopped riding Kelso in 1974 after he became arthritic.

Summary of Kelso's Racing Career*

1959

Race	Furlongs	Weight	Finish	Earned
Purse	6	120	1	$ 1,980
Purse	6	117	2	680
Purse	7	117	2	720

---

* Reprinted through the courtesy of *The Blood-Horse.*
tc Turf course.

1960

Purse	6	117	1	2,925
Purse	8	117	1	2,925
Arlington Classic	8	117	8	———
Choice Stakes	8½	114	1	36,320
Jerome Handicap	8	121	1	37,945
Discovery Handicap	9	124	1	18,290
Lawrence Realization	13	120	1	35,800
Hawthorne Gold Cup	10	117	1	88,900
Jockey Club Gold Cup	16	119	1	70,205

1961

Purse	7	124	1	6,500
Metropolitan Handicap	8	130	1	74,100
Whitney Stakes	9	130	1	36,400
Suburban Handicap	10	133	1	72,735
Brooklyn Handicap	10	136	1	73,320
Washington Park Handicap	8	132	4	7,500
Woodward Stakes	10	126	1	71,240
Jockey Club Gold Cup	16	124	1	68,770
Washington, D.C. International	12 tc	126	2	15,000

1962

Metropolitan Handicap	8	133	6	———
Purse	8	117	1	4,875
Suburban Handicap	10	132	2	21,040
Monmouth Handicap	10	130	2	21,830
Purse	8½ tc	124	1	3,250
Purse	8½ tc	113	4	420
Stymie Handicap	10	128	1	19,045
Woodward Stakes	10	126	1	74,880
Jockey Club Gold Cup	16	124	1	70,785
Man o' War Stakes	12 tc	126	2	22,960
Washington International	12 tc	126	2	15,500
Governor's Plate Stakes	12	129	1	35,100

1963

Palm Beach Handicap	7	128	4	1,480
Seminole Handicap	9	128	1	37,830
Widener Handicap	10	131	2	25,680
Gulfstream Park Handicap	10	130	1	70,500
J. B. Campbell Handicap	8½	131	1	71,337

Nassau County Stakes	9	132	1	17,745
Suburban Handicap	10	133	1	70,525
Whitney Stakes	9	130	1	36,270
Aqueduct Stakes	9	134	1	71,890
Woodward Stakes	10	126	1	70,720
Jockey Club Gold Cup	16	124	1	70,785
Washington International	12 tc	126	2	25,000

1964

Los Angeles Handicap	7	130	8	----
Californian Stakes	8½	127	6	----
Purse	9	136	1	9,750
Suburban Handicap	10	131	2	22,000
Monmouth Handicap	10	130	2	21,500
Brooklyn Handicap	10	130	5	----
Purse	9 tc	118	1	6,175
Aqueduct Stakes	9	128	1	70,005
Woodward Stakes	10	126	2	21,640
Jockey Club Gold Cup	16	124	1	70,590
Washington International	12 tc	126	1	90,000

1965

Purse	6	122	3	500
Diamond State Handicap	8½	130	1	14,202
Brooklyn Handicap	10	132	3	10,720
Whitney Stakes	9	130	1	35,360
Aqueduct Stakes	9	130	4	5,410
Stymie Handicap	10	128	1	17,842

1966

Purse	6	113	4	500

Age	Starts	1st	2nd	3rd	Earned
2	3	1	2	0	$ 3,380
3	9	8	0	0	293,310
4	9	7	1	0	425,565
5	12	6	4	0	289,685
6	12	9	2	0	569,762
7	11	5	3	0	311,660
8	6	3	0	2	84,034
9	1	0	0	0	500
Totals	63	39	12	2	$1,977,896

Secretariat. After Citation won the Kentucky Derby, the Preakness, and the Belmont Stakes in 1948, a quarter of a century passed before another horse won the Triple Crown. Until then, fourteen horses managed to win two of the three races. Then came Secretariat.

The ninth winner of the Triple Crown was a handsome chestnut colt with three white socks, a star, and a strip. Secretariat was bred by the Meadow Stud, owned by Christopher T. Chenery at Doswell, Virginia. He was foaled at the Meadow on March 30, 1970. Both the stud and the Meadow racing stable were then under the direction of Mr. Chenery's daughter, Mrs. John (Penny) Tweedy.

Secretariat started life with all the advantages. He was sired by Bold Ruler, a great race horse, sire of many stakes winners, and leading American sire from 1963 through 1969. Secretariat was out of Somethingroyal, whose 12 previous foals included 3 major stakes winners and 3 stakes-placed horses. She in turn was sired by *Princequillo, sire of 64 stakes winners. Secretariat himself had excellent conformation, extraordinary good health, and his dam's good temperament. He was raised at one of our best studs with the most competent help. When he went into training and competition he had a top trainer and jockey in Lucien Laurin and Ron Turcotte, his rider in all but three of his races. Secretariat almost always performed up to expectations. At his best he was electrifying and was compared to Man o' War.

Secretariat's first start was July 4, 1972, in a 5½ furlong race at Aqueduct race track. He was bumped at the start and ran fourth. Eleven days later he won a 6 furlong race by 8 lengths. Next he won an allowance race at Saratoga, the first time Turcotte rode him. Then he took the Sanford, the Hopeful, and the Futurity Stakes. He won the Champagne Stakes by 2 lengths but bore in, was disqualified, and placed second to Stop the Music. He took the Laurel Futurity by 8 lengths, and finished the season by winning the Garden State Stakes. Thus he won 7 of his 9 races and $456,404. He had demonstrated such clear superiority over the other two-year-olds racing in 1972 that he was named champion of his division and Horse-of-the-Year.

Mr. Chenery died on January 3, 1973. In order to pay great inheritance taxes and still keep Meadow Stud and Meadow Stable operating, the heirs needed a lot of money. They decided to syndicate Secretariat and their good four-year-old stakes winner, Riva Ridge. Mr. Seth Hancock of Claiborne Farm arranged the syndication. Secretariat was syndicated for $6,080,000—a record at the time. This was based on 32 shares at $190,000 each, each shareholder having the privilege to breed one mare to the horse every year. The Meadow retained 4 shares and 28 shares were sold to breeders in the United States, England, Ireland, France, and Japan. In addition, the Claiborne Farm received 4 shares for setting up the syndicate, and another share was given to Lucien Laurin, the trainer. The horse was to be raced at age 3 by the Meadow, then retired to stud as a four-year-old.

Secretariat at 3 years stood 16.1½ and weighed about 1,150 pounds. He was a handsome horse, very straight and correct in his leg position, short backed, deep chested, and heavily muscled over his arms and forearms and through his quarters.

He started his three-year-old career by winning the Bay Shore and the Gotham Stakes. In the Wood Memorial he came in third.

Then came the Triple Crown races. Secretariat set a new Kentucky Derby record, 1:59$\frac{2}{5}$, in beating Sham by 2½ lengths. He beat Sham (and all the others) again by 2½ lengths in winning the Preakness in 1:54$\frac{2}{5}$. His most awesome performance was his 31-length triumph in the Belmont Stakes. The fractional times were :23$\frac{3}{5}$; :46$\frac{1}{5}$; 1:09$\frac{4}{5}$; 1:34$\frac{1}{5}$; 1:59; 2:24—a world record for 1½ miles on a dirt track.

Three weeks after the Belmont Stakes, Secretariat was sent to Arlington Park for an invitational race, which he won easily by 9 lengths. At Saratoga in August, the crowd was stunned by Secretariat's loss to Onion in the Whitney Stakes.

The commercially sponsored Marlboro Cup—originally conceived as a match race between Secretariat and his stablemate, the four-year-old Riva Ridge—became an invitational handicap open to acceptance by the nation's best older horses. Secretariat and Riva Ridge finished one-two. The winning time of 1:45$\frac{2}{5}$ set a world record for 1$\frac{1}{8}$ miles.

Another upset followed. Secretariat went under by 4 lengths to Prove Out in the Woodward Stakes.

Secretariat was trained briefly on the grass, finishing his career with two turf races. He won the 1½ mile Man o' War Stakes by 5 lengths. Then he was sent to Woodbine, where, after opening up a 12-length lead in the Canadian International Championship Stakes, he galloped the final furlong and won by 6 lengths. The time for 1$\frac{5}{8}$ miles was 2:41$\frac{4}{5}$. Eddie Maple rode him in this race.

Secretariat won 9 races and $860,404 as a three-year-old: a record at the time. And once again he was Horse-of-the-Year.

A recapitulation of his racing career appears below.

Year	*Age*	*Sts.*	*1st*	*2d*	*3d*	*Unp.*	*Won*
1972	2	9	7	1	0	1	$456,404
1973	3	12	9	2	1	0	860,404
Total	(2)	21	16	3	1	1	$1,316,808

Secretariat entered stud at Claiborne Farm in 1974. Some of his first foals, sold as yearlings, gave him the rank of top sale sire in 1976 at the select summer sales. Six sold at Keeneland averaged $400,000.

The three sold at Saratoga averaged $333,333. By the end of 1981, fourteen sons and daughters of Secretariat had become stakes winners.

Forego. Horse-of-the-Year in 1974-75-76, Forego was a bay Thoroughbred gelding that, like Kelso, captured the hearts of racing fans. Everything about him was big—his physical size (over 17 hands), his desire to win, his sheer ability to do his job.

Forego was bred by the Lazy F Ranch, owned by Mrs. E.H. Gerry. He was foaled in 1970 at the Claiborne Farm, where Mrs. Gerry kept her brood mares. He was sired by Forli, an Argentine stallion that had been syndicated by Mr. Hancock of Claiborne and in which Mrs. Gerry owned a share. Forego's dam was Lady Golconda, a modest stakes winner by Hasty Road. Forego's female line was from the best Calumet Farm breeding. His second dam was Girlea by Bull Lea; his third dam was Whirling Girl by Whirlaway; his fourth dam was Nellie Flag, the first champion bred by Calumet and a daughter of American Flag by Man o' War.

Forego grew so big so fast that he was not raced at 2 years on the advice of his trainer, Sherrill Ward. At 3 he was fourth in Secretariat's Kentucky Derby. He had to be handled carefully all his life because of troubles with his ankles. His tendency to meanness led to the decision to geld him, and after the operation there were no more temperament problems. Forego won 9 of 18 races as a three-year-old, ending the season with victories in the Roamer and the Discovery Handicaps.

Forego was a mature, brilliant race horse by the time he was 4. He won 8 stakes races in 1974 from 7 furlongs to 2 miles. He showed all the Thoroughbred virtues—he was game, he could sprint, go a middle route, or stay 2 miles—and earned his first Horse-of-the-Year award.

For the next two years Forego continued as leader of the handicap division. Although he never managed to win all of the Handicap Triple Crown races in one season, he compiled a marvelous record. In four years Forego ran four times each in the Metropolitan, the Brooklyn, and the Suburban Handicaps. Of those 12 races he won 6, was second 4 times, and twice was third. He won the Woodward 4 times, the Carter and the Widener Handicaps twice each.

Sherrill Ward trained Forego for three years, then retired for health reasons at the end of 1975. Frank Whitely, Jr., trained the horse for the next three years. Heliodorus Gustines was Forego's usual jockey until mid-1976, when he was offered a contract by the Greentree Stable. From September 1976 until Forego was retired he was ridden by Willie Shoemaker, the leading American jockey.

It was Shoemaker who rode Forego to what was probably his most stirring victory—the 1976 Marlboro Cup Handicap. Assigned

137 pounds, and conceding 18 to 27 pounds to his rivals, Forego was far back in the running on a sloppy track. However, coming into the stretch he started to roll, made a tremendous drive through the final furlong, and won by a head in 2:00. Honest Pleasure, a very good three-year-old that had set a track record at Saratoga, was second under 119 pounds. Forego won 13 stakes races when carrying 130 pounds or more.

In 1977, after winning the Metropolitan and the Nassau County Handicaps during the summer, Forego suffered three defeats. However, he came back in September to win the Woodward (for the fourth time) under 133 pounds, giving 19 pounds to the runner-up.

Forego made only two starts as an eight-year-old. He won a 7 furlong allowance race at Belmont Park in June. Then on July 4, carrying 132 pounds on a sloppy track, he finished fifth in the Suburban Handicap. This was his last race.

The high regard in which Forego was held by knowledgeable racing people is shown by the comments made by the editor of *The Blood-Horse* when Forego's retirement was announced.

> There is a quality that manifests itself in stress of competition, in a market, a game, or a war. It is comprised of determination, and courage, and gallantry. It is called valor. It commands the respect of all, wherever found, in friend or foe, man or horse. Forego had it.*

Forego made his last public appearance in New York on September 16, 1978, when he led the post parade before the running of the Marlboro Cup Handicap. His former jockey, Heliodoro Gustines, rode him. Although two Triple Crown winners, Seattle Slew and Affirmed, were in the race, it was the old handicap champion that was greeted by the New York fans with prolonged and vociferous applause—both in the paddock and in front of the grandstand—as he led the post parade.

A recapitulation of Forego's racing career appears below.

Year	Age	Sts.	1st	2d	3d	Unp.	Won
1973	3	18	9	3	3	3	$188,909
1974	4	13	8	2	2	1	545,086
1975	5	9	6	1	1	1	429,521
1976	6	8	6	1	1	0	491,701
1977	7	7	4	2	0	1	268,740
1978	8	2	1	0	0	1	15,000
Totals	(6)	57	34	9	7	7	$1,938,957

*The Blood-Horse, July 17, 1978

Ben Nevis, a leading steeplechaser of the 1970s, coming over the third fence in the 1977 Maryland Hunt Cup. He won this race, then repeated his win in 1978. He was trained and ridden by Charles C. Fenwick, Jr., who also rode Ben Nevis to victory in the Grand National Steeplechase at Aintree, England, in 1980. Photo by Douglas Lees.

The 49th running of the Virginia Gold Cup, May 4, 1974, at Warrenton, Va. A crowd of 15,000 watched this 4-mile steeplechase over 22 timber fences. Photo by Douglas Lees.

The horses in this picture are taking the second jump of the Maryland Hunt Cup, a race of over 4 miles that includes 22 post and rail fences. The horse in the lead, Winton, won the Maryland Hunt Cup in 1945-46-47. He was ridden by his owner, Stuart Janney, Jr. Photo by Bert Morgan.

Some members of the Piedmont Hunt jumping the first fence in an old-fashioned point-to-point near Upperville, Va., on March 22, 1980, with the Blue Ridge Mountains in the background. Photo by Douglas Lees.

STEEPLECHASING IN AMERICA

Although very popular in England, steeplechasing makes up only a small part of Thoroughbred racing in the United States. Only five American race tracks—Saratoga, Belmont Park, Delaware Park, Meadowlands, and Monmouth Park—have offered steeplechase races in recent years.

Most steeplechasing occurs at hunt race meetings and at point-to-point meets. Hunt race meetings are recognized by, and run under the rules of, the National Steeplechase and Hunt Association. Races over brush, hurdle, and timber are carded, as well as a few flat races. Purses are offered and many professional jockeys and trainers are involved.

Point-to-points are held by hunt clubs to make money and to provide exciting sport for riders and spectators. Races are run over timber, hurdles, and brush and on the flat. Many offer only a trophy, but some offer purses. Many amateur jockeys and trainers and regular fox hunters participate. These point-to-point meets are the training ground for green horses and riders. Most of the top amateur jump riders as well as a number of the top professional steeplechase jockeys and trainers got their start in point-to-points.

The amateur flavor of the sport is maintained by having some races over jumps restricted to horses ridden by their owners, some races for lady riders, and old-fashioned point-to-points. The latter are cross-country races where fox hunters choose their own line between designated points, with no flags.

Some jumping races are run over timber (post and rail) fences. Hurdle races are over panels of light wood fencing with brush set in them, inclined "away" at an angle of 15° from the perpendicular. Brush jumps are frames of wood filled with cedar and brushed with the same material on the "take off" side. The height of the usual steeplechase obstacles is from 4'4" to over 5'.

Each of the obstacles on a steeplechase course is flagged. A small red or blue flag indicates the inside of the course, a small white flag indicates the outside; the obstacle is jumped between the flags.

The length of steeplechase races varies from 1½ to 4 miles. The minimum weight carried is 130 pounds.

Hunt race meetings and point-to-point meets are held mostly in Virginia, Maryland, Pennsylvania, New Jersey, Kentucky, Tennessee, South Carolina, and Georgia.

Mrs. Marion duPont Scott had a greater influence on steeplechasing than anyone else for over 50 years. She was the first American owner to have an American-bred horse win the Grand National at Aintree. Her stallion Battleship, a son of Man o' War, won that race in 1938. Since that time horses bred and raced by Mrs. Scott have frequently set the pace in the steeplechase world.

Every fall the Montpelier Hunt races are held at Mrs. Scott's estate in Virginia. (The mansion, Montpelier, was the home of President Madison.) Many years ago Mrs. Scott acquired the vast training and racing center at Camden, South Carolina, with schooling and training facilities for both flat horses and jumpers unmatched anywhere in the United States. The Carolina Cup races are held here each spring. The international steeplechase known as the Colonial Cup has been held at Camden since its inception in 1970. It is the richest steeplechase race in America.

THE AMERICAN SADDLEBRED HORSE

The development of the American Saddlebred paralleled that of the Standardbred. Both breeds resulted from a top cross of Thoroughbred stallions on a native mare foundation. In each breed the descendants of one stallion have constituted a family that has dominated the breed. Their respective histories are almost contemporaneous. Denmark, the Thoroughbred whose progeny founded the American Saddlebred breed, was foaled in 1839. Messenger, another Thoroughbred, reached this country in 1788; his great-grandson, Hambletonian 10, foundation sire of the Standardbred breed, was foaled in 1849.

Development of the Breed

The chief differences in the development of the American Saddlebred and the Standardbred stem from the native mares that were used and the goals which the breeders themselves had in mind. The original American Saddlebred Horse was born of necessity on the frontier, where riding was the chief means of transportation.
An easy, ambling gait was cultivated, and those horses that showed greatest proficiency in this direction were selected for breeding.

On the other hand, road and vehicle construction progressed most rapidly in the vicinity of the large eastern cities. Therefore the breeding of the trotters and road horses centered around New York City and Philadelphia, and the foundation mares were those that had proven themselves best adapted to trotting in harness.

Although horses were more extensively used for riding than for driving purposes in this country during the earlier period, the American Saddle Horse, in its present degree of development, is of more recent origin than the Standardbred. Selection has not been to a standard of performance only, but has also been based on ideals in type, conformation, and quality.

Breeders of American Saddle Horses first organized in 1891 under the name of the National Saddle Horse Breeders Association.

*Fiery Crags, a three-gaited champion campaigned years ago by the Dixi-
ana Farm, Lexington, Ky. A champion in Fine Harness as a young horse,
this gelding was converted to a three-gaited horse and was seldom defeated. He had the refinement, the conformation, and the square, balanced trot necessary for a top show horse. Trained and ridden by Charles
Dunn.* Photo by Rounds, courtesy Dixiana Farm.

*The slow gait, or stepping pace, as performed by the five-gaited stallion
Colonel Sport. This son of Kalarama Colonel was owned and shown by
the Nawbeek Farm, Paoli, Penna. He was ridden by Jimmie Robinson.*
Photo by McClasky.

The five-gaited horse at the rack. Mrs. Fred Van Lennep, owner of the Dodge Stables, Lexington, Ky., riding Blue Hawaii. Note that she is riding the horse on the curb rein and that only one foot is bearing weight at this flashy four-beat gait. Unretouched photo by McClasky.

My-My, the greatest five-gaited American Saddle Horse of the 1960s. Winner of the five-gaited championship stake at the Kentucky State Fair 1963–68, at the Ohio State Fair 1962–68, and at many other big shows. This 15.3-hand chestnut mare was sired by Beau Fortune and was out of the champion show mare Daneshall Easter Parade by Masked Marvel. She was owned by Miss Jolie Richardson, Atlanta, Ga. She was trained and ridden by Frank Bradshaw, Georgetown, Ky. Note the height of stride and the extreme flexion of the hock. Unretouched photo by Crane.

In 1899 the name was changed to the American Saddle Horse Breeders Association. At this time, 17 famous stallions were selected as the foundation sires of the breed. In 1902 this list of sires was decreased to 10 stallions. Then in 1908 all the names but one were eliminated, and Denmark was designated the sole foundation sire of the breed. Thoroughbred, Standardbred, Morgan, and ambling horses of unknown breeding were the strains upon which the American Saddle Horse breed was built. At the 1980 annual meeting of the association, the membership voted to change the name to the American Saddlebred Horse Association.

Denmark, the Foundation Sire

Denmark was named as the foundation sire of the American Saddlebred breed because 1,653 (55 per cent) of the 2,981 entries in the first volume of the stud book traced directly to him in the male line. Most of those horses traced through his son Gaines Denmark. In the first 4 volumes of the stud book, 7,311 (61.4 per cent) of the 11,977 entries traced directly to Denmark.

Denmark was a brown horse foaled in Kentucky in 1839. He is said to have been a consistent four-mile race horse. He was sired by the imported Thoroughbred stallion °Hedgeford and was six generations removed from Herod, one of the three important early sires in the development of the Thoroughbred breed. °Hedgeford, foaled in 1825, had been imported to New York in 1830 and later sent to Kentucky where he died in 1840.

Denmark was out of Betsey Harrison, a mare of Thoroughbred breeding owned by Samuel Davenport of Kentucky. Denmark traced eight times to Herod and six times to Eclipse.

When bred to the "Stevenson mare," a natural ambler, Denmark sired Gaines Denmark, his most prepotent son. This blending of the quality and stamina of the Thoroughbred with the easy natural gaits of Kentucky mares resulted in the American Saddlebred.

Saddlebred Horse Families

There have been two major families in the American Saddlebred breed. The Denmark family descends from Denmark, the foundation sire. The Chief family descenas from Mambrino Chief, foaled 1844, a great-grandson of imported Messenger. The Denmarks were known for exquisite finish and easy riding qualities, the Chiefs for brilliant action at the trot. Both families were crossed with Morgan blood and with easy-riding Kentucky mares. In the 19th century these families were more or less distinct. However, modern day American Saddlebred pedigrees show many crosses of these sire lines.

SOME IMPORTANT SIRE LINES IN THE AMERICAN SADDLEBRED HORSE

Denmark (1839)   The Foundation Sire
  Gaines Denmark (1851)
  |Washington Denmark (1855)
    |King William (1860)
      Black Eagle (1869)
        Black Squirrel (1876)
          Squirrel King (1882)
            Forest King (1894)
              My King
                Stonewall King (1920)
                  |Stonewall's Golden Dream
                  |Stonewall Premier (1949)

    |Crigler's Denmark (1872)
      Rex Denmark (1884)
        Rex McDonald (1890)
          |McDonald Chief (1896)
          | Independence Chief
          |Rex Peavine (1899)
            |Rex Firefly (1921)
            | |Sensation Rex
            | | Vanity's Sensation
            | |Sparkling Firefly
            | Sparkling Waters (1935)
            |Kalarama Rex (1922)
              |Kalarama Colonel (1938)
              | Colonel Sport (1942)
              |Society Rex (1937)
              |Kalarama Bittersweet (1937)
              |Royal Rex Sea
                Bobby Sea

  |Diamond Denmark (1858)
    Montrose (1869)
      King Lee Rose (1889)
        Guided by Love (1905)
          |AmericanBorn (1921)
          |My Own Love
            Sun Beau
              Beau Fortune (1941)

Mambrino Chief (1844)
  Clark Chief (1861)
    Harrison Chief (1872)
      Bourbon Chief (1883)
        Bourbon King (1900)
          Edna May's King (1918)
            Anacacho Shamrock (1932)
              Wing Commander (1943–1969)
                Flight Time (1962)
                  Lover's Time
            Anacacho Denmark (1930)
              Oman's Desdemona Denmark
          King's Genius (1924)
            Bourbon Genius (1933)
              Genius Bourbon King (1944)
                Valley View Supreme (1952)
                  Status Symbol (1968)
                  Supreme Sultan
            Ridgefield's Genius (1942)
              Truly Genius

American Saddlebred Horse Characteristics

The best American Saddlebreds are characterized by their high head carriage, their long, arched necks, and fine throats. They have high, refined withers and sloping shoulders. Their pasterns are long, sloping, and springy. Their feet are shapely but somewhat narrow. The top line is nearly level, the back and loin short, the croup level from hip to tail, and the tail attached high. The ribs are well sprung, but typically rather shallow.

The majority of American Saddle Horses measure from 15.1 to 15.3 hands and weigh about 1,100 pounds. Chestnut, bay, and brown are the most common colors. White markings are fairly common. A few grey, roan, and black horses also are seen. The best representatives of the breed show great style, quality and beauty, an alert temperament, and a flashy, animated way of going.

Gait Terminology

Natural gaits are those that are performed by a horse instinctively and without training. Examples are the walk, trot, and gallop, and, in some horses, the pace.

Acquired gaits are those which result from special training. The rack and the slow gait are examples.

A *diagonal gait* is one in which the legs move in diagonal pairs. The trot is an example.

A *lateral gait* is one in which the legs move in lateral pairs. The pace is an example.

Anacacho Shamrock, sire of Wing Commander *and many other winners for the Dodge Stables. Note the proud carriage of head and neck, the sloping shoulder, high withers, level topline, and good leg position typical of the best American Saddle Horses.* Photo by Horst, courtesy the Dodge Stables.

"*Free-going*" is a term applied when the gaits are performed in an effortless manner.

"*Laboring action*" is the term used when a horse's efforts on the move are obviously excessive.

"*Easy-gaited*" is the term applied when the rider's reactions to the various gaits are pleasant and enjoyable.

"*Hard-gaited*" is the term applied when the stride lacks spring and when the rider's reactions to the various gaits tire him quickly.

"*High-gaited*" and "*high-going*" are terms applied to the action when a horse folds his knees, flexes his hocks, and raises his feet high from the ground.

Gait Requirements in the Show-Ring

The gaits required of the three-gaited horse in the show-ring are the walk, trot, and canter. The gaits required of the five-gaited horse in the show ring are the walk, trot, slow gait, rack, and canter.

Wing Commander, greatest five-gaited American Saddle Horse of modern times and leading sire of the present day. Bred, owned, and exhibited by the Dodge Stables, Lexington, Ky. Trained and ridden by Earl Teater.
Photo by Horst, courtesy the Dodge Stables.

The walk. The walk is a four-beat gait that should be done with a long, prompt stride. Trueness of stride, both front and rear, and folding of knees and flexion of hocks as a horse pushes himself up into the bridle should be features of this foundation gait. The horse that dances and prances at the walk, tosses his head, and keeps up a constant duel with the rider's hands is neither a pleasure horse nor a show horse.

The trot. The trot is a diagonal, two-beat gait that lends itself to all sorts of road conditions and can be performed better than the pace or the rack on either soft or rough ground.

The five-gaited saddle horse should trot at speed and in form. It makes no difference how fast he goes, if he can maintain his form at speed. Speed is an asset on show day in competition with other gaited horses. If, as a result of being overridden, a gaited horse extends his chin, lands on his heels in front, leaves his hocks behind him, and turns in a sprawling, uncollected performance, then speed at the trot is no longer an asset but a liability.

The three-gaited horse should trot at moderate speed and always in form. He should fold his knees, flex his hocks, and go collectedly with a balanced stride. The kind of speed that calls for quarter boots should not be tolerated in three-gaited classes.

The slow gait. The slow gait used to be called the stepping pace. It is a slow, showy, ambling, four-beat gait with a broken rhythm. It differs from the true pace of the Standardbred pacer. The slow gait of the five-gaited horse is done slowly and with great style. The light harness pacing horse goes at tremendous speed, with so much roll to the body that the gait is most unpleasant to ride. When a five-gaited horse does the slow gait in competition he should be held to it and made to perform the gait properly. He should not be permitted to push forward and shift into a rack.

The rack. The rack is a fast, flashy, even-interval four-beat acquired gait. It used to be called the single-foot, a name that more nearly defines it because when the rack is properly executed only one foot bears weight at a time. The rack is a difficult gait for a horse, and some horses refuse to rack at all. Therefore they are kept as three-gaited horses. If a horse is to rack well, the track should be level and the footing fairly firm.

To have his head, neck, and legs properly set in performing the rack, a horse should go up against the curb bit. He should not be allowed to fall into a swinging, side-wheel pace, for the rack is distinctly a four-beat gait. "Paces in his rack" is a criticism of horses at the rack that display a tendency to pace and thus mix the two gaits. The gait mixing tendency of five-gaited horses is sharply discriminated against whether a horse mixes his rack with the trot or whether he tends to pace when he is asked to rack. "He can rack a hole in the wind" is a statement sometimes made by trainers who commend their horses for the speed they can display at the rack.

The canter. The canter is a three-beat gait, a restrained gallop, performed slowly and collectedly. The more slowly this gait is done, if performed with promptness, life, and exactness, the better. Hence the old saying "He can canter all day in the shade of an apple tree." Although done slowly the canter is not a lazy, listless, loose-jointed gait. The horse that looks as though he wants to run but restrains himself at the will of the rider and canters lightly at about six miles an hour is doing the canter properly.

A Leading Stud and Show Stable

The Dodge Stable, Castleton Farm, Lexington, Kentucky, was a leader in the production and showing of American Saddlebred Horses for over four decades. The owners were Mr. and Mrs. Frederick Van Lennep. Mrs. Van Lennep was born Frances Dodge. For many years the man in charge of the breeding, training, and showing was Earl Teater.

Wing Commander, the greatest five-gaited show horse of modern times, was bred, trained, and shown by the Dodge Stable. Campaigned all over the major horse show circuits, Wing Commander was undefeated from 1948 to 1953 inclusive. He won the five-gaited championship stake six times at the Kentucky State Fair. He died January 19, 1969.

Wing Commander was a dark chestnut with four white feet and a little white in his face. As a young horse he appeared rather tall and a bit narrow, not a picture-book horse. But the observer forgave any minor deficiencies in conformation when Wing Commander was in motion. He had blazing speed at the trot and rack, but still went in form. His slow gait was the true, showy, brilliant gait not often seen. The only gait assignment Wing Commander did not really like was to canter on the right lead. He would do it, but he sometimes objected. His speed and stamina and his high, square trot have been passed on to his sons and daughters.

The Dodge Stable had great success in producing show stock by breeding their former show mares to Wing Commander and other top stallions. Wing Commander made a notable sire record in the 1960s. At the 1966 Kentucky State Fair his get dominated the show. The first three places in the five-gaited stallion stake were won by his sons. Three other sons topped the amateur five-gaited stallion and gelding class. Two daughters were first and second among the fine harness mares. The three-year-old five-gaited stake and the weanling filly championship went to his get.

Mrs. Van Lennep died on January 24, 1971. The Dodge Stable was dispersed at public auction at the Tattersalls Sale Company, Lexington, Kentucky, on July 8, 1975. The 79 horses sold for almost $500,000.

THE MORGAN

Morgan horses may be regarded as the first American breed. All Morgans descend from one stallion, called by the name of one of his owners, Justin Morgan.

Foundation Sire

No definite proof about Justin Morgan's pedigree has ever been produced. It is believed that he was foaled near West Springfield, Massachusetts about 1789. The stud book lists as his sire a Thoroughbred stallion, True Briton. The dam is given as the Wildair mare. True Briton had been stolen from the Tory sympathizer Col. James DeLancey of New York, and taken to New England. Justin Morgan's maternal grandsire, Wildair, was a Thoroughbred stallion that had been imported by another James DeLancey, cousin to the first one mentioned.

Pedigree of Wing Commander

Sire/Dam	2nd Generation	3rd Generation	4th Generation	5th Generation
Anacacho Shamrock f. 1932 Undefeated 1940 on Pacific Coast	Edna May's King f. 1918 Champion at Ky. State Fair 1924 & 1926	Bourbon King f. 1900	Bourbon Chief f. 1883	Harrison Chief by Clark Chief (Chief)
				Belle by Latham's Denmark (Denmark)
			Annie	King by Harrison Chief (Chief)
				Daughter of Richilieu by Indian Chief (Morgan)
		Edna May	Rex Peavine	Rex McDonald by Rex Denmark (Denmark)
				Daisy 2d by Peavine 85 (Morgan)
			Lee Wood	Peavine 85 by Rattler (Morgan)
				Daughter of Warren Harris' Denmark (Denmark)
	Sally Cameron	Highland Squirrel King	Forest King	Squirrel King by Black Squirrel (Denmark)
				Stella French by Montrose 106 (Denmark)
			Nellie P.	Rockaway (Unknown. Reg. on petition of Mo. breeders)
				Daughter of Prairie Chief by Grey Eagle (Thoroughbred)
		Altadena	Prince Arthur	Highland Denmark by Black Squirrel (Denmark)
				Miss Humphreys by Black Squirrel (Denmark)
			Mania	Cecil Palmer by Cromwell Jr. (Denmark)
				Medica by Harrison Chief (Chief)
Flirtation Walk	King's Genius Champion at Ohio State Fair 1931–32–33 & at International 1930–31–32–33	Bourbon King	Bourbon Chief	Harrison Chief by Clark Chief (Chief)
				Belle by Latham's Denmark (Denmark)
			Annie	King by Harrison Chief (Chief)
				Daughter of Richilieu by Indian Chief (Morgan)
		Princess Eugenia	Chester Peavine	Rex. Peavine by Rex McDonald (Denmark)
				Miss Madison by Chester Dare (Denmark)
			Queen of Lincoln	Wood's Eagle Bird by King Eagle (Denmark)
				Daughter of Silver King (Unknown)
	Spelling Bee	King Vine	Rex Peavine	Rex McDonald by Rex Denmark (Denmark)
				Daisy 2d by Peavine 85 (Morgan)
			Bourbon Belle	Bourbon King by Bourbon Chief (Chief)
				Daughter of Eric Chief (Unknown)
		Not Registered	Red Light 2d	Lightfoot Brummel (Denmark)
				Daughter of Glenbrook (Unknown)
			Not registered	Happy Bell (Unknown)
				Untraced

Wing Commander f. 1943 Bred and Shown by the Dodge Stables

This pedigree shows the breeding of the most noted five-gaited saddle horse of modern times. Wing Commander was widely shown by the Dodge Stables and was undefeated in 1948–49–50–51–52–53. He won the Championship five-gaited stake six times at the Kentucky State Fair. His pedigree shows mild inbreeding to Bourbon King and Rex Peavine. Otherwise it is typical of the usual American Saddle Horse pedigree, a mixture of the known and unknown. Of the 32 horses in the 5th generation, 14 are of the Denmark family and 6 of the Chief family. Five of the 5th generation horses trace in the male line to Justin Morgan; six are of unknown breeding; and one traces directly to a Thoroughbred other than the antecedents of the Denmark and Chief lines. Both the sire and the dam of Wing Commander were good show horses. Note that the dam was a "short bred" mare on the bottom side of the pedigree.

As a two-year-old, Justin Morgan was taken to Randolph, Vermont by the man whose name he later bore. The dark bay colt matured to about 14 hands in height and a weight of 950 pounds. He died in 1821, about 30 years of age.

He was a most prepotent sire, passing his compact form, his spirit, and vigorous action to his get.

Justin Morgan's most important sons were Sherman, Woodbury, Bulrush, and Revenge.

Development of the Breed and Its Influence on Other Breeds

Morgans became the best driving horses and trotting race horses in the northeastern United States during the early and middle part of the 19th century. Justin Morgan's son Sherman sired Black Hawk, a stallion that became the sire of many good trotters. The best son of Black Hawk was Ethan Allan. He took a mark of 2:15 for the mile in defeating Dexter, a son of Hambletonian 10. With the advent of the larger Hambletonian horses, Morgans declined in popularity. However, many Morgan mares became the dams of Standardbred trotters.

The Morgan stallion Peavine, foaled in 1863 and sired by Rattler, a grandson of Black Hawk, appears in many American Saddlebred Horse pedigrees. Indian Chief, a grandson of Black Hawk, is another name found in American Saddlebred Horse pedigrees. Both Peavine and Indian Chief are in the ancestry of Wing Commander, the leading American Saddlebred sire of modern times.

The dam of Allan F-1, foundation sire of the Tennessee Walking Horse breed, was Maggie Marshall. She was sired by Bradford's Telegraph by Black Hawk.

Whereas the Standardbred horse caused the popularity of Morgans to decline, the automobile almost brought an end to the breed. There was no longer a demand for road horses.

The Morgan Horse Register and Morgan Horse Club

Col. Joseph Battell of Middlebury, Vermont, after many years of assembling information, privately printed in 1894 *The Morgan Horse and Register,* Volume I. The Morgan Horse Club was formed by a group of Morgan breeders in 1909. The Club incorporated and took over the Register in 1927. Horses could be registered under several different conditions until 1948. At that time the stud book was closed to all horses except those produced by stallions and mares already registered. In 1971 the organization became the American Morgan Horse Association.

The United States Morgan Horse Farm

In June, 1906 the U.S. Department of Agriculture began a

Waseeka's Nocturne, five times grand champion under saddle at the National Morgan Horse Show. Trained and ridden by John Lydon for Mrs. D. D. Power, Waseeka Farm, Ashland, Mass. As premier stallion at the Waseeka Farm, Nocturne has been one of the most consistent sires of high-quality, good-moving Morgan horses in America. Photos courtesy Mrs. D. D. Power, saddle photo by Freudy.

Waseeka's Nocturne

Morgan breeding program at Burlington, Vermont to promote, preserve, and improve the Morgan breed. This project was moved in 1907 to the farm located at Weybridge near Middlebury, Vermont that had been donated for the purpose by Col. Battell.

The U.S.D.A. bought seven mares and two fillies. The stallion used was General Gates, a great-grandson of Ethan Allan. He was bred by Col. Battell. Two of the mares had been purchased in Kentucky. They were daughters of Harrison Chief, but their dams were of Morgan breeding.

The U.S. Morgan Horse Farm was turned over to the University of Vermont in July, 1951. The Morgan breeding program has continued most successfully.

The Morgan stallion Parade and his son Broadwall Drum Major that toured the United States with the Lippizaner horses from the Spanish Riding School of Vienna. Parade was Grand Champion at the 1955 National Morgan Horse Show. He and his son have won many classes for harness pairs for their owner J. C. Ferguson, Broadwall Farm, Greene, R.I. In this photo they are driven by Mr. Ferguson, accompanied by his wife, to a basket phaeton in a Cavalcade Americana class. Photo by Freudy courtesy J. C. Ferugson.

The Modern Morgan

Since World War II the numbers of Morgan breeders and Morgan horses have increased greatly. The breed is widely distributed over the United States, but is outranked numerically by all the other breeds of light horses except the Hackney.

Most typical Morgans are from 14.1 to 15.2 hands in height and weigh from 900 to 1,150 pounds. They are compact, fully made, muscular, smooth horses. They often have a rather cresty neck, great slope to the shoulder, and good quality bone. Most Morgans have snappy action and a spirited but tractable disposition. Chestnut, bay, brown, and black are the usual colors with limited white markings.

Morgan horses are not specialists. They are good, versatile, general purpose horses. They can be used in harness, or under saddle, with English or Western tack. Some live their lives as cow

Merry Go Boy, first at the National Tennessee Walking Horse Celebration, Shelbyville, Tenn., as a weanling, yearling, two-year-old, and three-year-old, and Grand Champion in 1947 and 1948. As a sire this black stallion did much to improve the quality and conformation of Tennessee Walking Horses. He was owned by the S.W. Beech Stables, Lewisburg, Tenn., where he stood at a $400 fee. Photo by Les Nelson.

ponies in the Western cattle country. Many serve as pleasure riding horses all over America.

Morgan breeders who boast of the versatility of their breed should remember that structurally correct underpinning and the ability to go a good trot are basic ingredients in the make-up of any high-class horse. Sometimes they have stressed other features to the detriment of the breed.

THE TENNESSEE WALKING HORSE

The Tennessee Walking Horse originated within an area of about 14 counties in the middle section of Tennessee more than a century ago. It did not come into great public notice, however, until after the organization of the Tennessee Walking Horse Breeders Association at Lewisburg, Tennessee in 1935. The establishment of the Tennessee Walking Horse National Celebration at Shelbyville, Tennessee in 1939, and the annual staging of this big show also helped to popularize the breed.

Development of the Breed

Breed-building sires and dams of the Tennessee Walking Horse breed have had pedigrees that traced to the Thoroughbred, the Standardbred, the Morgan, and the American Saddle Horse. For many generations the breeders of Tennessee Walking Horses selected their breeding stock with the aim of breed improvement always in mind. The best representatives of the breed today may boast such characteristics as the endurance that was typical of their Thoroughbred and Standardbred ancestry, the docility and the balanced conformation of the Morgan, and the style, finish, and quality of the American Saddlebred. As a result of the mingling of these various breed influences the modern Tennessee Walking Horse has been developed as a separate breed entity.

The Tennessee Walking Horse has been bred for utility. In the beginning this horse was asked to do three tasks. He was used for riding, for driving in light harness, and for tilling the fields. He had to fit into a program of sound farm economy. He was a saddle horse, a driving horse, and a work horse.

Today, however, the Tennessee Walking Horse is most often used as a riding horse, a pleasure mount for those who seek diversion and recreation in the saddle on bridle trails and in the open field. Walking Horses are seen regularly in the show arenas at our large horse shows where their distinctive gaits have won them recognition.

Foundation Sires

The horse most responsible for the establishment of the Tennessee Walking Horse as a breed was the Standardbred stallion Allan F-1. He was foaled in Kentucky in 1886 the property of E. D. Herr. Allan F-1 was sired by Allandorf, a grandson of George Wilkes that was the most famous son of Hambletonian 10. The dam of Allan F-1 was a mare of Morgan breeding named Maggie Marshall. She was sired by Bradford's Telegraph by Black Hawk by Sherman by Justin Morgan.

Allan F-1 was sold with his dam to George F. Fly of Elyria, Ohio. When the colt went into training he was inclined to pace. Because his owner wanted trotters, the colt was returned to Kentucky, and was sold for $355 to go to Tennessee. He eventually got to the stable of James Brantley who liked his tendency to do the running walk. In the hope of producing good plantation horses Mr. Brantley bred Allan F-1 to his best walking mare, Gertrude. Gertrude traced through her dam to Gifford Morgan. In 1906 Gertrude produced Roan Allen F-38 by Allan F-1.

Roan Allen F-38 was a roan horse with flaxen mane and tail, a blazed face, and hind stockings. Since the great majority of Tennessee Walking Horses trace to Allan F-1 through Roan Allen F-38, many people regard Roan Allen F-38 as the real foundation sire of the breed.

Present Day Blood Lines

The two leading sires of Tennessee Walking Horses of modern times, Merry Go Boy and Midnight Sun, traced directly in the male line to Allan F-1. Merry Go Boy was out of Wiser's Dimples. This mare was sired by an American Saddlebred Horse, but her dam was a daughter of Allan F-1. Inasmuch as the Tennessee Walking Horse Breeders Association of America permits breeders to use artificial insemination, both Merry Go Boy and Midnight Sun had many get. The male line of descent is shown below.

> *Allan F-1*
> Roan Allen F-38
> | Merry Boy
> | Merry Go Boy
> | Wilson's Allen
> | Midnight Sun

Walking Horse Characteristics

The typical Tennessee Walking Horse stands about 15.2 hands in height and weighs 1,000 to 1,200 pounds. The best specimens of the breed are balanced in conformation, are attractive about their heads, and stand squarely on clean, hard legs. They can do a flat-foot walk, a running walk, and a canter. There is a wide range in color—chestnut, black, roan, white, bay, brown, gray, and sometimes palomino. White markings are very common, especially on roan horses.

The breed still needs refinement and finish. Coarseness appears too frequently. The set of the underpinning needs improvement. Long backs, steep croups, splay-footedness, and sickle hocks occur too often.

Walking Horse Gaits

In the show ring Tennessee Walking Horses have to perform at the walk, the running walk, and the canter. The walk is a four-beat gait. The horse should move with a long, true, prompt stride at least four miles per hour.

The running walk has the same sequence of hoof beats as the flat-footed walk, but the cadence is much faster. The running walk is characterized by a much greater overstep than is seen in the ordinary walk. That is, the hind foot is grounded much more in advance of the front hoof print on the same side than it is in the flat-footed walk. Most horses of show calibre overstep three feet or so and move two to three times as fast as they do at the walk. Many horses nod their heads considerably when at the running walk. Their ears move back and forth and some horses even click their teeth. The gait is a very free and easy motion, comfortable for the rider and easy on the horse. The tremendous overstride gives a smooth, gliding sensation. The running walk can be performed over most any kind of surface. For this reason it was a very useful gait for the plantation horse used by overseers of field labor in the South in the old days.

The canter is a three-beat gait, a restrained gallop. It should be a smooth, collected, graceful gait. Some riders of Tennessee Walking Horses lift and pump a horse's head so much that the canter becomes entirely too artificial.

The principal show for horses of this breed is the National Tennessee Walking Horse Celebration held annually at Shelbyville, Tennessee.

THE APPALOOSA

Horses with the distinctive color patterns found in Appaloosa horses have been known for centuries. They are depicted in the art of ancient China, the Middle East, and Egypt. Such horses probably reached Spain by way of North Africa when the Moors took over the country. Early Spanish explorers to the New World

Mighty High, grand champion mare 1967 National Appaloosa Horse Show, Walla Walla, Wash. Sired by High Hand and out of Ayoka. Owned by Carl Gene Miller, Morton, Ill. Photo by Johnny Johnston.

Capay Oak Chip, first prize two-year-old and champion junior gelding 1967 National Appaloosa Horse Show. Sired by Bright Chip and out of Montana Bells. Owned by Capay Rancho, Orland, Calif. Photo by Johnny Johnston.

brought horses to Mexico and the southwestern part of what is now the United States. Indian tribes from the Northwest likely stole or captured horses from the Southwest. When Lewis and Clark made their expedition they found the Nez Percé Indians riding useful horses many of which had distinctive spotting patterns.

The Nez Percé Indians were located mainly along the Snake and Clearwater rivers in territory that now is included in southeastern Washington, northeastern Oregon, much of Idaho, and even Montana. They used their horses for war, for buffalo hunting, for travel, and for racing. They are said to have practiced selective breeding and the castration of inferior stallions.

In the Nez Percé country was a small stream called the Pelouse, or Palouse, that flowed into the Snake River. Early white settlers came to call any spotted horse belonging to an Indian along this stream a Palouse or an Apalousey. The present breed name of Appaloosa derives from this usage.

When some of the Nez Percé revolted and were forced off their tribal lands that had been guaranteed by the treaty of 1855 and when Chief Joseph, following a long and arduous retreat with his people, surrendered to prevent total annihilation, the tribe was exiled to Oklahoma. They had some 3,000 horses, about one-half of which were Appaloosas. These horses were captured by General Nelson Miles, taken to Fort Keough on the Yellowstone, and sold. The Appaloosa thus became a "lost breed."

An article on Appaloosas that appeared in the January, 1937 issue of *The Western Horseman* created interest among a number of horsemen in forming a breed society. Claude J. Thompson of Moro, Oregon who had been breeding Appaloosas for many years did the preliminary organizational work. The Appaloosa Horse Club was incorporated December 30, 1938, and Mr. Thompson served as president until 1948. World War II curtailed the activities of early members of the club. Following the war, George B. Hatley of Moscow, Idaho, the club secretary, and Dr. Francis Haines of Lewiston, Idaho, the vice-president worked on the stud book. The first volume was published in 1948. The registrations were closed to foundation stock August 1, 1949. The first All-Appaloosa Show was held June 20, 1949. Since that time the interest in breeding and using Appaloosas has increased greatly. Registrations increased from 612 in 1949 to 27,992 in 1979.

Appaloosas find great favor in the rugged cow country of the western United States for use as cow ponies. Some Appaloosas are raced, mostly at short distances. Many are used for pleasure riding under Western tack and for competitive events featured at western horse shows. They are hardy, rugged, tough horses with a lot of stamina.

Jesse Redheart, great-grandnephew of Chief Joseph of the Nez Percé, in full regalia on an Appaloosa. Photo courtesy *The Western Horseman.*

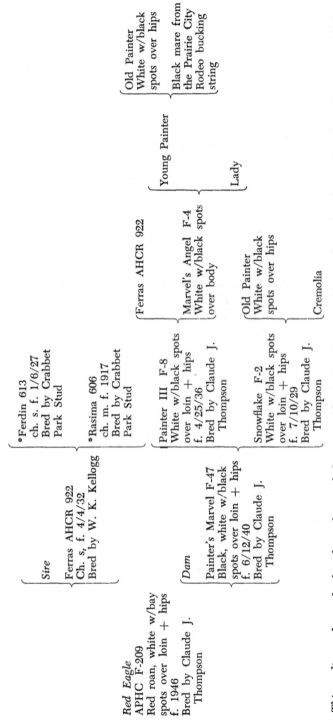

This pedigree shows the breeding of one of the most influential stallions in the Appaloosa breed. It also shows how some of the Appaloosas in Vol. I of their Stud Book resulted from crosses with Arabians. Old Painter was the horse on whose blood the Appaloosa Horse Club was founded by Claude Thompson. Red Eagle, bred by Mr. Thompson, was sold to John Derek for a movie that was not made. He then was sold to Thomas L. Clay, 1001 Ranch, Lincoln Co., Nevada. Red Eagle was National Champion in 1951 and has sired four National champions. Red Eagle died May 17, 1971, aged 25.

Crystal Curtain, first prize yearling filly 1967 National Appaloosa Horse Show. Sired by Dragon Seed and out of Soo Cerise. Owned by A. L. Learner, Danville, Calif. Photo by Johnny Johnston.

The most typical Appaloosas measure about 15 to 15.2 hands in height, and weigh 1,000 to 1,150 pounds. Distinctive features are the white sclera of the eye, the parti-colored skin around the lips and nostrils, and the fine, thin mane and tail.

Several major color patterns plus variations and combinations are found. The Appaloosa Horse Club does not favor any pattern over another. Among the typical color patterns are:

A horse having dark roan or solid-colored fore parts, but white with dark "squaw spots" over the loin and hips.

A white horse with spots over the entire body.

A horse having dark roan or solid-colored fore parts with white over the loin and hips.

A horse having dark base color with various sizes of white spots or specks over the body.

A horse having mottling of dark and white covering the body.

Some color patterns may not be apparent at birth. Some patterns vary a bit in appearance with the season of the year and length of hair coat.

The Quarter Horse as a roping horse. Photo by Dixon, courtesy the Bateman Ranch.

The working Quarter Horse in action. Frank Albright riding Cindy, a champion cutting horse, at the Bateman Ranch, Knox City, Tex. Photo by Dixon, courtesy the Bateman Ranch.

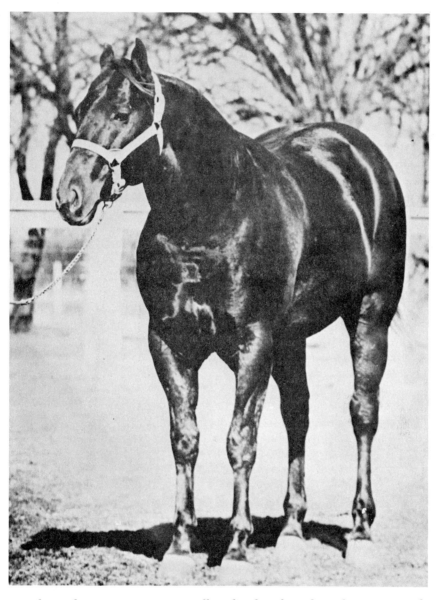

Hired Hand, a Quarter Horse stallion bred and used on the King Ranch, Kingsville, Texas. He was sired by Old Sorrel, the foundation sire of the King Ranch Quarter Horses. Hired Hand died July 18, 1970, aged 27, and was buried next to Old Sorrel in the Santa Gertrudis Division of the King Ranch.
Photo courtesy the King Ranch.

THE QUARTER HORSE

No breed of horses in the world has increased in numbers so much in recent years as the American Quarter Horse. Quarter Horses find wide acceptance all over America as pleasure riding horses under Western tack. Thousands are used as stock horses on cattle ranches. Some are trained as polo ponies, and many are raced at short distances. These many uses indicate the typical Quarter Horse characteristics—level headedness, agility, speed, and stamina.

The American Quarter Horse Association was organized in March, 1940. It was re-organized to include some rival associations in March, 1950. Thus, the Quarter Horse, as a breed with an organization of breeders and a stud book, is quite new. It is in many respects still in its formative stages. Many of the leading Quarter Horses of the day are half-Thoroughbred or at most only one generation removed from Thoroughbred breeding.

However, as a strain of working stock horses and short distance race horses, the Quarter Horse dates to colonial times in this country. The so-called American Quarter Running Horse was known in Virginia, Maryland, and the Carolinas, and always appeared in frontier areas as the country opened up to the west. The principal development of the breed as we know it today occurred in Texas and the Southwest.

Important Early Breeders

William Anson of Christoval, Texas was about the first really noted improver of the Quarter Horse. He not only bred, used, and raced Quarter Horses, but also studied their history and blood lines. An important stallion he used was Harmon Baker by Peter McCue.

W. T. Waggoner of Vernon and Fort Worth, Texas had one of the largest ranches in that state and one of the best bands of Quarter Horses. When the stud book was formed "Waggoner bred" was considered pedigree enough.

Coke Roberds of Hayden, Colorado and Dan Casement of Manhattan, Kansas were other noted early breeders.

Of the breeders of 50 years ago that are still active today the King Ranch at Kingsville, Texas is the best known. The King Ranch has carried on a very scientific program of line-breeding with their horses. The stallion Old Sorrel, foaled in 1915, was the foundation sire of the King Ranch Quarter Horses. He was a grandson of Peter McCue. The King Ranch has sold Quarter Horses to Brazil, Argentina, and Australia. Horses of their breeding have gone to studs in many states.

The champion Quarter Horse stallion Poco Bueno. In stud for many years at the Waggoner Ranch, Vernon, Texas, Poco Bueno sired 36 AQHA champions. He died November 28, 1969, aged 25, and was buried on the ranch. Photos by Stryker.

Poco Bueno

Foundation Sires

When the American Quarter Horse stud book was established, 18 of the first 19 registration numbers assigned to horses in Volume I were saved for living horses that had proved themselves as outstanding sires of offspring of the Quarter Horse type. The first number was reserved for the stallion that was named Grand Champion at the Southwestern Exposition and Fat Stock Show at Fort Worth in 1941. This horse was Wimpy P-1, foaled in 1936 and bred by the King Ranch. He was a double grandson of Old Sorrel.

Most Influential Early Sire

Peter McCue was the most influential sire in the early development of the Quarter Horse. Of the 19 foundation sires, 7 traced directly to Peter McCue in the male line. About one-fifth of the horses in the early volumes of the stud book descended directly from this stallion.

Peter McCue was bred by Samuel Watkins of Petersburg, Illinois, and was foaled in 1895. Peter McCue was registered as a Thoroughbred by the Jockey Club. His sire was given as Duke of the Highlands, a Thoroughbred stallion owned by Mr. Watkins. Notwithstanding this fact, the American Quarter Horse Association believes that Peter McCue was sired by the Watkins-owned Quarter Horse stallion, Dan Tucker, and that is how his breeding appears in Quarter Horse pedigrees. Peter McCue's dam was Nora M., a daughter of the Thoroughbred stallion Voltiguer. Peter McCue was raced in the Middle West. He did stud duty in Texas and Oklahoma, and eventually was owned by Coke Roberds, Hayden, Colorado.

SOME MAJOR SIRE LINES IN THE QUARTER HORSE BREED

Traveler Line

Traveler (1878–1910)
  Little Joe (1904–1929)
    Zantanon (1917–1941)
      King (1932–1958)
        Poco Bueno (1944–1969)
          Poco Tivio (1947–1976)
          Poco Dell (1950)
          Poco Pine (1954–1974)
        Royal King (1943)
        Small Town Dude
          Blondy's Dude (1957–1980)
        Tabano King (1956)

Shiloh and Peter McCue Line

Shiloh (1844–1874)
  Old Billy (186?)
    Whalebone (1868)
      Locks Rondo (1880–1897)
        Little Rondo (1895–1915)
          Yellow Jacket (1908–1934)
            Cowboy (1927–1946)
            Hard Twist
            Blackburn (1927–1949)
    Cold Deck (1868?)
      Barney Owens (1871?)
        Dan Tucker (1887–1912)
          Peter McCue (1895–1923)
            Hickory Bill (1907–1923)
              Old Sorrel (1915–1945)
                Little Richard (1922–1950)
                  Peppy (1934–1965)
                Solis (1923–1936)
                  Wimpy P-1 (1936–1959)
                    Bill Cody (1944)
                      Joe Cody (1952)
                Hired Hand (1943–1970)
                  Hired Hand's Cardinal (1949)
                    Cardenal Chico (1955)
                      Mendigo (1960)
                        El Pobre
                Silver King (1937)
                DoubleDiamond
                  Two D Two
                    Two Eyed Jack (1961)
              Harmon Baker (1907–1925)
                Dodger (1924–1941)
                  Pretty Boy (1928)
                    Pretty Buck (1942)
                      Snipper W (1946)
            Buck Thomas (1921)

Joe Blair Line

Joe Blair (TB)
  Joe Reed (1921–1947)
    Joe Reed II (1936)
      Leo (1940–1967)
        Leo San
          Mr. San Peppy (1968)
        Croton Oil (1955)

Three Bars Line

Three Bars (TB) (1940–   )
| Lucky Bar (TB)
| Impressive (1969)
| Rocket Bar (TB) (1951)
| Rocket Wrangler (1968)
| Sugar Bars (1951)
| Otoe (1960–1971)
| Otoe's Hand
| Lightning Bar
| Doc Bar (1956)
| Steel Bars (1953)
| Triple Chick (1955)
| Three Chicks (1959)
| Three Ohs (1966)
| Alamitos Bar (1959)
| Bar Flower (1962)
| Tonto Bars Gill
| Tonto Bars Hank (1958)
| The Ole Man (1963)

Top Deck Line

Top Deck (TB) (1945)
| Moon Deck (1950)
| | Jet Deck (1960–1971)
| | | Jet Smooth (1965)
| | | Easy Jet (1967)
| | | Flaming Jet (1971)
| | Top Moon (1960)
| | | Lady Bug's Moon (1966)
| | | Bugs Alive In 75 (1973)
| | | Moon Lark (1976)
| Go Man Go (1953)
| Duplicate Copy (1962)
| Rebel Cause (1958)

Leading Breeders and Sires of AQHA Champions

Through 1979 the leading breeder of AQHA champions was Howard Pitzer, Ericson, Nebraska, whose stallion Two Eyed Jack was the leading sire of AQHA champions. Two Eyed Jack was a great-great-great-great-grandson of Peter McCue. H.J. Wiescamp of Alamosa, Colorado, was the second ranking breeder. The Waggoner Estate of Vernon, Texas, ranked third. Their late stallion Poco Bueno and his son Poco Pine were tied for second place on the list of sires of AQHA champions.

Two Eyed Jack, many times grand champion Quarter Horse and leading sire of AQHA champions and show Register of Merit qualifiers. He is pictured here at 14 years of age. Owned by Howard Pitzer, Pitzer Ranch, Ericson, Nebraska. Photo by Alfred Janssen III.

The Thoroughbred stallion, Three Bars, leading sire of racing Quarter Horses from 1949 through 1968. Owned by Sid Vail, Victorville, Calif. Photo courtesy The Quarter Horse Journal.

Quarter Horse Racing

Quarter Horse racing has grown as the breed has increased in numbers. The American Quarter Horse Association registered 137,090 horses in 1980—far more horses than were registered by any other breed society. During the same year 20,551 horses started in 13,777 recognized Quarter Horse races for total purses of $38,641,432.

Most Quarter Horse racing is conducted in the western and southwestern states, as well as in Canada and Mexico. Although the breed gets its name from the ability to run a quarter of a mile, only 820 (5.95%) of the 13,777 races run in 1980 were at that distance. Almost one-fourth of the races were at 400 yards, and one-third were at 350 yards.

Leading Sires of Racing Quarter Horses

Most racing Quarter Horses are largely Thoroughbred in their breeding. The leading sires are Thoroughbred stallions or horses with several Thoroughbred crosses close up in their pedigrees.

Three Bars, a Thoroughbred foaled in 1940, was one of the most influential sires of racing Quarter Horses. For over 20 years he topped the lists of sires of money winners and sires of Register of Merit performers. The sons of Three Bars, from both Thoroughbred and Quarter Horse mares, have made him the leading sire of sires. Three Bars was sired by Percentage and was out of Myrtle Dee by Luke McLuke. He was owned by Sid Vail, Victorville, California.

Other important sires of racing Quarter Horses have been Top Deck, Depth Charge, Spotted Bull, Rocket Bar, Custus Rastus, Azure Te, Aforethought, and Jack Straw—all of them Thoroughbreds. Go Man Go by Top Deck and Johnny Dial by Depth Charge were from mares of at least some Quarter Horse blood. Both were top racing Quarter Horses and both became influential sires. The sons, grandsons, and further male descendants of Top Deck have been very important in the world of Quarter Horse racing.

Quarter Horse Characteristics

Most Quarter Horses measure from 14.2 to 15.2 hands in height, and weigh 1,050 to 1,250 pounds. Bay, brown, chestnut, and dun are common colors. Some roans, greys, and blacks appear.

There is considerable variation in body conformation. Some breeders prefer a racy type, others a thicker made horse. Of all our breeds Quarter Horses are typically the most muscular. Great muscular definition is often seen over the arms and forearms, and through the stifles, thighs, and gaskins. The typical Quarter Horse has strong jaws, clean throat, low head carriage, and a well-balanced conformation. Quarter Horses often move with a low, pointing, rather short stride at the walk and trot.

Common faults are coarseness, short, straight necks, low withers, long backs, high hips, and crooked hocks.

The best racing Quarter Horses have been largely Thoroughbred in their breeding, with most of the good Thoroughbred characteristics strongly marked in their make-up.

BREEDS OF PONIES

The term "horse" in American horse shows designates animals over 14.2 hands, except registered Appaloosas, Arabians, Morgans, Palominos, Pintos, and Quarter Horses which may be under that measurement. The term "pony" designates any animal 14.2 hands and under with the exceptions noted above. In some European countries the division between horse and pony is set at 14 hands.

Shetland Pony

The smallest of our breeds is the Shetland pony. The American Shetland Pony Club sets a height limit of 11.2 hands, or 46 inches. The majority of ponies in the Shetland Islands are considerably smaller.

The Shetland pony breed originated hundreds of years ago on the rough, rocky Shetland Islands located north of Scotland and west of Norway. The climate of the islands is often damp and cold. Pasture and hay are the principal feeds. The ponies that developed there had to be extremely hardy to survive.

In their native land the ponies were used as pack animals to haul peat that was used for fuel. About the middle of the 19th century some Shetlands were taken to England for work in the coal mines.

At about the same time, some of the larger landowners on the islands began to breed their ponies more systematically to improve their stock. The stud established by the Marquis of Londonderry on the Island of Bressay was an important source of good breeding ponies.

The Shetland Pony Stud Book Society was formed and Volume I of the stud book published in 1891. Stud books also were established in the United States in 1888, in Canada, and in the Netherlands.

The Shetland pony on the Islands is still a pony of drafty proportions, shortlegged, heavy-boned, and full-middled. The ponies imported to the United States prior to World War I were of this type. A few such ponies are found today.

The Shetland type that has evolved in this country in the last 50 years has great quality, presence, and personality, and a distinctive trot showing height of stride and flexion of knees and hocks. Perhaps the pony most responsible for propagating the refined American type was King Larigo, a noted show pony of the 1920s. He became an outstanding sire for his breeder George A. Heyl of Washington, Illinois. Curtiss Frisco Pete, the leading Shetland breed class winner and top sire of the 1950s–1960s, was a direct descendant of King Larigo. The American Shetland has a thinner neck, more sloping shoulder, narrower body, more nearly level top line, and more springy action than the Island type. Probably 90 per cent of the Shetlands in the United States are of the American type. Almost all colors are found—spotted, chestnut, black, brown, bay, grey, white, palomino, silver dappled.

Through the years the Shetland pony has become very popular all over the United States. One reason for the expansion of the breed has been its ready acceptance as a child's mount. Surefooted, docile, and an easy keeper, the Shetland can be kept in rather small quarters. Many are kept for children on the outskirts of cities as well as on farms.

Curtiss Frisco Pete, six times champion stallion at the Shetland Pony Congress, Waterloo, Iowa. Premier stallion at the Fernwood Farm, Barrington, Ill., he was the leading sire of halter class winners four times and of performance ponies five times. Photos courtesy Fernwood Farm.

Curtiss Frisco Pete

In horse shows Shetland classes may be divided according to height, one class open to ponies 10.3 hands (43 inches) and under, the other for ponies over 10.3 and not exceeding 11.2 hands (46 inches).

Ponies in harness are shown to a small viceroy buggy at a "Park Pace" and a "Smart Trot." At a park pace the pony should trot slowly and collectedly with medium height and reach of stride. A pony at a smart trot should show more brilliance, height, and flexion. The forearm should be raised at least to horizontal position and the hocks should be well flexed. Excessive speed is neither required nor expected.

In classes for roadster Shetlands the ponies are shown to a roadster cart and are rigged with a snaffle bit, overcheck, running martingale, and trotting boots. They are driven at a jog, a road gait, and at speed.

Shetlands under saddle may be shown with English or Western tack according to class specifications.

Coed Coch Hillstream, Welsh riding pony stallion sired by Bwlch Hill Wind and out of Coed Coch Penwn. At the dispersal of the Coed Coch Stud in Wales in 1978, this pony was sold for 2,000 guineas to Mrs. Clay Camp, Keswick, Virginia. Photo from the National Welsh Pony Yearbook, courtesy Kathy Huber.

Coed Coch Llwydrew, grey Welsh pony owned by Mrs. William C. Cox, The Oaks, Cohasset, Mass., shows the long, straight, powerful stride of good Welsh ponies at the trot. Photo by Freudy.

Welsh Pony

Next to the Shetland, the Welsh pony is the best known in America of the many pony breeds developed in Great Britain. The ponies running over the hills and mountains of Wales have a long complex historical background. The native stock on occasion would be improved by an Arabian stallion turned out to run with the mares. Over the years several rather distinct types evolved such as the Welsh mountain pony and the Welsh cob.

Until very recent times the Welsh pony has not been bred or used widely in the United States, and never was promoted as was the Shetland. In 1956 only 351 ponies were registered by the Welsh Pony Society of America. Registrations during 1978 numbered 475 head.

Welsh ponies in the United States may not exceed 14.2 hands. Since they are larger than Shetlands they move more like a horse, and make excellent intermediate mounts for children not yet large enough to ride a full-sized horse with ease and comfort.

Welsh ponies find special favor as hunter ponies. Many successful U.S. Pony Club Teams have been mounted on Welsh ponies at their rallies. Welsh ponies are hardy, spirited, strong, proud-going ponies. Any color except piebald or skewbald is permitted in the breed.

American horse shows divide Welsh ponies into "A" and "B" sections. Ponies in "A" sections must not exceed 12.2 hands, those in "B" sections are over 12.2 but not over 14.2 hands.

Six performance class sections are offered. Welsh pleasure ponies are shown under saddle or in harness. In the roadster pony section the ponies are driven at a jog, a road gait, and at speed to a small bike. They are rigged with a snaffle bit, overcheck, martingale, and quarter boots. Classes for roadster ponies under saddle sometimes are offered, also. Ponies in the formal driving section are shown without any special equipment at an animated, natural trot and an animated walk to a small four-wheeled buggy. In the Welsh fine harness pony section the ponies are brought out in light

Wennol Beckan, Welsh pony owned by Mrs. William C. Cox, The Oaks, Cohasset, Mass. Blue ribbon winner at Piping Rock and other big shows in the East. Photo by Freudy.

Poinsettia, champion Hackney pony at Devon, the Ohio and Illinois State Fairs, American Royal, and the International Livestock Exposition in 1966. Owned by Lydia Luhman Pederson, Clover Leaf Farm, Caledonia, Ill. Jack Kooyman, whip. This red bay mare was sold in 1967 to Arthur Birtcher, Santa Ana, Calif. Photo by McClasky.

harness with snaffle bit and overcheck to a small viceroy buggy. They are shown at an animated park trot and at an animated walk. They should move in a fashion similar to that of a Fine Harness horse. The last section is for Welsh hunter and jumper ponies. A good Welsh pony ridden by an accomplished hunter-seat rider shows a long, reaching, powerful stride with great impulsion and driving power off the hocks. The last section is for Welsh ponies in draft harness. In this section the ponies are shown naturally, with long mane and tail, wearing heavy draft type harness with collar and breeching, hitched to a four-wheeled wagon (or a cart for singles), at a working trot and flat-footed walk. Utility is stressed for ponies, harness, and wagon.

Some Important Breeders

For over half a century the Coed Coch stud, situated in the Denbighshire hills in the north of Wales, was the most influential Welsh pony breeding establishment. Miss Margaret (Daisy) Brodrick started breeding Welsh ponies there in 1924. She kept a very high quality stud until her death in 1962. She left Coed Coch to Lieutenant Colonel E.W. Williams-Wynn, whose family had been horse breeders in Wales for several centuries. Nearly 200 ponies were maintained. Representatives of the stud became noted show winners in Great Britain; they were sold throughout the British Isles as well as to North America and Australia.

Coed Coch ("the Red Wood," in English) was best known for its Section A or Welsh Mountain ponies, but they also produced excellent Section B ponies of greater size and also some top-quality riding ponies. Almost every Welsh pony breeder of consequence in the United States has used ponies with Coed Coch bloodlines.

Following the death of Lt. Col. Williams-Wynn the Coed Coch stud was sold by his heirs to pay the death duties. The dispersal sale held in 1978 realized £184,453 for 219 ponies, an average of £842. Mrs. Clay Camp of Keswick, Virginia, got the good grey riding pony stallion, Coed Coch Hillstream, for £2,000 at this sale.

Among American breeders of recent years Mrs. J. Austin duPont of Liseter Hall Farm, Newtown Square, Pennsylvania, was one of the most prominent. Mrs. duPont's ponies frequently dominated the Welsh pony breed classes at the Devon horse show at Devon, Pennsylvania. Her four-in-hand of Welsh ponies hitched to a Brewster brake won the four-in-hand division of the driving marathon at Devon, the largest of American outdoor horse shows.

Connemara Pony

Connemara ponies have been bred on the west coast of Ireland for many years, but have been known in the United States only since the 1950s.

The native ponies developed on the wild mountains and hills of western Ireland had to subsist under difficult conditions. They grazed on gorse and heather and lived all year in the open. As a result, the Connemara ponies that survived had great hardiness, constitutional vigor, and stamina. Infusions of Thoroughbred and Arabian blood were occasionally made by turning out such stallions to run with the mares.

The Connemara Pony Breeders Society with headquarters at Galway, Eire, was formed in 1923. Each year the Society buys about a dozen promising colts and turns them out on the hills. They have also at times introduced small Thoroughbred and part-Arabian stallions in some sections of Connemara.

The American Connemara Pony Society was formed in 1956, and in 1959 put out their stud book with 155 entries. Registrations during 1979 numbered 81 purebreds and 35 half-breds.

Connemara ponies range in height from 12.2 to 14.2 hands.

Connemaras in action. The winning Hunt Team at the 1965 Bridlespur Hunter Trials owned by Mr. and Mrs. Clarkson Carpenter, Jr., Three Creek Farm, St. Charles, Mo. The ponies pictured here are Tre Awain Tinkerman, Jenna Johnson, up; Tourbillon, Laura Carpenter, up; and Tre Awain Nameless, Betsy Lewis, up. The stallion Tourbillon was champion at the 1966 Midwest Connemara Breeders' Show and Connemara division of the Bridlespur Hunt Horse Show, St. Louis. Photo by Gulick courtesy Mrs. Clarkson Carpenter, Jr.

They average about 14 hands. Almost all colors except piebald and skewbald are found. Grey and dun are common, as well as bay, brown, and black. Chestnut is not a typical color in the breed. Connemaras are big enough to carry an adult in the hunt field, but tractable enough for teen-age riders.

The most brilliant show jumper in Ireland in recent years has been the bay gelding Dundrum. He is an overgrown first-cross Connemara sired by a Thoroughbred stallion, Little Heaven, that had been turned out by the Connemara Pony Society. Dundrum measures just over 15 hands. Owned and ridden by Tommy Wade he won the King George V trophy at the White City Show, London, in 1963. Dundrum has jumped as high as seven feet two inches in puissance classes.

A first-cross Connemara named Little Model has carried the famous English dressage rider, Mrs. V. D. S. Williams, to many victories. Little Model was out of a Connemara mare, but was sired by the Thoroughbred stallion Little Heaven. Mrs. Williams rode Little Model in the dressage competition in the 1960 Olympic Games at Rome. In 1961 Mrs. Williams riding Little Model placed third in the European Dressage Championship at Aachen.

In the United States, Connemaras are shown in the style of hunter ponies. They appear in classes for pony hunters under saddle, pony hunter hacks, pony working hunters, and, of course, in jumping classes.

Probably the largest single exportation from Ireland to America was a group of 54 head sent over in 1958 by Stanislaus Lynch.

Hackney Pony

The Hackney breed discussed in Chapter 7 also comes in pony size. These ponies are registered with the American Hackney Horse Society. Hackney ponies are used almost exclusively as driving ponies in heavy harness. For horse show purposes Hackney pony classes are divided into two height divisions. One is for ponies 13 hands and under, the other for ponies 13 but not exceeding 14.2 hands.

Hackney ponies are presented with a short mane and tail docked quite short. They are driven with either a Liverpool or elbow bit and a side bearing rein. The usual show vehicle is a small viceroy buggy except in gig classes and four-in-hand classes. Hackney ponies are driven at a park pace and at a smart trot. Excessive speed is not required or desired.

Hackney ponies should be balanced in conformation, refined about their fronts, lean, and clean in bone and joints. Sharp withers, sloping shoulders, short backs and couplings, rounding ribs, level croups, and heavily muscled thighs should be evident. Folding of the knees and flexing of the hocks characterize the high stride of good Hackney ponies.

In motion, at either a park pace or a smart trot, height, length, and trueness should be features of the stride. The length of the toes and weight of the shoes should not be so great that action is artificialized. The trot of the Hackney pony should be a God-given trot rather than a man-made gait.

A top Hackney pony with his extremely high-stepping trot and high spirits can give a brilliant, dashing show in harness. Occasionally Hackneys will be seen under saddle in children's classes. However, the temperament and high action of most Hackneys render them unsuitable for such work. It is a mistake for parents to mount their children on such ponies because a smooth polished performance is virtually impossible.

Mr. Sandman, Harness Pony champion at many major shows in the 1960s for Mrs. Victoria Armstrong, ABC Farm, Brampton, Ontario. Later owned by the Charnigan Farm, Topanga, Calif., he became a very successful sire. He died in 1977 when almost 25 years old. Photo by Budd.

Harness Pony

In American horse shows the division for Harness Ponies is most often filled with ponies of Hackney breeding. However, a harness pony in performance classes may be any breed or combination of breeds with long mane and undocked tail. The maximum height for harness ponies is 12.2 hands (50 inches). These ponies are shown with a Liverpool bit to a small viceroy buggy or to a miniature side rail buggy of the fine harness type. They are driven at a park pace and at a smart trot and are expected to have all-around action. As is true of Hackney ponies when they appear in ladies's, amateur, and junior exhibitor classes they must be driven in the half-cheek, appear to have perfect mouths, should stand quietly while remaining checked up, and back easily.

Noble Kalarama, an American Saddlebred stallion that was a champion in fine harness. Pictured here at 20 years of age, he demonstrates the proud, lofty carriage and the high, balanced trot shown by top Fine Harness Horses. He is driven here by Jack Thompson. Photo by John R. Horst.

10

Horse Breeding

The prospective horse breeder should be a good judge of horses, if he is to make intelligent selection of his foundation stock. He should have as much horse handling experience as possible. He should recognize the problems and handicaps associated with the production of horses.

The investment required to start any horse breeding enterprise is high in comparison to costs with other livestock programs. Grade mares cost more than grade sows. Purebred mares cost more than purebred sows.

The turnover in the horse business is slow in comparison to that in cattle, sheep, or hog projects. A mare's pregnancy lasts approximately eleven months. Two or three more years must elapse before her foal can be useful for any job. In contrast, if one is breeding sheep or swine, the ewes and sows can be bred, their offspring born, grown, fed, and marketed in eight to ten months.

The element of risk is greater in handling pregnant mares and brood mares with foals than in caring for pregnant cows, sows, or ewes and their produce. The soundness of the offspring as a determining factor in the success of a horse breeding program is much more important than it is in cattle, sheep, and swine production.

The rate of reproduction in horses is low in comparison to that of other kinds of livestock. Under average farm conditions only 50 to 60 per cent of the mares bred produce living foals. About 8 to 10 per cent of the foals born do not survive. The average brood sow raises over 7 pigs per litter and does so twice a year.

SELECTION OF BREEDING STOCK

The horse breeder has three bases upon which to select animals for breeding purposes.

Individuality and Performance. Most breeders try to select
stallions and mares with good conformation, quality, soundness,
breed character, and way of going. Furthermore, they seek horses
that have shown that they can do their job well. Outstanding race
horses produce a larger percentage of superior racing offspring
than do mediocre race horses. The best saddle show horses produce more high-quality foals than do plain saddle horses.

Pedigree. Prospective breeding stock should also be considered
as representative of an ancestry. If a stallion has been sired by a
good horse from a good brood mare both of which consistently have
produced offspring that could do their job well he is more likely
to sire good foals himself than is a horse from poor parents. The
immediate ancestry should be considered. Noted great-grandpar-
ents are relatively unimportant. It is wise to remember when selecting stallions and mares for breeding purposes that inheritance
is from the ancestry through the parents to the progeny.

Progeny. The real test of the value of breeding stallions and
brood mares is the level of excellence found in their progeny. This
is the best single basis for choosing breeding stock. Brood mare
owners who want to improve their stock try to patronize stallions
whose get have demonstrated their ability to do well in their field
of service. If a mare's first three foals have been disappointing, it
is unlikely that any future foals will prove to be more satisfactory.

When young fillies are purchased as prospective additions to
the brood mare band or when colts are bought as future sires, they
have to be selected on their individuality, performance, and pedigree. But when mature horses are considered, their progeny offer
the best basis for selection or rejection.

SOME HORSE BREEDING TERMS

Breeding. Breeding can be defined as an attempt to regulate
the progeny by selecting the parents with the aim of improving the
stock. All those who wish to be successful in horse breeding must
have the goal of improvement constantly in mind.

The term breeding sometimes is used in reference to the blood
lines or ancestry of a horse, sometimes to the sexual mating.

Breeder. The breeder of a horse is the person who owned the
horse's dam at the time of mating. The breeder determined the
mating and caused it to be made. (In the United States the Jockey
Club rules state that the breeder of a Thoroughbred horse is the
person who owned its dam at the time the horse was foaled.)

Stud. A stud is a horse breeding establishment or breeding
farm. Sometimes the term is used more specifically in reference to

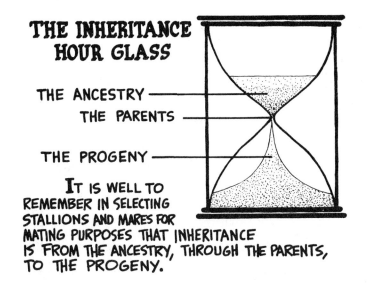

THE INHERITANCE
HOUR GLASS

THE ANCESTRY ————

THE PARENTS ————

THE PROGENY ————

IT IS WELL TO
REMEMBER IN SELECTING
STALLIONS AND MARES FOR
MATING PURPOSES THAT INHERITANCE
IS FROM THE ANCESTRY, THROUGH THE PARENTS,
TO THE PROGENY.

the collection of brood mares and stallions kept for breeding purposes at such an establishment. In the western part of the United
States, the term stud frequently is used colloquially as synonymous
with studhorse or (breeding) stallion.

Breed of livestock. A breed of livestock is a group of animals
of common origin within a species that have distinguishing characteristics not found in other members of the same species. Generations of selective breeding have so fixed these characteristics that
they are rather uniformly transmitted to successive generations. Today a strain of animals usually is not regarded as a breed unless
there is a pedigree registry association of breeders of those animals.

Registry association. A livestock registry association or breed
society performs many functions, among which may be: establish-
ing rules of registration; issuing registration certificates to qualified
stock; keeping a stud book or herd book; promoting the breed by
means of a breed journal, advertising, show, and sales.

Pedigree. A pedigree is a record of an animal's ancestry.

Pedigree Registration Certificate. A Pedigree Registration Certificate is the official written record of an animal's ancestry issued by
the breed registry association and bearing its official seal. The information given may include most or all of the following: name
and registration number of the animal; date of birth; color markings; photograph; tattoo identification; name and number of the
sire and dam and, sometimes, several generations of ancestors;
breeder's name and address; and names and addresses of subsequent
owners. Unless the registration papers are officially transferred fol-

Meadowlands, p, 3, 1:59⅖. A fast pacer with very good conformation, Meadowlands represents the best in Standardbred blood lines. He was sired by Adios, the leading sire of speed, and was out of Maggie Counsel, the dam of six horses with records under 2:00. Photo courtesy William B. Murray.

lowing the sale of a registered animal, the buyer really does not have title to the animal.

Purebred. A purebred horse is registered or eligible for registration in the stud book of his breed. The degree of purity of breeding depends on the eligibility rules of the registry association. Purebred horses are most frequently of a distinctive and useful type. They are descended from a long line of ancestors especially selected for this useful type by the men who founded and developed the breed.

Crossbred. A crossbred horse is one whose sire and dam are purebreds belonging to different breeds. The term crossbred is frequently used in reference to a horse sired by a purebred stallion and out of a high-grade mare of another breed. An example of cross breeding in horses is the use of Thoroughbred stallions on draft mares to produce heavy-weight hunters. Another example is the

PEDIGREE OF THE THOROUGHBRED STALLION
SECRETARIAT

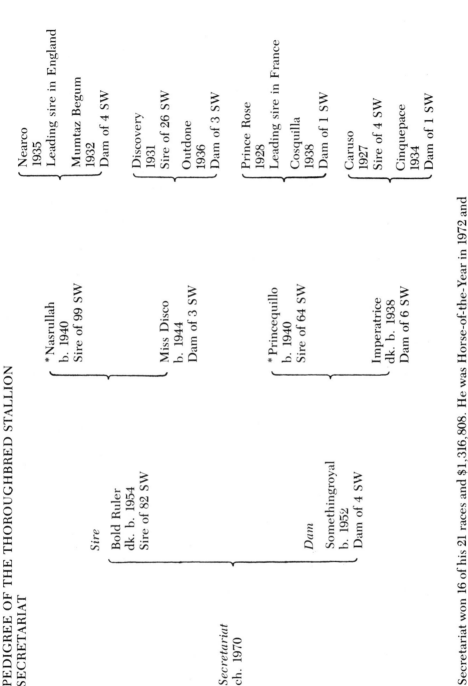

Secretariat won 16 of his 21 races and $1,316,808. He was Horse-of-the-Year in 1972 and again in 1973, when he won the Triple Crown. His sire, Bold Ruler, sired 82 stakes winners. His dam, Somethingroyal, produced 3 other stakes winners. Such a combination of individuality and performance together with demonstrated breeding ability in the immediate ancestry is what breeders seek when selecting a stallion for breeding purposes.

cross of Arabians on Welsh ponies to provide large hunter ponies for children not yet ready for big horses.

Grade. A grade horse is one bearing the marked influence of one or more generations of pure breeding. Grades usually are sired by purebred stallions and are out of mares of somewhat mixed breeding.

Scrub. A scrub is an animal that bears no evidence of improved breeding.

Grading-up. Grading-up is the process of improving horses by the continued use in successive generations of good purebred stallions of the same breed. In the days of the horse cavalry and horse-drawn artillery, the U.S. Army Remount fostered the grading-up of horse stock in many parts of the country by making Thoroughbred

Grey Flight, leading dam of Thoroughbred stakes winners in modern times. Sired by °Mahmoud and out of Planetoid by Ariel, Grey Flight was purchased for $35,000 by Mrs. Henry Carnegie Phipps's Wheatley Stable at the 1946 Saratoga yearling sale. She became a stakes winner of $68,990. Then she became a brood mare for Mrs. Phipps at the Claiborne Farm, Paris, Ky. Nine of her first 12 foals became stakes winners, and her daughter Misty Morn has produced five stakes winners. In 1967 Grey Flight, aged 22, was bred to Bold Ruler. Photo by "Skeets" Meadors.

stallions available to mare owners for breeding purposes.

Full brothers (sisters). Full brothers (sisters) have the same sire and same dam.

Half-brothers (sisters). As the term is used by most horsemen, half-brothers (sisters) are horses out of the same dam but sired by different stallions. Horses sired by the same stallion but from different dams should be referred to as being "by the same sire" rather than as "half-brothers." American Thoroughbred breeders always adhere to this usage, as do all British horsemen and cattlemen.

Brothers-in-blood. The relationship of brothers (sisters)—in-blood may result from any one of three kinds of matings:

1. The same stallion bred to full sisters.
2. Full brothers bred to the same mare.
3. Full brothers bred to full sisters.

The pedigrees of brothers-in-blood are identical after the first generation.

Family. The term family is used rather loosely in reference to a group of horses within a breed all of which trace to the same outstanding ancestor. In some breeds families are traced to a noted stallion; in other breeds families are traced in the female line to an outstanding mare.

Dams. The female line of ancestors is traced through the dams. The mother of a horse is called his dam. His second dam is his maternal granddam. His third dam is the dam of the second dam, and so on.

Prepotency. Most often used in reference to males, prepotency means the ability of an animal to transmit well-defined characteristics uniformly to his offspring.

Inbreeding. Inbreeding may be defined as the mating of animals that are more closely related than the average of the population from which they are selected. The intensity of inbreeding may vary, depending upon the closeness of the relationship between the mated relatives. Real close breeding, such as full brother to full sister, sire to daughter, dam to son, is not often practiced by horse breeders. As a general rule such close inbreeding should be attempted only by the expert, the master breeder with extremely sound stock.

Inbreeding purifies the genetic make-up of the animals. The result may be good or bad. Therefore, desirable as well as undesirable animals are produced by this system of mating. Offspring from inbred parents, more often than offspring of non-related parents, are likely to receive the same hereditary factors from their sire and dam. As a result, animals from an inbred line can be expected to produce offspring more uniform in their breeding ability than non-inbred stock.

Linebreeding. Linebreeding is a mild form of inbreeding in which an attempt is made to keep the animals closely related to an outstanding ancestor in the pedigree. Linebreeding is fairly common in some breeds of horses, though not followed to the same extent as it is in the breeding of purebred cattle, sheep, and swine.

Pedigree of the Quarter Horse stallion SIXTEEN TONS

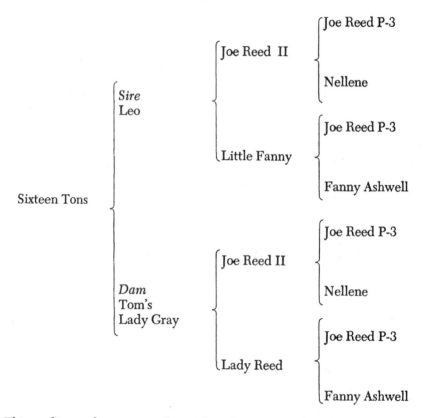

This pedigree shows very close inbreeding. Note that the sire and the dam were brother- and sister-in-blood. Both of them were sired by Joe Reed II and were out of full sisters.

Pedigree of the Standardbred Mare LULU PATCH

Lulu Patch
ch. filly
f. 1964
Bred by
P. D. McAtee
Calgary,
Alberta

Sire
Brino Patch A

The Peter Patch

Berton Patch
by Dan Patch

Bessie Directum

Eunice Patch

The Peter Patch

Berton Patch

Bessie Directum

Peppy Patch

Berton Patch

Bessie Directum

Dam
Gipsy Patch

Brino Patch A

The Peter Patch

Berton Patch

Bessie Directum

Eunice Patch

The Peter Patch

Berton Patch

Bessie Directum

Peppy Patch

Berton Patch

Bessie Directum

Alberta Patch

The Peter Patch

Berton Patch

Bessie Directum

Peppy Patch

Berton Patch

Bessie Directum

This pedigree shows much more intensive inbreeding than is
generally practiced or practicable among horse breeders.

II

Stallion Management

The stallion has more influence than any other single horse on the success of the breeding operations of a stud farm. Therefore, careful supervision of the stallion is basic to successful stud farm management.

METHODS OF BREEDING

In the western part of the United States many horse breeders practice pasture breeding. Many pony breeders use this method, also. The stallion is run on pasture with a small band of mares for three to five months. Usually very high percentage foal crops are obtained by pasture breeding. The horses are living under the most natural conditions, and the mares are mated many times.

However, hand breeding is the most common method of breeding horses. The mare in heat is brought to the stallion, and one mating is permitted. If the animals involved are of considerable value, and if the stallion owner wants to breed his horse to many mares, hand breeding is the rule.

AGE AT TIME OF FIRST SERVICE

As a practical matter most stallions are four years old when first used for breeding service. Well-grown yearlings are capable of mating. Two- and three-year-old colts sometimes are bred to mares. But most young horses are in training for their job—racing, showing, pleasure riding, working cattle. Serious training and competition cannot usually be combined successfully with a heavy breeding season.

NUMBER OF MARES BRED TO A STALLION

A stallion's age and his fitness for breeding service have an in-

Ribot, twice winner of the Prix de l'Arc de Triomphe, grazes in one of the stallion paddocks at the Darby Dan Farm, Lexington, Ky. Photo by the author.

fluence on the number of mares he breeds. A two-year-old colt, if used, is bred to about a dozen mares. Most Thoroughbred stallions in their first season at stud after being retired from racing are limited to about 20 mares. The following season they may be assigned 35 to 40 mares.

The length of the breeding season also determines how many mares a stallion may breed. If his stud service is limited to three months, he cannot breed as many mares as he could during a six-month season.

The number of services needed per mare will also influence the total number of mares a stallion can breed.

The classic example of a stallion used for extremely heavy breeding service is Hambletonian 10, the foundation sire of the Standardbred breed. Hambletonian 10 was in the stud for 24 seasons. He was bred to 1,908 mares, and got 1,331 foals (69 per cent). In 1864 he was bred to 217 mares.

The great English Thoroughbred stallion Hyperion was in the stud for 13 years. He got 368 foals from 471 mares (78 per cent).

Some years ago the Greentree Stud, Lexington, Kentucky gave

These stallion barns at the Darby Dan Farm, Lexington, Ky., are the home of °Ribot, Sword Dancer, Summer Tan, Chateaugay, and other stallions owned by John W. Galbreath. Photo by the author.

full details of their breeding season records in an advertisement in *The Blood-Horse*. The figures are reproduced here because they illustrate the accomplishments of one of the great stud farms of America using young stallions, mature stallions, and a classic race horse that turned out, most unfortunately, to be of low fertility.

Fertility Record of Greentree Stallions, 1954°

	Mares Bred	No. of Covers	Examined In Foal	Per Cent In Foal
Tom Fool	18	44	16	88.8%
One Hitter	15	37	14	93.3%
Bimelech	39	79	29	74.3%
Shut Out	37	81	25	67.5%
For 1954	109	241	84	77.0%

Tom Fool and One Hitter were making their first seasons in stud.
Bimelech in his past five full seasons (1950 eliminated because he was injured at mid-season) covered 185 mares and 149 or 80.5% were reported examined in foal.

———————
° As reported in advertisement in *The Blood-Horse*, November 27, 1954, page 1,246.

The fireproof stallion barn and farm headquarters at the Castleton Farm, Lexington, Ky., is the home of the World's Champion harness horse, Bret Hanover, p, 4, TT 1:53⅗. Castleton Farm and the Dodge Stables have long been noted for their Standardbreds, American Saddle Horses, and Hackney ponies. Photo by the author.

Shut out in five seasons covered 191 mares with 139 (72.2%) examined in foal.

Capot is not included in the above figures. He is a horse of limited fertility. In his first four seasons at stud he has been bred to 40 mares that were kept on his book for the full season. Of these, 12 (30%) have been examined in foal.

A study of the Greentree figures will show:
1. Well supervised stallions in good condition when bred to mares in good health will get 75 per cent or more of their mares in foal.
2. On the average between two and three breeding services are required per mare.
3. On the average between two and three breeding services are required for each pregnancy.

FREQUENCY OF SERVICE

Most men who handle stallions prefer to use the horse only once a day for breeding service. A popular stallion with a full book of mares may have to be used two or three times a day during the peak of the breeding season. He should have a day of rest at least once a week, more frequently if possible, to permit full maturation of the sperm cells. The range of fertility and of sex drive is rather wide. If a stallion is of low fertility, the number of his mares should be reduced, and each mare bred should be given more services.

In the 1920s the greatest Clydesdale stallion in Scotland was Dunure Footprint. He was an extremely virile and fertile stallion. During the breeding season two men cared for this horse, one in the day time, one at night. At the peak of his popularity as a sire, Dunure Footprint is reliably reported to have bred mares in one instance every two hours for three days and four nights. This example of frequent service should be understood as the exception, not the rule. The best stud farms prefer once a day breeding service.

HANDLING STALLIONS AT TIME OF SERVICE

Before mating, the mare should be teased by the stallion to be sure she is in heat. Some Thoroughbred stallions are so high-strung that another calmer horse is used as a teaser. The mare should be restrained by hopples, a nose twitch, or a breeding stall to afford greater safety to the stallion and his handler. On most stud farms the stallion's penis and mare's external genitals are washed with mild soap suds and rinsed prior to service. The mare's tail is wrapped with a bandage.

The stallion, controlled by a bridle with a lead shank, is brought up behind the mare, and when fully ready is allowed to mount the mare.

At the time of ejaculation the stallion's tail flags up and down. If there is any question about a complete service, rapid return of desire after the stallion dismounts indicates that he did not ejaculate. Occasionally one may encounter a stallion that gives a false service, and does not ejaculate until the second time he mounts the mare.

If a stallion is inclined to bite, he should be muzzled or the mare's neck, withers, and back should be covered with a blanket or gunny sack. If the stallion is quite large and the mare small, a breeding roll should be used. This is a padded, leather covered roll 4 to 6 inches in diameter by 15 to 20 inches in length. As the

The outstanding race horse and sire, Tom Fool, in one of the large stallion paddocks at the Greentree Stud, Lexington, Ky. Winner of the Handicap Triple Crown, Tom Fool has become an excellent sire. Buckpasser and Tim Tam are among his noted get. Photo by "Skeets" Meadors.

stallion mounts the roll is placed between the mare's buttocks and the stallion just above the penis. In this position it limits the entry of the stallion and thus prevents possible vaginal and cervical lacerations, especially in maiden mares.

Following service the stallion is again washed and is returned to his stall.

The first time a young stallion is mated he should be handled by an experienced stud man. An old, quiet, experienced mare fully in heat should be used, if possible. The man handling the stallion should remain calm and patient. Once a colt has successfully bred a mare he rarely has trouble thereafter. But sometimes a young stallion can be difficult, awkward, and quite exasperating the first time he breeds a mare.

If the mare is quite tall in comparison to the stallion, she should be stood with her hind feet in a slight depression so the stallion will have the advantage of having his hind feet on higher ground when he mounts.

When help is limited, the use of a breeding stall for the mare keeps the mating from being so acrobatic and simplifies the job of the man handling the stallion.

FEEDING AND MANAGING THE STALLION

The stallion should be kept under the most natural conditions possible. A large box stall, 15 feet by 15 feet, or larger, should be provided. The stallion should be stabled where he can see other horses. He should not be isolated.

A paddock of about two acres in size is a valuable facility in caring for a stallion. If the stallion's stall opens directly on to his paddock, he can go in and out at will. Of course the stallion paddock should be strongly fenced. It should be separated from other paddocks by a laneway so that horses in adjacent fields and paddocks cannot fight over the fence.

Green growing forage is extremely valuable in maintaining a high degree of fertility in the stallion. Therefore, every effort should be made to keep a thick stand of grasses and legumes growing in the stallion paddock.

The chance to run free in his paddock helps to keep the stallion calm and contented. Such freedom is especially valuable for a nervous, high-strung, hot-blooded horse.

During the breeding season the stallion should maintain his condition. He should not lose weight. If he is to be bred to many mares, he should be fed as a horse at hard work. This means he should get at least one pound of grain for every 100 pounds he weighs. Oats are the principal, and, on some farms, the only grain fed. Other stud managers prefer a mixture of oats with a little corn, wheat bran, and soybean meal.

In addition to the grain the stallion should be given at least 1¼ pounds of good quality hay for every 100 pounds he weighs. Some horsemen feed as much hay as the stallion will eat. At least one-half of the hay should be a legume such as alfalfa or red clover. The legumes are relatively high in protein, vitamin, and mineral content compared to straight grass hays.

Regular exercise helps to maintain good physical condition in the breeding stallion. Some horses take considerable exercise in their paddocks. However, most successful stud managers set up a regular exercise schedule for their horses. Starting some six weeks before and continuing through the breeding season the stallion can be ridden for five or six miles every day. Harness horses can be driven. In bad weather a stallion can be exercised for 30 minutes on a longe line at the walk, trot, and gallop.

As mentioned previously, the number of mares bred to a stallion and the frequency of breeding service must be adjusted according to his age, his fitness, his degree of fertility, and the length of the breeding season.

SOME CAUSES OF LOW FERTILITY IN THE STALLION

Many factors affect fertility. Some possible causes of low fertility include:

1. Poor general health and condition as a result of improper feeding, negligent care, and faulty management.

2. Excessive masturbation. Most stallions masturbate at some time. Rarely do they indulge in this practice to the extent of limiting their fertility, if they have been managed according to the program discussed in the preceding section. Stallions that masturbate to excess usually become very rank and produce rather thin semen with a low number of sperm cells. Stallion rings of various sizes are available. One of these rings slipped over the end of the stallion's penis prevents masturbation. However, improving management practices is a preferable method of treatment.

3. Disease and injury. Severe illness accompanied by high fever may render a stallion at least temporarily infertile. A kick in the scrotum may have the same result.

4. Heredity. In some breeds of horses there are family lines that are known to produce animals of low fertility. Whether it is advisable to propagate such animals must be decided by the horse breeder.

5. Worry and anxiety. Though it is doubtful that horses are subject to the same strains, stresses, and neuroses as humans, an excessively high-strung, nervous temperament may impair the fertility of a stallion. This condition is most likely to be encountered among Thoroughbreds. Such a stallion should be in the company of other horses and should be kept on a regular regimen. A teaser stallion should take his place in teasing mares.

STALLION SEMEN

The surest test of a stallion's fertility is the production of a high percentage foal crop. However, a fairly good indication of probable breeding results may be obtained from a laboratory examination of his semen.

A regular practice on big horse farms is to examine the stallion's semen prior to the breeding season and occasionally during the season. Among the points to be noted are the volume, the sperm count, the pH value, the motility of the sperm cells, and their morphology. The color and consistency of the semen and the presence of red blood cells and pus cells are also considered.

The volume of semen stallions ejaculate at one time may range from 40 to 320 c.c. Most stallions of the light breeds produce less than 150 c.c., the volume for many stallions ranging from 60 to 90 c.c., or approximately two to three ounces. When an examination of the entire ejaculate is to be made the stallion is permitted to mount a mare in heat but his penis is directed into an artificial vagina.

The normal average sperm count for stallion semen is 60,000 sperm cells per cubic millimeter.

The normal pH reaction is from 7.3 to 7.8. An acid reaction below seven is definitely abnormal.

When normal semen is examined under the microscope the sperm cells are seen to be lashing their tails and moving vigorously across the field. The length of time this active motion is maintained varies directly with the degree of fertility. If a stallion's semen still has active cells an hour after collection, his level of fertility is higher than one whose sperm cells lost their motility in a short time.

Specialists in horse breeding have found that in normal stallion semen over 90 per cent of the sperm cells will be of normal shape. If there are 200 abnormal sperm cells per 1,000, the stallion is of low fertility. If one-half the sperm cells appear abnormal in the microscopic field, the stallion for practical purposes is sterile. Stained slides are made for morphological study under the microscope.

The first two or three services after a period of sexual inactivity may contain a large number of abnormal sperm cells. For this reason many stud managers make a couple of semen collections or breed the stallion to one or two grade mares at the start of the breeding season before they use the horse on their good mares. If the horse is of normal fertility, his subsequent semen production will be satisfactory.

Stallion semen is approximately 97.62 per cent water and 2.38 per cent solids. Of the solids, about 60 percent are protein.

The techniques of handling and preserving stallion semen have not been perfected to the high degree attained in handling bull semen. Artificial insemination can be practiced with horses, but is not yet so widely used as it is with cattle. Some horse breed registry associations in the United States do not at this time accept for registration foals conceived as a result of artificial insemination. Other associations do permit this method of reproduction which may in the future become more widely accepted.

12

Brood Mare Management

Horse breeding is an art practiced for 5,000 years. However, problems associated with reproduction still remain to perplex and plague the practical horseman.

THE BREEDING SEASON

Horse breeding has become a seasonal activity in some regions largely because of economic and geographic reasons. Mares of all types kept under ordinary farm conditions in the United States and on a reasonably high plane of nutrition exhibit reproductive phenomena throughout the year. Foals are born in all months. But most breeders of Thoroughbreds and Standardbreds, as well as those of other light breeds, prefer early spring foals so that the young horses will be well developed when they are put into training for racing, showing, or other uses at 1½ to 2 years of age. Hence, the breeding season for horses in many areas is limited to the late winter, spring, and early summer.

Since the mare's pregnancy is about 340 days, if a mare is bred in the spring and conceives, she will foal the following spring. Spring foals have the advantages of warm weather, sunshine, grass, and exercise. In general, there is lower foal mortality in spring than in winter. Winter foals often cause troublesome management problems. Late summer foals may be handicapped by the fly and short grass season. Fall foals are always small in their age group for two or three years, and are less likely to meet with ready sale.

ESTRUS AND THE ESTRUAL CYCLE

Mares experience a regular, rhythmical sexual cycle. This estrual cycle takes about 21 days on the average. Although there is considerable variation, each mare tends to follow her own pattern.

When during the cycle there is sufficient amount of the hormone estrogen present the mare comes into estrus, or heat. The heat period on the average lasts about 5 days. Then the mare is out of heat for 16 days. The accompanying tables illustrate the range of duration of estrus and the estrual cycle. Both the cyclic changes and the heat period tend to become much more regular in spring and early summer than they were in the winter time.

Table 1° Duration of Estrus in Draft and Light Mares

Type of Mare	No. of Mares	No. of Periods	Duration of Estrus (Mean days)	Range of Duration of Estrus (days)
Draft	40	127	5.2	1–14
Light	35	69	5.5	1–37
All	75	196	5.3	1–37

° From Table 7, p. 28, Missouri Agr. Exp. Sta. Res. Bul. 329

Table 2° Length of the Estrual Cycle in Draft and Light Mares

Type of Mare	No. of Mares	No. of Cycles	Length of Cycle (Mean days)	Range of Length of Cycle (days)
Draft	37	63	20.1	10–29
Light	18	27	22.0	13–37
All	55	90	20.7	10–37

°From Table 10, p. 30, Missouri Agr. Exp. Sta. Res. Bul. 329

Table 3° Length of the Interestrual Period in Draft and Light Mares

Type of Mare	No. of Mares	No. of Periods	Length of Period (Mean days)	Range of Length of Period (days)
Draft	37	71	14.9	7–27
Light	18	35	16.0	5–33
All	55	106	15.3	5–33

°From Table 13, p. 32, Missouri Agr. Exp. Sta. Res. Bul. 329

To the practical horseman, the variations noted in the tables point up the importance of regular, systematic teasing of all mares during the breeding season to determine when they are in heat and when they should be mated.

Thoroughbred brood mares and foals on the well-managed pastures of the Calumet Farm, Lexington, Ky. Note that the fence corners are rounded. Photo by "Skeets" Meadors.

Estrus comes from the Greek word meaning frenzy which very well describes the actions of some mares in heat. Among the indications of heat are an obvious desire, a relaxation of the external genitals, winking of the lips of the vulva, frequent urination, a mucous discharge from the vagina. The mare in heat will usually be quiet, relaxed, and passive in the presence of a stallion.

To determine their condition, mares are teased by a stallion at the stall door, or at a teasing pole, or in a breeding stall.

Some physiological changes in the genital tract may indicate that a mare is in heat. Cervical tone is a rather reliable indication of estrus. There is a gradual relaxation of the cervix one to two days before heat, and complete relaxation can usually be observed at the time of ovulation.

Both rectal and vaginal temperatures are slightly higher during heat than interestrus, and those of mares nursing foals are higher than those of dry mares.

The highest vascularity and, hence, the reddest color of the

Breeding stall in the stallion barn at the Castleton Farm, Lexington, Ky.
Photo by the author.

mucosa of the vagina and cervix can be observed at the approximate time of ovulation. The least vascularity is noted between the fifth and tenth days of interestrus.

A horseman with training and experience may be able by means of manual examination per rectum of the mare's ovaries to feel the changes in the development of the follicle on the ovary as the mare comes into heat.

"Split" estrus is sometimes observed. This phenomenon is characterized by an initial heat period of one or more days, followed by a non-receptive period usually of one to two days duration, and a subsequent return of heat for one or more days. "Split" estrus in itself is not deleterious to fertility, although the cause of divided heat periods is not fully understood. Ovulation usually does not occur in mares exhibiting "split" estrus until after heat has reappeared. Hence, under practical breeding conditions where the common practice is to cease trying mares after they have apparently gone out of heat, a condition of "split" estrus in a mare might result in a disappointing breeding record.

"Physiological" estrus, or "silent" heat, is accompanied by the ovarian, uterine, and vaginal changes characteristic of psychological estrus, but receptivity, or sex-desire, is absent. The incidence of "silent" heat and of post-estrual ovulation is undoubtedly small in the entire mare population, but these phenomena probably account for some part of the low foaling percentages reported from various parts of the world. Estrus is the only guide to the time of mating under most stud farm conditions. Hence, ovulation in the absence of heat symptoms, or heat with the absence of ovulation, will very likely result in failure to conceive.

"Silent" heat and post-estrual ovulation do not, in themselves, prevent conception providing the development of follicles and the time of ovulation are observed by rectal palpation. A large percentage of mares bred while unwilling to accept the stallion even though they are nevertheless in "physiological" heat as determined by examination will conceive.

There is a tendency for breeding irregularities and deficiencies to appear in certain family lines of some breeds of horses. While this problem is of interest to the physiologist and geneticist, it is questionable whether it is advantageous to the horse breeder to propagate lines of stock which exhibit such irregularities.

Thoroughbreds grazing on the rolling pastures of the Sagamore Farm, Glyndon, Md., owned by Alfred Gwynne Vanderbilt. Photo by Winants Bros.

OVULATION AND OVARIAN CHANGES

Ovulation refers in a broad sense to the development of the ovum, or egg cell, and ovarian follicle and the discharge of the mature egg cell by the rupture of the follicle in the ovary. Follicular growth is accompanied by the secretion of the hormone estrogen which gradually induces estrus, or heat. For most successful breeding of a species in which the heat period is relatively long, as it is in the mare, a knowledge of the time of ovulation is of major importance. It is highly desirable for the mating to occur near the time of ovulation because neither the egg cell nor the spermatozoa live a long time in the genital tract of the mare. A horseman who has an intimate knowledge of equine anatomy and sufficient training can determine the condition of the ovaries by palpation per rectum.

The ovaries of the mare are kidney- or bean-shaped and vary greatly in size and shape. Age, the stage of the estrual cycle, and pregnancy affect their conformation, but they are usually from 4 to 9 cm. in length and 2.5 to 5.0 cm. in thickness. One ovary may be larger than the other. The position of the ovaries is not constant. In most mares they are located in the sub-lumbar region of the abdominal cavity ventral to and 8 to 15 cm. posterior to the kidneys and 5 to 12 cm. from the median plane. During pregnancy the ovaries are drawn downward, and by 10 to 12 weeks are on a level with the pubis. With age and succeeding pregnancies the ovaries tend to move ventrally.

Ovulation in the mare occurs most usually from one to two days before the end of her heat period. On some big Thoroughbred breeding farms that have expert veterinary supervision mares are bred only after manual examination per rectum has shown that the follicle on the ovary is about to rupture and release the ovum or that ovulation has already occurred.

PREPARATION FOR BREEDING

Mares should be in good flesh but not fat at breeding time. They are usually in the best condition for breeding when they are on good pasture and after they have begun to shed their hair in the spring. Mares that have been stabled part of the time will start to shed earlier in the spring than will mares that have run out. Open mares that have been in the fields all winter and that have had good hay at all times and enough grain to maintain thrifty condition will come to the breeding season in excellent condition.

Large breeding farms usually require a health certificate be-

Blue grass pastures are a basic part of the horse production program at the Greentree Stud, Lexington, Ky. Photo by "Skeets" Meadors.

fore breeding an outside mare to their stallions. Therefore, if a mare is booked to a prominent stallion, a veterinarian must examine her.

TEASING MARES

Regular teasing of the mares to be bred should be started before the breeding season begins. Although there is considerable range in estrual cycles, each mare follows a fairly regular pattern, and this should be learned. Ordinarily the heat periods in January and February will be longer and somewhat more irregular than those later in the season. Maiden mares should be carefully initiated to the teasing process so that they will relax and show their true condition in the presence of the stallion.

The teasing may be done over a stall door, at a teasing pole, or a breeding stall. Control and safety of the mare and stallion and safety for the handlers should be considered. It is important to know the mare's temperament and to follow a regular routine program of teasing in order to note gradual changes in response.

As mentioned previously, a small percentage of mares may fail to show signs of heat. Sometimes these mares will show to be in heat when run with other mares in the field, but not when tried by the stallion. More often they prove to be a special problem to the horseman. They have to be examined by means of a vaginal speculum and by ovarian palpation per rectum to determine when they are in condition to be bred. A systematic plan of examining these mares must be followed.

Some mares with foals will not show heat. A vaginal speculum may have to be used, but some of these mares may react to the stallion if they are teased in a different location or if a twitch is used on them.

In some instances a mare may be neither very receptive nor very antagonistic to the teaser. Examination may reveal her true condition. If a mare was once thought to be in foal, great care should be used in determining her status before breeding her again. Signs of temper and irritation must be differentiated from heat symptoms because abortion may occur if an already pregnant mare is bred. Mares have been bred and a few weeks later have produced a foal from the previous year's mating, but there is always danger of abortion under such conditions.

BREEDING PRACTICES

Actual breeding practices vary all the way from pasture breeding to the highly supervised mating on a Kentucky Thoroughbred farm with a veterinarian in attendance. The more valuable the animals involved, the greater the care. When sanitation and safety are considered, some if not all of the following practices will be followed.

After the mare has been teased and found to be in heat her hindquarters are washed and rinsed, and her tail is wrapped with a roller bandage. Sometimes lubricating jelly is put about the vulva, especially with a maiden mare. The mare is stood facing a wall and two to three feet away from it. She is held by two men, one on each side, and each holding a lead strap. If the stallion is valuable and the mare the least bit unruly, the mare is hobbled. A nose twitch is applied to the mare, and is held by the man on the near side. A piece of canvas or burlap put over the mare's withers will prevent injury from a possible bite by the stallion. The stud horse is brought up behind the mare and when ready is allowed to mount. During service the mare is steadied by the holders. After the mating is over the mare is unhobbled at once and is led around for a short time to prevent straining.

If a stallion habitually gives a very close cover, it may be advisable to hold a breeding roll against the mare's buttocks and above the penis of the stallion whenever he is bred to a small mare or to a filly at her first mating.

Although some stud farms make a practice of impregnating mares following natural service, the value of this practice is debatable. It consists usually of filling a gelatin capsule with semen taken from the stallion when he dismounts, and placing this capsule through the cervix into the uterus with the rubber-gloved hand. Sometimes a glass syringe with tubing attached is used. Extreme sanitation must be observed. Impregnation may have some real advantage if a stallion does not cover closely, or if a small stallion is bred to a large mare.

PRECAUTIONS WITH MAIDEN MARES

Experienced horsemen feel that some of the troubles in handling maiden mares at time of service may be eliminated by the following procedure. The mare is teased and handled as if she were actually to be bred except that hobbles are not used. The mare is stood in position facing a wall, twitched, and held by two men. Her left fore leg is strapped up securely with a leather strap equipped with a buckle that allows quick release. (A stirrup leather will do.) Then the teasing stallion is allowed to mount but not to breed the mare. The mare's fore leg is released so she can more easily bear the stallion's weight. After one or two such experiences the mare will ordinarily be much more willing to accept the regular breeding stallion.

Another common practice with mares being bred for the first time is to have the veterinarian break the membrane that partially occludes the opening to the vagina. The vaginal speculum or gloved hand is used and there is less hemorrhage and bruising of tissue than if the stallion eliminates the membrane at the first breeding.

RE-BREEDING FOLLOWING FOALING

Breeding mares at their foal heat period (about nine days after the birth of the foal) is not recommended by most horsemen. Reasons sometimes advanced for the practice are that some mares do not come into heat when suckling foals, or at least do not show to the teasing stallion. If the mare has foaled late in the season she may have to be bred at her foal heat or left unbred for the year.

Actually, however, research investigators and the records of many Kentucky Thoroughbred nurseries show that only about 50 per cent of the mares bred at their foal heat conceive. If a mare happens to be infected when bred on the ninth day, even though she conceives she is apt to abort as a result of infection. Another reason for questioning the wisdom of breeding during the foal heat is that a week to ten days is often not enough time for a mare's genital tract to return to normal.

The weather conditions the week after foaling may be the deciding factor. If the mare can be on grass and can exercise, she will recover much more rapidly than she will if confined to the stables, as is often the situation in bad winter weather.

As a general rule, mares should not be re-bred until their second heat period after the birth of the foal, that is, when the foal is about 30 days old.

When a mare has suffered a difficult delivery, or has retained the afterbirth, or has produced a dead or diseased foal, she should be examined by a veterinarian. Such a mare should not be bred at the foal heat, but should be medically treated and returned to normal condition before she is re-bred.

DISEASES OF THE GENITAL TRACT

Some diseased conditions of the genital tract are plainly shown by abnormal discharges that adhere to the tail and buttocks. If there is any question about breeding health, infections in mares can best be determined by bacterial cultures. Such examinations should be made before the breeding season commences, and the specimens should be obtained when the mare is fully in heat.

Disease organisms most frequently encountered are: *Streptococci, Staphylococci, Bacterium coli, Pseudomonas aerugenosa,* and *Aerobacter aerogenes.* These bacteria may be introduced accidentally at the time of breeding, or foaling, or examination.

Some older brood mares have an altered conformation of the pelvic outlet where the vulva is nearly horizontal instead of vertical. This faulty conformation coupled with a lack of muscle tone about the vulva draws air and foreign materials into the vagina, thus maintaining an infected condition. Veterinarians can remedy this condition to a large extent by suturing or clamping the upper part of the vulva. This operation will noticeably reduce infertility by preventing further windsucking and introduction of infection. Mares that have been so sutured must usually be opened up before mating and always before foaling to prevent serious tearing of the tissues. Following service they are re-sutured.

THE PREGNANT MARE

After mating, if fertilization takes place and pregnancy is established, the mare usually does not come back into heat. This failure to come into estrus is the first sign of pregnancy. Many pregnant mares show a change in their behaviour toward other horses and people. Most have an increased appetite. The belly enlarges gradually and this change is quite evident in five or six months. In late pregnancy the foal can sometimes be seen to move after the mare takes a drink of cold water.

Several tests for pregnancy can be made. Horsemen trained in the technique can palpate the foetus through the wall of the rectum. This manual examination is probably most easily done at about 25 to 60 days after breeding. A biological test that can be done only from about 50 to 90 days after breeding involves injecting blood serum from the mare into immature female rats, and later noting the effect of the hormones in the blood on the reproductive tract of the test animals. A chemical test involving urine from the mare can be conducted only after 100 days have passed since the mare was bred.

The length of gestation in the mare varies considerably, but will average 340 days. If a mare carries her foal for a year or longer, the foal often is large and somewhat clumsy and helpless. A foal born two or three weeks before the due date is somewhat premature. If a perfectly normal foal arrives three or four weeks before he is expected, in all probability the mare conceived to a mating before the last one noted for her. Such a situation can occur, but is not usual. On the average, stallion foals will be carried 1½ to 3 days longer than fillies.

On big stud farms the pregnant mares are simply kept on pasture most of the time. However, the privately owned saddle mare can be ridden practically up to the day she foals. Good judgment must, of course, be used, but mild regular exercise will keep the mare in better physical tone than complete idleness.

DEVELOPMENT OF THE FOAL EMBRYO

The accompanying table shows the stage of foetal development at each month of the mare's pregnancy. Note the large growth of the embryo during the last quarter of gestation. The mare must be well fed at this time. Her nutritional needs are greater, especially for protein and mineral, as is pointed out in the next chapter.

Weight and Dimensions of Unborn Foal[*]

End of Month	Length, Poll to Root of Dock	Weight	Stage of Development
1	1¼ in.	Minute	All internal organs present.
2	3–3¾ in.	Minute	Limbs distinct. Sex recognizable. There is about 1 oz. of fluid inside the membranes.
3	5 in.	4½–6 oz.	The villi or tufts of the outer membrane are forming, and so are the hoofs. Ends of cannon bones ossifying.
4	8–9 in.	2 lb.	Some fluids present in foetal stomach. First traces of hair round lips. Union between maternal and foetal systems complete.
5	9–15 in.	4 lb. 4 oz.	Traces of hair above eyes and on tip of tail. External sexual organs formed.
6	22 in.	12 lb. 12 oz.	Hair much more apparent.
7	23–25 in.	29¾–34 lb.	Mane growing.
8	27–29 in.	36–42 lb.	Hair all along spine.
9	30–33 in.	51–57 lb.	Short hairs all over body. Might just survive if born now.
10	34–37 in.	64–74 lb.	Coat and long hairs fully grown.
11	43 in. and upwards	85–107 lb.	Milk molars through gums. Sometimes nippers also.

THE FOALING MARE

During the 11th month of pregnancy the mare's udder enlarges. The rather waxy material in the dry udder is forced out and beads of wax may form on the teats a day or two before the mare foals. The wax may leave and milk run from the udder in some cases before the foal is born. Relaxation of the mare's pelvis,

[*] From Mares, Foals and Foaling, by Friedrich Andrist, translated by Anthony Dent. J. A. Allen & Co., London

depression of the croup muscles on either side of the tail, slight elevation of the tail, and enlargement and relaxation of the lips of the vulva are other signs of rapidly approaching parturition. Just before foaling the mare may be nervous, paw the bedding in her stall, break out in a sweat, lie down and get up once or twice. The attendant should not disturb the mare, but should observe her from a place where he cannot be seen.

The natural place for a mare to foal is on a good, clean pasture. But for valuable breeding stock and for late winter and early spring foals a large foaling stall should be made ready. Every effort should be made to keep this stall clean and disinfected. Near at hand such supplies as soap, buckets, tail bandages, antiseptic solution, cotton, navel paint and powder, bulb syringe or enema can and hose, and hot water should be available.

Large stud farms always have a man on duty at night during the foaling season. When this attendant finds that a mare is going to foal he washes the mare's hindquarters and her udder, and wraps her tail. Then he leaves the mare alone unless she later requires help in delivery.

A normal foaling is usually accomplished in from 15 to 30 minutes and when the mare is lying down on her side. A wrong presentation of the foal, however, may be serious, and indicates an immediate need for a veterinarian.

The appearance and rupture of the allanto-chorion or outer foetal membrane is a sign of immediate foaling. From 1½ to 3 gallons of straw colored fluid may be present. The attendant can usually soon tell if the foal is in the normal position with the front feet extended, the head extended between the legs, and the foal's back up against the top of the pelvic canal of the mare.

If the foal is large and the delivery slow, the attendant may pull downward on the foal's legs in the direction of the mare's hocks. This assistance should be given only when the mare labors.

Sometimes a foot of the foal may be bent backwards or may extend up instead of out through the vagina if the elbow catches on the brim of the mare's pelvis. An attendant may be able to rectify the position. Extreme cleanliness should be observed. A veterinarian should be called and, if possible, the mare should be got up and kept walking slowly. This reduces the tendency to labor.

Sometimes the foal may be upside down. In such a case, veterinarians recommend that the mare be made to rise and stand for a few minutes. Often when she lies down again a normal position of the foal has been attained. If not, this procedure should be repeated while waiting for the veterinarian to arrive.

A caudal or backwards presentation may occur in one or two per cent of the deliveries. A very rapid birth is desired in such circumstances because the navel cord may break too soon and the foal may smother before it is born.

Fortunately for the horseman, the vast majority of mares foal easily and without trouble.

After the mare foals she may be given a drink of tepid water and a bran mash. The mare's hindquarters should be sponged off and the stall cleaned and rebedded. The after-birth usually is passed within a short time after the foal is born. If the after-birth has not come away within three hours a veterinarian should treat the mare and remove the placental membranes. A retained placenta will lead to internal infection and founder in the mare.

CARE OF THE NEW-BORN FOAL

The first duty of the attendant after the foal has been born is to make sure that the foal can breathe. Any membranes and fluid around the nostrils should be removed at once. The foal can be rubbed with towels to dry him off.

The umbilical cord of a foal is about as long as the foal is tall and may remain intact until the mare gets up and turns toward the foal. Sometimes the cord breaks when the foal makes his first struggling efforts to rise. Sometimes the cord must be broken by hand. More blood can pass to the foal if the cord is not broken right away. After thoroughly cleansing his hands, the caretaker grasps the cord with both hands and breaks it two or three inches from the foal's body. Because the stump of the navel cord offers an avenue of infection, it should be dipped in a glass containing a ten per cent tincture of iodine solution. Formalin, metaphen, merthiolate, or one of the sulfonamides may be used for treating the navel. Promptness of treatment is essential. A drying powder should be dusted on the stump of the navel cord several times daily until it has dried and dropped off.

A common practice on many stud farms is to give the new-born foal an intramuscular hypodermic shot of 1 gram of streptomycin and 400,000 units of penicillin to prevent diseases. Some horsemen also give a tetanus shot.

The foal should not be hurried in his efforts to rise. A normal, vigorous foal will be up in ten minutes to an hour after birth. Nor should the caretaker worry unduly about getting the foal to nurse. The nursing instinct is probably the strongest basic impulse with which mammals are born. Occasionally a young mare with her first foal may be a bit nervous and may have to be held when the foal first nurses, but this it not usual. If a mare's udder is quite swollen and tender, she might have to be restrained the first day so that the foal can nurse more easily.

Foals at birth usually weight between six per cent and ten per cent of the weight of their dams. Thus most foals of the light breeds of horses weigh between 60 and 120 pounds.

When the weather permits, the mare and foal may be turned out to pasture each day. Judgment must be used. If the mare runs a great deal or if the sun is very hot, the new foal may become exhausted. However, moderate exercise on pasture is a prime factor in restoring normal condition to the mare's reproductive tract. Where the mare and foal can be turned out, the mare will have recovered in five or six days. On the other hand, if the mare has been confined for the week following foaling, the owner should not consider breeding her during the foal heat because in all likelihood her uterus will not have returned to normal.

CARING FOR THE ORPHAN FOAL

An orphan foal presents a special problem to the horseman. Sometimes it is possible to get a nurse mare to raise the foal. Many orphan foals have been saved and well grown by nursing a milk goat. If the foal must be bottle-fed by hand, a satisfactory mixture is skim milk plus one teaspoonful of Karo syrup per ounce. Four to eight ounces of this mixture at body temperature should be given every two hours. The amount fed and the feeding intervals can be gradually increased. Many orphan foals have been raised on milk replacers sold by most feed companies for raising dairy calves. Absolute cleanliness of all feeding and mixing utensils is imperative. The orphan foal should be encouraged to eat grain as soon as possible, usually at two to three weeks of age.

TWIN FOALS

Twin foals constitute practically an abnormal pregnancy in the mare. The vast majority of twin pregnancies terminate in an abortion.

The following figures, because of the large numbers of mares involved, have some significance. This information comes from a report in *Animal Breeding Abstracts;* Volume 19, No. 4, December 1951. The data for this report were obtained from records of four government stud farms in Poland.

Of 8,252 mares that conceived to first service, multifoetation occurred in 266 mares. The results of these multiple pregnancies were as follows:

199 aborted both foetuses

21 produced 2 still-born foals

13 produced 1 living and 1 dead foal
17 produced 2 weakly foals
16 produced 2 viable foals

Thus about ⅕ of 1 per cent of the pregnancies resulted in successful living twins.

DISEASES AND INFECTIONS OF THE NEW-BORN FOAL

Constipation. Many foals seem to have difficulty in passing the meconium, or foetal manure. Laying back the ears, switching the tail, raising the hind legs, and straining are common symptoms of constipation. The colostrum has laxative properties, but sometimes, especially when considerable milk has run from the mare's udder prior to foaling, an enema is needed to start the foal's bowels. One or two quarts of mild soap suds and warm water may be given by means of an enema can with hose. The enema should be repeated until the normal soft, pasty manure replaces the hard, black pellets of meconium. Many stud farms make a regular routine practice of giving an enema to all new-born foals. This practice pays because it prevents constipation. Constipated foals will not nurse.

Diarrhea. Diarrhea or scours often occurs in the young foal when the mare comes into the foal heat about nine days after foaling. When the mare is in heat her temperature rises and her milk may change somewhat. A dose of two ounces of castor oil given as a drench will usually stop the scours in the foal. The mare's feed should be reduced and her udder milked out by hand. The foal's hindquarters should be washed and greased with vaseline to prevent galling and blistering.

Another possible cause of scours in the young foal is eating manure. Stalls and paddocks should be kept as clean as possible.

Navel ill. Most infectious diseases of foals are caused by one of three specific organisms, *Shigella equirulis, Streptococci,* and *Bacterium coli.* The presence of these organisms in the foal results in a septicemia or unhealthy condition due to pathogenic bacteria and their associated poisons in the blood. Chills, profuse sweating, irregular intermittent fever, and great prostration may accompany the septicemia. Losses from these infections formerly were difficult or impossible to prevent. However, mortality has been greatly reduced since the development and wide use of antibiotics.

Veterinarians on Kentucky stud farms and at the University of Kentucky have found that about 40 per cent of the diseased foals examined have been infected with *Shigella equirulis.* This organism causes the so-called sleeper or dummy foals. Such foals are either in a semi-comatose condition or, if able to rise, walk drunkenly. The disease appears early in life and is very rapidly fatal, often within three days. Streptomycin has proved effective in some cases, but close observation of the young foal and prompt treatment, if trouble arises, are necessary.

About one third of the infections of foals are streptococcic. Foals infected with *Streptococci* live two or three weeks, sometimes longer. Fever and tenderness of joints, swelling of joints, diarrhea, and failure of the navel to dry properly may be symptoms of this infection. Very close observation of the foal and early treatment with the sulfonamides and penicillin may save the foal.

Bacterium coli infection by itself does not cause a large percentage of deaths among foals, but it may complicate other infections. Loss of equilibrium, inability to rise or to control voluntary movements may be typical of *Bacterium coli* infections. Aureomycin has given good results in some cases where treatment was begun early.

Prevention is the best precaution against these "navel ill" diseases. All horse breeders should follow these recommendations:

1. Breed only those mares whose genital tracts are free from infection.

2. Use all sanitary measures at time of mating.

3. Keep the foaling stall as clean and sanitary as possible before, during, and after parturition.

4. Treat the umbilical cord promptly after the birth of the foal, and continue the use of drying powders until the stump of the cord dries up and drops off.

5. Isolate any infected foal and disinfect any contaminated premises.

Jaundice. The loss of foals from hemolytic icterus, or jaundice, is probably more common than many horsemen realize. Sometimes during pregnancy the mare may become sensitized against the red blood cell type of the foal. This incompatibility of blood types results in the production of antibodies in the mare's blood. The antibodies also appear in the colostrum milk for 12 to 24 hours after foaling. When the foal nurses his dam the antibodies cause the agglutination (clumping together) of the red blood cells of the foal. A jaundiced condition develops in 12 to 24 hours, or less, if the foal nurses strongly. The mucous membranes become quite pale and yellowish. Death comes in two days or less.

If the red blood cell types of the mare and the stallion to which she is bred are incompatible, then the foal is certain to get jaundice if allowed to nurse. When facilities for blood testing are not available it may be assumed that, if a mare's foal from a given mating has developed jaundice, another foal by the same sire would also be afflicted.

However, when it is known that the blood types are incom-

Some of the large bluegrass paddocks at the Calumet Farm, Lexington, Kentucky, one of the most successful Thoroughbred breeding and racing establishments in America. Photo by "Skeets" Meadors.

patible or when the jaundice is noted early, the foal may be saved by preventing it from nursing its dam. The foal should be muzzled and the mare milked out by hand at frequent intervals for 24 hours. The foal may be bottle-fed skim milk to which has been added one teaspoon of karo syrup per ounce. He should be given four to eight ounces of this mixture every two hours.

In cases where the jaundiced condition has started to develop, blood transfusions with blood that has been cross matched and found compatible may save the foal. Close observation of the foal is necessary, if early and effective treatment is to be given.

Rheumatic arthritis. Rheumatic arthritis is a non-infectious, non-contagious, severely crippling disease that may affect the older foal or weanling. This disease affects the muscles, tendons, and joints. There may be swelling of joints and loss of condition. After the acute stage has passed a chronic condition follows in which ring-bones, contracted feet, and rough joints are commonly seen. Foals so affected are usually worthless for racing or showing, but may be salvaged for breeding purposes depending on their condition.

SOME CAUSES OF LOW BREEDING EFFICIENCY

Extremely well-managed stud farms in the United States sometimes get foals from 75 to 85 per cent of the mares that are bred. The national average is probably from 50 to 55 per cent. Figures reported for French Thoroughbred mares bred in 1963 and foaling in 1964 indicate a live foal crop of 61.5 per cent.

The relatively low reproductive rate of horses is one of the serious economic problems in the horse business. Some possible causes of low breeding efficiency are:

1. Improper or inadequate teasing of the mares.

2. Estrus without ovulation. This may occur in late winter and early spring.

3. Failure to detect heat in the mare.

4. Failure to mate the mare at the optimum time.

5. Failure to mate the mare frequently enough.

6. Disease or infection of the genital tract of the mare.

7. Early abortion. About ten per cent of the pregnancies end in abortion at about 80 days.

8. Low fertility of the stallion.

9. Tendency of both stallions and mares that have been shipped long distances to require a year to adjust and acclimatize.

ABORTION

About 10 per cent of the mares that become pregnant do not produce live foals.

Some of the possible causes for abortion are:

1. Twin pregnancy. Most twin foals are aborted or are born so prematurely as to have no chance of survival.

2. Moldy, spoiled feed, contaminated water, and poisons.

3. Fatigue brought on by transporting the mare a great distance.

4. Failure of the placenta to become attached to the uterus. This results in abortion during the first month of pregnancy.

5. Hormonal failure or imbalance. During the fifth month, the production of progesterone (the hormone responsible for the maintenance of pregnancy) shifts from the corpus luteum on the ovary to the placenta. If this shift is not complete, the lower level of progesterone being produced may result in the termination of the pregnancy by abortion.

6. Virus. Equine rhinopneumonitis is an acute, highly contagious upper respiratory disease of horses caused by equine herpesvirus type 1. When it strikes young animals they contract fever, coughs, and runny noses. Pregnant mares usually do not show visible clinical symptoms, but equine rhinopneumonitis causes them either to abort

or to produce foals that die soon after birth. Vaccines are now available for immunization against this disease.

   7. Contagious equine metritis (CEM). This venereal infection appeared during the late 1970s in some Thoroughbred studs in Great Britain, Ireland, France and Australia; it was introduced into the United States by some imported horses. The disease is transmitted at the time of mating and by inadequate hygienic procedures in washing the mare and stallion at time of service. Infected mares abort at the 40 to 60 day period, and generally are lost to breeding for the year. Thus the stud farm may suffer devastating losses. Strict control of imports and interstate transport, along with international cooperation of veterinarians and disease laboratories, brought the disease under control by 1980.

WEANING

   On most stud farms, brood mares and their foals are run on pasture for a few months. The mares are fed grain to encourage their milk production, and grain is provided in foal creeps so that the foals may eat at will undisturbed by their dams.

   Many horsemen wean foals at 5 to 6 months of age. By this time the milk secretion of the mares has decreased markedly, and the foals are eating about one pound of grain for every month of age. Some people wean all the foals at one time, moving the mares out of sight and sound. Others prefer interval weaning, where one or two mares are removed from the pasture each week until all of the foals have been weaned.

   In a mare whose foal is weaned at 5 to 6 months, the udder will dry up readily if the mare's feed is limited. If the udder does swell, it can be rubbed with camphorated oil.

13

Feeding Horses

"The eye of the master fattens his cattle."

The individual horse is the unit in horse feeding. Hogs may be fed from a self-feeder. Steers eat from the same feed bunk. Fattening lambs go to the same hay rack and feed troughs. But horses usually are fed as individuals. Horses probably differ more in their temperament and their feed requirements than do other livestock.

Feeding horses is both an art and a science. The science aspect is knowing the nutritional requirements of horses, the nutritional value of feed ingredients, and putting together a properly balanced ration. The art consists of knowing what to feed, when to feed it, and the amount of feed needed to meet each horse's individual requirements. Thus we might paraphrase the old saying printed at the head of this chapter and say, "The eye of the master fattens his horses."

SOME FUNDAMENTAL CONSIDERATIONS IN FEEDING

1. Good horsemen feed horses according to their individual needs.

2. Good hosemen feed according to the job the horse is doing. Horses ridden four hours a day obviously have different nutritional needs from those ridden two hours a week.

3. Horses should be fed for long time efficiency. Hogs are fed and sent to market at five months of age. Horses often are with their owners for years. Hence they must be fed to develop maturity, remain in good health, have stamina, and stay serviceably sound.

4. Only feeds of good quality should be fed. Moldy, spoiled feed and hay can kill horses.

5. A variety of feeds should be used. Though many horses have been kept on oats and timothy hay, some variety in the ration

makes it more palatable, stimulates the appetite, and is more nearly adequate from the nutritional standpoint. Of course, commercially mixed horse feeds and pelleted feeds are composed of a variety of ingredients.

6. Feeding times should be regular and punctual. Horses are creatures of habit. A nervous, high-strung horse can be upset when his routine is disrupted.

7. Feed should be given in rather small amounts, two or three times a day, not all at once.

8. Changes in rations should be made gradually to avoid digestive troubles.

9. Availability of feeds is another factor to consider. Horses are fed many different kinds of grains and hays in various parts of the world. Those available in an area may be fed even though not the most suitable.

10. Suitability is another consideration. Timothy hay is an excellent roughage for mature geldings. Alfalfa hay would be more suitable for weanlings and yearlings because it has much more digestible protein, minerals, and vitamins needed for growth and development.

11. Cost of the feed must be considered by every horseman. All horse owners know that the feed cost is the major cost in keeping horses.

THE HORSE'S DIGESTIVE SYSTEM

A basic knowledge of the digestive system of the horse helps the horseman to understand the complexities of feeding.

The horse has a simple stomach with a capacity of about four gallons. This compares to the 40-gallon compartmented stomach of the cow.

Much digestion, mainly by bile and pancreatic juice, takes place in the small intestine. This part of the tract is about 70 feet long and 3 inches in diameter and has fluid contents. Enzymes break feed stuffs into usable nutritional constituents. Amylase converts starches to sugars, lipase changes fats to fatty acids and glycerol, and trypsin helps the work of protein digestion. Carotene is converted to Vitamin A. Much absorption of these end-products of digestion takes place through the small intestine wall.

The large intestine consists of the caecum (three feet long, one foot in diameter, contents semi-liquid), the large colon (twelve feet long, ten inches in diameter, contents semi-liquid), and the small colon (ten feet long, four inches in diameter, contents solid).

Much cellulose digestion occurs in the caecum or "water gut." Micro-organisms convert cellulose to fatty acids. The micro-organisms also are associated with the synthesis of B-complex vitamins and amino acids.

A continuation of bacterial digestion occurs in the large colon, which is usually distended with partially digested feed, and more nutrients are absorbed.

In the small colon the undigested parts of feed are formed into the characteristic balls of manure.

The digestive tract of the horse, in comparison to that of the cow, does not permit the use of large quantities of dry roughages. The horse is better adapted to grain feeding and the consumption of young growing grasses rather than dry, coarse roughages. In his natural habitat the horse had the opportunity to graze almost continually and he is made for the continual consumption of small quantities of feed.

THE NEED FOR NUTRIENTS

Horses require nutrients, as do other animals, for
1. Growth.
2. Repair of worn-out body tissues.
3. Energy to maintain body temperature.
4. Energy for vital body functions.
5. Energy for the production of movement and external work.
6. Reproduction.
7. Milk production.

To satisfy these requirements horse rations must supply water, protein, energy, minerals, and vitamins.

Good horsemen formulate their rations to meet the specific requirements of the animal. They consider the age, sex, phase of reproduction, and amount of use or work.

GRAINS AND GRAIN BY-PRODUCTS FED TO HORSES

The nutritional requirements of horses can be met by using a variety of grains and roughages. No one grain or one type of roughage is best. A brief discussion of the common grain feeds follows.

Oats. Analysis:		
Digestible protein	9.4 %
Total digestible nutrients	70.1 %
Calcium	0.09%
Phosphorus	0.33%
Nutritive ratio	1:6.0

Oats are the leading horse feed in America, and next to corn

the most widely grown. On the average oats contain about 30 per
cent hulls, and the standard weight is 32 pounds to the bushel.
However, real good feeding oats should test 40 pounds to the
bushel. They should break sharply in the teeth and taste like good
oat meal. Oats are considered to be the safest grain to feed to horses
because the hulls make the grain bulky. Oats, therefore, form a
loose mass in the digestive tract and are easily digested. Because
of the relatively high protein content, oats make a balanced ration
for mature horses when fed with a grass hay such as timothy.

Corn. Analysis:	Digestible protein	6.7 %
	Total digestible nutrients	80.1 %
	Calcium	0.02%
	Phosphorus	0.27%
	Nutritive ratio	1.11

Corn is the leading grain crop grown in the United States. It
is the great energizing, heat-giving, fat-furnishing feed for livestock, and is used extensively in the Middle West as a horse feed.
Ear corn is safer to feed than shelled corn because horses must eat
it more slowly. When mixed with other grains corn is usually
coarsely ground. Although somewhat spoiled corn can be fed to
hogs it is very dangerous to feed to horses. Corn has less digestible
protein and minerals than oats. Consequently, corn is not so suitable as oats for young growing horses, if it is the only grain fed.
Not only is corn relatively low in protein content but also a large
part of the protein in corn lacks the essential amino acids. Corn
fed with alfalfa hay or a good mixed hay makes a balanced ration
for mature horses. With a balanced ration it takes 15 per cent less
corn than oats to keep horses in condition. Corn often is lower in
cost than oats, feeding value considered.

Barley. Analysis:	Digestible protein	10.0 %
	Total digestible nutrients	77.7 %
	Calcium	0.06%
	Phosphorus	0.40%
	Nutritive ratio	1:6.8

Barley is used extensively as a horse feed in the Western states,
Canada, Great Britain, Europe, Asia, and North Africa. Barley
grains are hard and small. They should be rolled or coarsely ground
and mixed with bulk feeds.

Wheat bran. Analysis:	Digestible protein	13.3 %
	Total digestible nutrients	66.9 %
	Calcium	0.13%
	Phosphorus	1.29%
	Nutritive ratio	1:4

Wheat bran is the coarse outer covering of the wheat kernel. It is twice as bulky as oats. Horses like it. Bran is mildly laxative, and for this reason is often fed to horses in the winter months when their ration is composed largely of dry grain and hay and lacks the succulence furnished by pasture during the grazing months. Many horsemen who run rental riding stables give a bran mash to their horses on idle days. Bran and corn are approximately equal to oats and corn when fed with mixed clover and timothy hay.

PROTEIN CONCENTRATES FED TO HORSES

The various legume meals are excellent horse feeds. Rich in protein, phosphorus, and B-complex vitamins, the protein concentrates are universally used to help balance horse rations. No more than one to two pounds per day of any protein concentrate should be fed to a horse.

Linseed meal. Analysis:

Digestible protein	30.7 %
Total digestible nutrients	70.3 %
Calcium	0.44%
Phosphorus	0.94%
Nutritive ratio	1:3

The old-fashioned kind of linseed meal was fed to add "bloom" to the horse's coat and to regulate bowel function. Most linseed meal available today is made by the solvent process and contains no more than 0.5 per cent fat.

Soybean meal. Analysis:

Digestible protein	42.0 %
Total digestible nutrients	78.1 %
Calcium	0.29%
Phosphorus	0.64%
Nutritive ratio	1:0.9

Soybean meal is widely used in balancing horse rations, and it has the highest biological value of the protein supplements for horses.

Cottonseed meal. Analysis:

Digestible protein	43.0 %
Total digestible nutrients	65.2 %
Calcium	0.21%
Phosphorus	0.96%
Nutritive ratio	1:1

Cottonseed meal has been used in horse rations in the south. In the southwest and western range country many horses are fed cottonseed cake or cottonseed meal cubes.

ROUGHAGES FED TO HORSES

Hays vary greatly in feed value. Most horsemen prefer early cuttings for horse hay. Variations in nutritive content may result from variety and species of the hay, soil type, soil fertility, rain fall, topography, air temperature, amount of sun, harvesting method, stage of maturity when cut, and length of time in storage.

Timothy hay. Analysis:

Digestible protein	4.2 %
Total digestible nutrients	51.7 %
Calcium	0.41%
Phosphorus	0.21%
Nutritive ratio	1:11.3

Timothy hay has long been one of the most popular roughages for horses because of its clean fragrant odor and freedom from dust and mold. Although not so nutritious as some of the legumes, timothy (as well as many other grass hays) makes a good roughage, especially for mature horses.

Alfalfa hay. Analysis:

Digestible protein	10.9 %
Total digestible nutrients	50.7 %
Calcium	1.47%
Phosphorus	0.24%
Nutritive ratio	1:3.7

Good quality alfalfa hay is an excellent source of protein, calcium, carotene, and B-complex vitamins. To be of good quality it must be green, leafy, and free from dust and mold. Alfalfa hay is particularly valuable for young growing horses and horses in the breeding herd. Because alfalfa consumption usually does result in somewhat softer manure and greater urination, alfalfa is not widely used as the *only* roughage fed to horses in training for racing. However, many of the top race horse trainers do feed some alfalfa hay to their horses.

Good Mixed grass-legume hay over 30% legumes Analysis:

Digestible protein	7.2 %
Total digestible nutrients	49.5 %
Calcium	0.90%
Phosphorus	0.19%
Nutritive ratio	1:5.9

Mixed grass-legume hays, such as timothy and red clover, are widely grown and in many areas are the major hays produced for horses. They usually make excellent roughages.

Silages. Sometimes on a farm where corn silage or grass silage is produced to feed to cattle, the silage may be fed to horses on the farm. Most horses have to learn to like silage. Usually grain must be sprinkled over the silage before horses will eat it. If fed, silage must be of the best quality. It is not the roughage of choice for most horsemen.

PROPORTION OF GRAIN AND HAY FED TO HORSES

Mature idle horses can be maintained satisfactorily on good pasture, salt, and water during the summer, or on good hay, salt, and water during the winter. When horses are used regularly under saddle or in harness they need a more concentrated source of energy, and must be fed some grain.

The following recommendations should be regarded merely as guide lines to be varied according to each horse's need and the severity of his job.

Idle   Chiefly or entirely on roughage, unless it is of poor quality, in which case grain should be fed.

At light work (1 to 3 hours per day)

$\begin{cases} .4 \text{ lb. to } .75 \text{ lb. grain} \\ 1.25 \text{ lbs. to } 1.5 \text{ lbs. hay} \end{cases}$ for every 100 lbs. of body weight

At medium work (3 to 5 hours per day)

$\begin{cases} .75 \text{ lb. to } 1 \text{ lb. grain} \\ 1 \text{ to } 1.25 \text{ lbs. hay} \end{cases}$ for every 100 lbs. of body weight

At hard work

$\begin{cases} 1 \text{ to } 1.4 \text{ lbs. grain} \\ 1 \text{ lb. hay} \end{cases}$ for every 100 lbs. of body weight

SUCCULENT FEEDS FED TO HORSES

During the winter months, or whenever they are not on pasture, horses relish succulent feeds such as carrots, rutabagas, or apples. Though their feeding value is not particularly high, these feeds offer variety and palatability, and stimulate the appetites of horses being kept on a dry, monotonous ration. They should be chopped into pieces small enough for a greedy horse to eat without choking. In all probability apples and carrots are much more frequently fed to privately owned pleasure horses than to horses in large public or professional stables.

Some horsemen soak dried beet pulp in water until it swells, then mix it with their grain ration to provide bulk and succulence to a dry winter ration.

ENERGY IN HORSE RATIONS

The energy portion of a horse ration consists of the carbo-
hydrates and fats supplied in the grain portion of the ration and
from roughages. As the amount of work a horse performs increases,
the energy requirement also increases. The capacity of the digestive tract of the horse is limited. Consequently, the working horse
may not be able to eat enough pasture or hay to meet its needs.
It must be fed a grain concentrate. The grain part of the ration
must be increased in proportion to the work expended, and the
roughage part decreased, to provide the energy requirements. The
suggested total digestible nutrients content for horse rations is a
minimum of 55 per cent. As work increases, energy requirements
increase. Some rations may contain 65 per cent or more total digestible nutrients for maximum horse performance.

PROTEIN IN HORSE RATIONS

Protein is necessary for the formation of all tissue, hair, hoofs,
skeleton, and blood. It is also needed for the replacement of worn
tissues. The protein value of a feed is determined by its amino acid
content and how well it meets the horse's needs. The horse can get
some of its amino acid needs from the micro-organisms in the
caecum. However, high quality protein rations should be fed,
especially to foals whose caecum may not yet have many micro-
organisms present for bacterial synthesis.

Protein requirements are greatest for young growing horses,
and are gradually reduced from youth to maturity. Pregnant mares
need extra protein to maintain themselves and at the same time
develop the fetus adequately. Mares nursing foals need additional
protein to support a high level of milk production. These varying
requirements are reflected in the following table.

Suggested Protein Requirements of Horses

	Protein %
Foals	20–22
Yearlings	13–14
Two-year-olds	10–12
Mature	10
Pregnant mares	12–14
Lactating mares	13–15

VITAMINS IN HORSE RATIONS

Vitamins are organic substances that are necessary for the

utilization of various nutrients in the ration. Not much experimental work in horse nutrition has been conducted, but horses are believed to have vitamin requirements somewhat similar to those of other livestock. Fancy, mysterious, and expensive vitamin mixes are not necessary. Most good quality commercially mixed horse feeds include vitamin supplements.

Vitamin A. Carotene, the precursor of vitamin A, is found in green hays and young pasture grasses and legumes. After 90 days storage most hays lose much of their carotene. Therefore, adding Vitamin A to rations of horses not on pasture makes sense. Vitamin A deficiency may result in reproduction failures, night blindness, poor hoof development, and other disorders. However, horses kept under natural conditions are not likely to suffer any deficiency.

Vitamin D. Vitamin D is needed for proper absorption and use of the calcium and phosphorus in rations. Horses living a natural life are exposed to direct sunlight and will not be deficient in this vitamin.

Vitamin E. Vitamin E is found in young, growing green grasses and in the germ of most grains. Practical rations, therefore, contain a liberal amount of vitamin E. Some horsemen believe this vitamin is beneficial to the breeding performance of stallions and mares.

Vitamins of the B-complex. Thiamine, riboflavin, niacin, pantothenic acid, and vitamin B-12 are believed by some research workers to be essential. Most of them are synthesized in the caecum of the horse, and are present in adequate amounts in practical horse rations. The colostrum milk is much richer in the B vitamins than later milk produced by the brood mare. If the B vitamins are deficient, horses show anorexia, nervousness, incoordination behind, loss of weight, and weakness.

MINERALS IN HORSE RATIONS

Minerals are needed for the development of the teeth and the skeleton, and are essential components of tissue and blood. They also are needed in various enzyme systems. A horse's mineral needs are influenced by the level of soil fertility and the subsequent quantities and ratios of minerals in the grains and roughages grown on that soil and consumed by the horse. Horses are believed to require 13 minerals—calcium, phosphorous, sodium, chlorine, iron, copper, cobalt, iodine, manganese, potassium, zinc, magnesium, and sulfur. However, fancy, mysterious, high-priced mineral mixtures are not necessary. Most good quality commercially mixed horse feeds include an adequate mineral supplement.

Calcium and phosphorus. Calcium and phosphorus are especially important for proper skeletal development of young growing horses. After horses mature these minerals are needed for maintenance of bony structures, for various body functions, for fetus development, and lactation. Three requirements must be met for proper calcium and phosphorus utilization.

1. Sufficient calcium and phosphorus must be fed. If there is any doubt, dicalcium phosphate should be offered free choice in a mineral box on pasture. It can be mixed with salt to encourage consumption.

2. A suitable ratio between calcium and phosphorus must be provided. The ratio ideally is about 1:1.

3. An adequate amount of vitamin D must be supplied. Horses in direct sunlight get plenty of vitamin D.

Salt. Common salt (sodium chloride) is one of the least expensive items the horseman has to buy. Common grains and hays lack salt, so it must be provided, and should be constantly available to horses. Iodized salt should be used, especially in iodine-deficient areas. Most horsemen find that feeding trace mineral salt is the easiest and least expensive way to provide the other essential minerals that are needed in rather minute amounts. Although salt blocks are widely used, granulated salt is more readily available to horses and will be consumed in greater amounts. Horses will take up to three ounces of salt each day. However, in hot weather or when they are worked hard, horses lose large amounts of salt in their sweat. At such times they need and will eat more salt.

WATER

Water is essential for most body functions and is a major constituent of the blood. Horses will drink ten to twelve gallons of water a day. Their water consumption will vary with the air temperature, the work they are doing, and the kind of ration they are fed. Horses fed legume hays drink more water than when they are fed only grass hays. Horses on pelleted feeds drink more water than they do when fed conventional grain and hay rations.

The water supply should be clean and fresh. Water buckets and water tanks should be kept clean. Horses can be given water before, during, or after meals or can have water free choice, available at all times. However, when horses have been ridden or driven and have become hot they should not be given water until they have been cooled out. Watering a hot horse may cause laminitis, or founder.

PELLETED HORSE RATIONS

In recent years many livestock feed companies have developed completely pelleted horse feeds. A soft, one-half-inch pellet is easily chewed by horses and is readily eaten. Pelleted feeds are only as good as their ingredients. Only well balanced, clean, nutritious feeds should be so processed.

For the owner of one or two horses, pelleted feeds have a number of advantages over conventional grains and hays. Pelleted feeds result in increased gains and increased feed efficiency. This may be due partly to the fact that the ingredients are ground before being pelleted, and, consequently, when they disintegrate they provide more surface area for the action of digestive enzymes and are more completely utilized. Pelleted feeds reduce feed waste, especially waste of hay. Pelleted feeds eliminate dustiness. They require less storage space, less labor, less handling. They permit a nutritionally balanced ration with the proper feed additives. Hence, pelleted feeds are the answer to the feeding problems of many small stable owners. A change from conventional to pelleted rations should be made gradually.

THE ROLE OF PASTURES IN HORSE PRODUCTION

Good pastures form the basis for successful horse production. The Blue Grass areas of Kentucky and Virginia and the excellent pastures around Ocala, Florida, give evidence that the best horses in America are grown on good pastures.

Pastures offer many advantages to horsemen.

1. Good pasture is the cheapest, most economical feed for horses. The feed cost can often be reduced one-half when horses are on pasture.

2. Pasture is the most natural, most nearly adequate feed for all kinds of horses.

3. The extensive use of pastures reduces the labor cost of handling horses.

4. Pasture permits the exercise needed by horses for the development of sound underpinning. No show-ring winners or race track champions have been raised in confinement.

5. Keeping land in pasture prevents soil erosion and builds up organic matter in the soil.

6. Horses on pasture drop their manure on the land, not in stalls that have to be cleaned.

7. Pastures promote greater animal health and are more sanitary than stables.

8. The opportunity to run free on pasture promotes greater contentment and mental balance in horses, especially those that are hot-blooded.

All horsemen should make the greatest possible use of pastures. Idle horses, brood mares, young growing horses, and stallions are best kept on pasture the major part of the time. Recommendations for seeding, fertilizing, and maintaining pastures can be obtained from any County Agricultural Extension Agent.

PASTURE MANAGEMENT

The main causes of poor pasture are depleted soil fertility, poor grazing management, and unfavorable climatic conditions. The first steps in pasture improvement are to conduct soil tests and then to apply the lime and fertilizers required to raise the fertility to a level adequate to grow good pasture.

Horses must use grass in the growing state for the best results. As forages mature there is a steady decrease in their protein content, digestibility, and palatability. Horses spot graze. They eat one part of a pasture and not another. Therefore, during a favorable growing season pastures must be mowed to increase their productivity and help to control some weeds. The regrowth after clipping is more palatable, digestible, and nutritious.

Horses do not graze close to their droppings. Pastures should be dragged with a chain harrow to break up the piles of manure.

Probably the key to the successful establishment and maintenance of good pasture is to keep a legume in the pasture. The pasture mixture should have at least one grass and one legume. The legumes increase the dry matter produced, stimulate the grass and thus reduce weed growth, and increase the palatability and nutritional quality of the pasture.

In a grass-legume mixture, the two grow better than either one alone. A mixture is adapted to diverse soil conditions. A mixture of plants provides a better balanced feed and a better distribution of feed through the grazing season.

Many pasture mixtures are used. The choice depends upon geographic location, topography, soil fertility, and use. In deep, fertile, well-drained soils alfalfa and brome grass make an excellent horse pasture. Timothy and red clover pasture is good for about two years. In parts of Missouri and Kentucky, Kentucky blue grass and Korean lespedeza make a good pasture combination. Sweet clover adds more nitrogen to the soil than most other legumes. When used in a pasture mixture it must be reseeded every year to keep the stand satisfactory. Ladino clover makes an excellent addition to pastures in some parts of the country.

Blue grass pastures are the most common permanent pastures for horses in the northern part of the United States. Many of these fields are badly managed. They would be improved by adequate fertilizing, reseeding, less concentrated grazing, and the addition of a legume to the seeding mixture.

In Florida, important pasture grasses include Coastal Bermuda, Pensacola bahia, and pangola. Bluestem pastures are a feature of Kansas agriculture. Buffalo and grama grasses are important in the Southwest. Horsemen use the species and varieties of grasses that do best in their localities.

Horses are destructive grazers. They have two sets of teeth and graze the forage shorter than do cattle. Horses tear the turf by their hoofs, especially on sandy soils or on wet, heavy soils. Horses denude some areas by frequent traffic. For example, they may walk alongside the fences, gather around gates or water troughs or on windy knolls. Also, on many farms, horses are "pastured" essentially the year around. Hence they have more opportunity than cattle to destroy pastures. This more or less continual grazing leads to overgrazing some areas, loss of desirable mixtures of plant species, and increased parasitism of the horses.

Horse farms typically are low users of fertilizers. Cattlemen can see the difference between mediocre and superior pasture in the milk pail under the dairy cow or in the weight gains of beef cattle. It is more difficult for horsemen to appreciate the value of pasture because so many factors other than feed influence the winning of a race or a show.

However, the proper use of lime and fertilizer would promote earlier spring grazing, later fall grazing, more abundant mid-summer grazing even in drought, and would upgrade the quality of the horse diet.

In addition to a good growth of forage, the other essentials for a horse pasture are good fencing, shade, and water. Barbed wire fences are dangerous and should not be used to enclose horses. Plank fences are the best, but often are too expensive. Woven wire fencing is widely used. Often an electric wire fence can be strung up to keep horses from damaging the permanent fencing.

If natural shade is not available in a pasture, a shed should be provided so the horses can get relief from the hot sun and perhaps get away from the flies. A three-sided shed in a pasture can also serve as a wind-break and shelter from severe winter storms, if horses do not have the protection afforded by woods.

A water supply in the pasture not only is a labor-saving device for the owner but also a benefit to the horse. He can drink whenever he wants or needs water.

FEEDING STALLIONS

Because the performance of the stud horse affects the entire horse production enterprise, the breeding stallion should be fed wisely. If a single horse is going to be favored, perhaps it should be the stallion in service.

A stallion should have access to a paddock of two acres or more. This provides the opportunity to exercise and also the green growing forage that is most helpful in maintaining a high degree of fertility.

If a stallion has a large book of mares, he should be fed, during the breeding season, as a horse at hard work. That is, he should be given 1 to 1.4 pounds of a well-balanced grain ration for every 100 pounds of body weight. In addition, he should get all the high quality mixed hay he wants. At least one-half of his roughage should be a legume. Special care should be taken to provide enough protein and vitamins.

FEEDING BROOD MARES

Brood mares do best when kept on pasture most of the time. Unless the pasture is extremely plentiful most horsemen feed two to four pounds of oats to their mares daily. As a mare's pregnancy advances during the fall and winter months her nutritional requirements increase. Also at this time most pastures provide only exercise. The greatest growth of the foal embryo occurs during the last three months of the gestation period. Consequently the mare needs to be especially well fed during late pregnancy.

The big drain on brood mares comes during their lactation period. Some mares undoubtedly give over 50 pounds of milk a day at the peak of their production. Pasture is the most natural habitat for mares and foals, and excellent pasture will maintain them. Unfortunately, most pastures fall short of an excellent rating. Therefore, to ensure the best growth of the foal and the greatest milk production from the mare, grain should be fed. The amount will vary with the individual situation, but 12 pounds per day is not uncommon.

FEEDING FOALS, YEARLINGS, AND TWO-YEAR-OLDS

Most foals will start to eat some grain when they are one to two weeks old, if their dams are being fed. Of course, their principal food is their mothers' milk. Many foals will double their birth weight during the first month, and will have tripled their birth weight by the end of the second month. The growing gains are the cheapest gains an animal makes. Therefore, many good horsemen provide a creep in the pasture where foals can eat grain undisturbed by the mares. When a mare and foal are stabled part of the time, the mare can be tied up in the stall while the foal is fed individually. Foals should be eating five to six pounds of grain daily by the time they are weaned at five to six months of age.

Good quality legume hay and good pastures should be the basis for feeding weanlings, yearlings, and two-year-olds. Pastures are indispensable for growing young stock.

On many Thoroughbred farms in the Blue Grass the yearlings are fed more grain than any other horses on the place—12 to 14 pounds of oats a day plus all the hay they will eat. This is not an extravagant practice. The young growing horse makes the most efficient use of his feedstuffs. The growing gains are the cheapest.

In the 1920s, Professor J. L. Edmonds of the University of Illinois conducted a series of feeding experiments with Percheron fillies. These young draft fillies were fed from weaning time until they were broke to harness work as two-year-olds. Professor Edmonds's feeding trials showed that it took almost twice as much grain and three times as much hay to produce each pound of gain the second winter (when the fillies changed from yearlings to two-year-olds) as it did during their first winter when they became yearlings.

The conclusion to be drawn from this work is that it pays to feed foals, weanlings, and yearlings liberally. Horsemen cannot starve young stock and produce show-ring winners, fast race horses, or satisfactory pleasure horses.

14

Horse Parasites and Common Diseases

Parasites are one of the chief sources of loss in livestock production. Horsemen, cattlemen, sheepmen, and swine producers—all have their own difficulties in working out a plan of management that will control parasites, but all agree that it does not pay to feed them. Therefore, the best stockmen try to kill the parasites so that all the feed goes to the livestock.

More than a hundred different kinds of parasites infest horses. Parasites, both external and internal, sap the energy, reduce the strength, and decrease the efficiency of a horse, no matter what his job may be. Not only does parasitic infestation result in unthrifty appearance; it may cause indigestion, colic, or stoppage of blood vessels or embolism. The following brief discussion of parasites is not meant to be all-inclusive; it is intended to summarize some useful facts concerning some of the most common and troublesome parasites infesting horses.

EXTERNAL PARASITES

Horse lice and mites are the most common external parasites to be found on horses. Unlike some of the internal parasites, they spend their entire lives on their hosts. Horse lice do not infest animals other than horses, asses, and mules.

Horse Lice

Two kinds of lice infest horses, the sucking louse (Haematopinus) and the biting louse (Trichodectes). Sucking lice, which are thought to do the most harm, are a little more difficult to eradicate. These two kinds of lice have similar life histories.

LIFE HISTORY Lice can live only a few days when removed from their natural host. Their eggs, commonly called nits, are laid

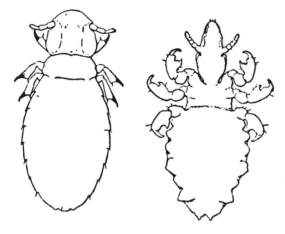

Two species of lice that infest horses. Left: Biting louse. Right: Sucking louse. Lice do their greatest damage to horses and colts in winter, when the animals are confined in close quarters and the parasites can spread easily. Courtesy Frank Thorp, Jr., Dr. Robert Graham, and C. O. Mohr.

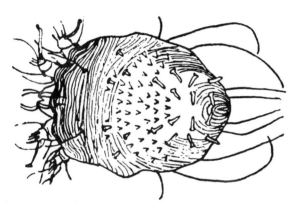

Sarcoptic mange mite. This parasite burrows into the skin, and soreness and wrinkling result. Mange is communicable to other animals and to man by direct contact. Courtesy Dr. Robert Graham.

on the hair, to which they are firmly attached. Ten to twenty days are required before the nits hatch. The newly hatched nits reach sexual maturity and lay eggs when they are about eleven or twelve days old. Long hair, commonly found on horses in winter, favors the development and spread of lice. Lice spread most easily through direct contacts and through hair carried on grooming utensils. Tufts of infested hair removed while rubbing or grooming animals, as well as harness, blankets, and other stable equipment, can, through contact, infest horses free from lice.

SYMPTOMS OF LICE INFESTATION Biting lice live by feeding on the external layers of the skin, hair, and exudates. Sucking lice actually puncture the skin of the host and suck blood. When not feeding, lice move about on the skin and annoy the host. The itching sensation causes the lousy animals to rub, bite, and kick in an endeavor to dislodge the pests. If lice are present in great numbers, the hair coat becomes rough, and patches of skin are stripped of hair by frequent rubbing.

Lice can be detected with little difficulty by pulling a tuft of hair and holding it against direct sunlight. The regions of the horse's body usually inhabited by lice are the sides of the neck, croup, flanks, and under the jaws. A heavily infested horse, however, may have lice on all parts of its body.

TREATMENT FOR HORSE LICE   One treatment will kill all live lice but will not destroy the eggs. Therefore, for permanent relief, a second treatment should be given seven to fourteen days later.

Dipping affected horses in a special tank is the best means of controlling lice, if the weather is suitable. Thorough spraying will also eradicate lice. Dusting powders may hold lice in check, but are not so effective as dipping or spraying. Among the safest effective drugs used to eliminate horse lice are rotenone, toxaphene, and synergized pyrethrins.

Oils and greases commonly used as insecticides on hogs will destroy horse lice, but are not recommended for horses because they remove hair and injure the skin.

Mites (Sarcoptes, Psoroptes, Chorioptes)

Mange or scabies of horses is a specific skin disease caused by small mites which live on or in the skin. The mites, about a fortieth of an inch in diameter, are so small that a microscope must be used to identify the species. The general contour of the body of a mite is oval and the mature parasite has four pairs of legs. Mites spend their entire lives on the host.

LIFE HISTORY OF MITES (SARCOPTES, PSOROPTES, CHORIOPTES) The life cycles of the three types of mites are virtually the same, varying only in detail. The female mite lays her eggs in the channel she makes in the skin. From ten to twenty-five eggs are laid in approximately two weeks. Soon after this the female mite dies. Incubation of the egg takes from three to ten days, and the young mites develop to maturity in ten to twelve days.

SYMPTOMS OF MANGE MITE   The sarcoptic mite is the one most commonly found in horses. This parasite burrows into the upper layer of the skin and forms channels in which it mates and reproduces. In the early stage of sarcoptic mange the only symptoms noticeable are areas of irritation or inflammation. Although any portion of the body may become affected, the withers, sides of the neck, shoulders, and head are the most common regions. The burrowing of the mites causes an intense pruritis or itching of the skin. An infested horse tries to get relief by rubbing against objects, by biting the itching areas, and by constantly twitching its skin. It is not uncommon to have scales form over infested areas.

Treatment of all three types of horse mange is the same, the object being to put some noxious agent on the troublesome parasite. Dips such as lime-sulfur, nicotine-sulfate and lindane are recommended. Frequent and thorough applications are necessary. In generalized cases, dipping in an especially constructed tank is necessary. Four to six dippings at intervals of one week usually eradicate the mites. The job is one for a veterinarian.

INTERNAL PARASITES

Bots

There are three species of botflies: the chin or throat fly, the common botfly, and the nose botfly. The throat and common botflies are the most widely distributed of the three species.

LIFE HISTORY   All three species lay their eggs on the hair of horses from July to September. The eggs are glued to the hair on parts of the body indicated by the names of the different species. After larvae of the common botfly hatch, they enter the mouth and burrow into the mucous membrane of the tongue. After molting, these larvae become attached to the pharynx and later enter the stomach. They require about one month to travel from the mouth to the stomach, where they are attached during the fall and winter months. It is not unusual to find two hundred to six hundred bots firmly attached to the stomach lining. The throat and common bots leave the body directly with the manure, but the nose bot reattaches to the rectum and the anus before it finally passes out. The bots pupate in the ground and emerge as adult flies during the summer months to lay their eggs on the hair of the horse; thus the cycle is repeated.

SYMPTOMS OF BOT INFESTATION   Horses that have large numbers of bots in their stomach may suffer from digestive disturbances and colic. The hooks of the bots imbedded in the wall of the stomach, as well as their spines on the body surface, cause irritation. Large numbers of bots result in unthriftiness and may even obstruct the opening at the junction of the stomach and the small intestine. While nose bots are attached to its rectum, a horse may show signs of pain and itching and rub itself against the stall in an effort to get rid of the parasites.

TREATMENT FOR BOTS. Carbon disulfide is the classic treatment for bots. The proper dosage is 6 drams (24 c.c.) for each 1,000 pounds of live weight. The drug is given by means of a stomach tube and because of its toxic properties should be administered by a veterinarian. One or two treatments should be given in late fall

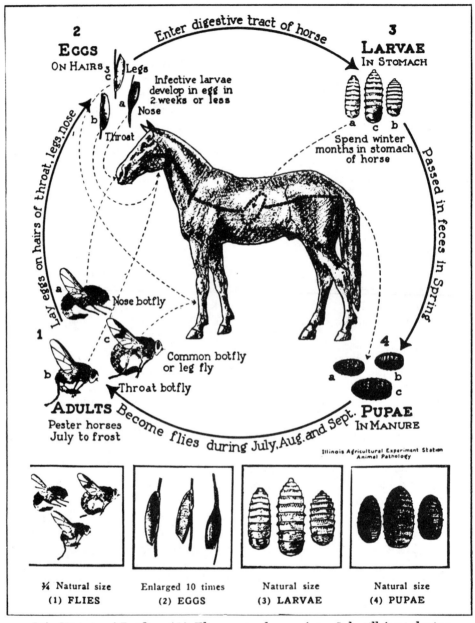

Life History of Botflies. (1) *Flies pester horses from July till frost, laying their eggs on the hairs of the nose, throat, jaws, breast and legs.* (2) *Larvae develop in the eggs in two weeks or less and enter the digestive tract.* (3) *Larvae spend the winter months in the stomach, where they are a drain on the animal. In the spring they pass out in the manure.* (4) *In the ground, pupae develop from the larvae. During July and until September, these pupae becomes flies which start the life cycle all over again.* Courtesy Dr. Robert Graham.

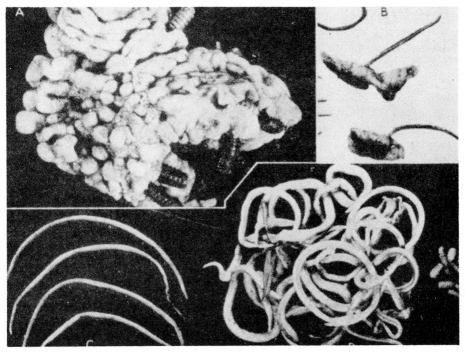

Three common internal parasites of horses. (A) Bots attached to the inner wall of a horse's stomach. Note nodules and tumors caused by these parasites. The tumors are the result of bots of several years' standing. Chronic thickening of the stomach wall interferes with normal digestion. (B) Palisade worms of the strongylus species. These and other palisade worms bury their heads in the lining of the intestines and cause extensive inflammation. (C) Large intestinal roundworms (ascarids) live unattached in the intestines and cause intestinal catarrh, indigestion, and unthriftiness. (D) Large intestinal roundworms and bots expelled by the same treatment. These parasites were passed by one horse a few hours after treatment. Many more were passed on successive days. Photographs courtesy Dr. Robert Graham.

or winter. Horses to be treated with carbon disulfide may be given water but no grain or hay for 24 hours prior to treatment. All feed should be withheld for five hours after the drug has been given.

In recent years other drugs effective against bots have been developed. A piperazine-carbon disulfide complex, known commercially as *Parvex*, though somewhat less effective than carbon disulfide, is relatively non-toxic. The dosage is one ounce per 100 pounds of body weight. Its use for strongyle and ascarid control at other times of the year carries the added advantage of eliminating bots. Removal of bot fly eggs on the hairs of horses' legs by clipping the hair may also aid in bot control.

Large Intestinal Roundworms (Ascaris equorum)

Large intestinal roundworms are more common and do much more damage to young horses than to mature horses.

The mature roundworms (or ascarids) are yellowish white in color, cylindrical in shape, and six to twelve inches long, tapering toward both ends. In the horse this worm is found chiefly in the upper part of the small intestine and less frequently in the stomach and other parts of the intestinal tract. A single horse may be host to hundreds of large intestinal roundworms. The ascarid of the horse does not infest other animals.

LIFE HISTORY   The female ascarid lays large numbers of eggs in the intestine of the host. These eggs, which cannot be seen with the naked eye, pass out in the manure, each covered with a thick shell which protects it. Under favorable conditions of temperature and moisture, the eggs on the ground or in the manure undergo certain changes before they become infective. They must spend two weeks or more outside the host before they become infective to susceptible animals. The appearance of the embryo or tiny worm in the eggs marks the infective stage, but the infective egg remains dormant until swallowed by the host. The infective eggs hatch in the intestinal tract and the live embryos leave the shells. The young worms then burrow into the walls of the intestines to enter the blood stream and migrate to the liver, the heart, and the lungs, where they undergo further changes. About one week elapses from the time the young worms are liberated in the intestinal tract until they are present in the lungs in great numbers. The young worms move up the windpipe and are swallowed. Upon reaching the intestine for the second time, the young worms develop into mature worms in about two or three months.

SYMPTOMS OF ROUNDWORMS   Ascarids in the intestinal tracts of foals and yearlings may cause digestive disturbances such as colic. As a result of irritation to the walls of the intestines, a catarrh accompanied by a diarrhea alternates with the passage of hard, dry feces coated with mucus. Toxins or poisons may kill horses that are heavily infested with roundworms. Heavily parasitized horses often have harsh, dry, dull hair coats and every action suggests a lack of vitality.

TREATMENT FOR ASCARIDS.   Because ascarids are so damaging to young growing horses, good horsemen try to raise their young stock free of these large roundworms. Treatments are recommended at 8, 16, 24, 32, and 40 weeks of age. Carbon disulfide, piperazine adipate, and *Parvex* (piperazine-carbon disulfide complex) are among the drugs most commonly used. Recommended dosages should be carefully observed. Once they reach maturity horses develop a sort of immunity to ascarids, and the worms do not establish themselves in the mature horse.

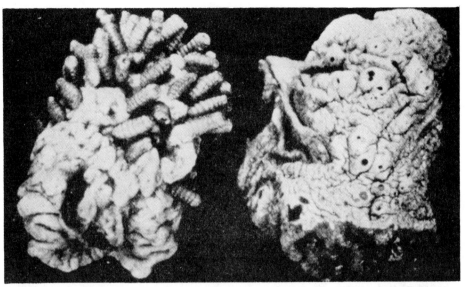

Injury to wall of stomach from Bots. Bots attached to the stomach may puncture the lining and cause thickened folds to develop as a result of chronic inflammation. Courtesy Dr. Robert Graham.

Strongyles or Palisade Worms

Palisade worms (strongyles) of horses and mules are small roundworms, commonly called red worms, palisades, or bloodworms. They are probably as deadly in their attacks as any parasites that infest horses.

Colts are more susceptible to attacks by strongyles than are older horses. These parasites are much smaller than the large roundworms, varying in length from a third of an inch to two and a half inches. They also differ from the former in that the adult worms are usually attached to the mucous membrane lining of the intestine by means of a mouth (supplied with suckers and sometimes with teeth) which is connected to the body of the parasite by a threadlike neck. Some bloodworms are free, however, in the fecal content.

LIFE HISTORY OF STRONGYLES Eggs of the strongyle are laid in the intestinal tract of the host and pass out with the manure. When conditions are favorable the eggs hatch in a day or so in the manure on the ground. The liberated larvae feed on the manure to which they have access, undergo two changes, and reach the infective stage in a short time. It takes the young worms about a week to reach the infective stage under favorable conditions, but a much longer period is necessary during the cold months, or during weather which is not conducive to their development. Moisture must be present for their development and enough is ordinarily

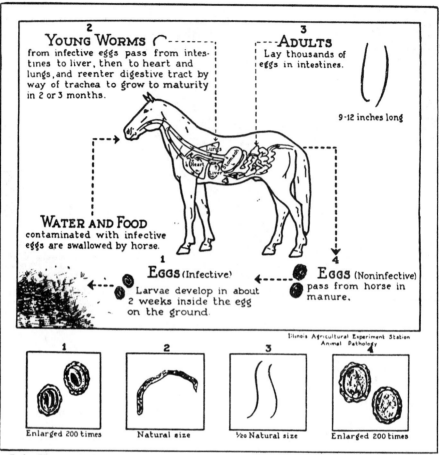

Life History of Large Roundworms of Horses. (1) Infective eggs, with larvae developed inside each one, are swallowed by the horse in feed and water. (2) The young worms that hatch from the eggs pass from the intestines to the liver, then to the heart and lungs, and re-enter the digestive tract by way of the windpipe to grow to maturity. (3) Adult worms in the intestines lay thousands of eggs. (4) Noninfective eggs pass from the horse in the manure. Within a few weeks, larvae develop within the eggs. When the horse swallows them the cycle starts all over again. Courtesy Dr. Robert Graham.

found in horse manure. Although direct sunlight is injurious to the hatching larvae, in the infective stage, the young worms are resistant to adverse weather conditions such as cold, heat, and dryness, and can remain viable in pastures for a long time.

After reaching the infective stage, the larvae, when there is enough moisture supplied by dew or rain, migrate up the stems of grasses and remain there. Grazing horses pick them up, and they pass into the large intestine, where they may develop into mature parasites. This part of the life cycle is not definitely known, as many of the larvae are known to migrate through the internal organs and tissues and have been found in practically every organ of the body. It is an established fact, however, that in the mature or adult stage they are found attached to the mucous membrane lining of the large intestine of horses, mules, and foals, where they lay eggs and begin their life cycle over again.

SYMPTOMS Horses mildly infested with strongyles may not show diagnostic symptoms. Anemia, weakness, emaciation, and general unthriftiness mark advanced cases. In heavy infestations, animals may suffer intermittent or persistent diarrhea or constipation, the hard, dry feces being covered with slimy mucus. The diarrhea is the result of the chronic irritation of the intestine.

Strongyles injure the walls of the intestine, to which they are firmly attached as they suck blood and tissue juices. They attach themselves by sucking a portion of the intestine into their mouth. Like ascarids, strongyles also produce primary toxins or poisons which may prove fatal.

The migration of strongyles to body tissues brings about serious conditions. It is not uncommon for one type of strongyle to lodge in the mesenteric arteries, causing a stoppage of the circulation which results in death.

TREATMENT FOR STRONGYLES. One of the most effective treatments to eliminate strongyles is to keep horses on a low-level dosage of phenothiazine. This consists of giving each horse two grams of phenothiazine powder on his feed each day for 21 days each month. This low-level treatment is more effective in reducing strongyle infection and, therefore, pasture contamination, than a therapeutic treatment of 2.5 grams per hundredweight two to four times a year.

Thiabendazole is very effective against all strongyles. It has a wide margin of safety. The dosage of 50 mg. per kilogram is given at six to eight week intervals.

Other treatments for strongyles include various piperazine preparations, cambendazole, mebendazole, pyrantel, and dichlorvos.

Pinworms (Oxyuris equi)

Pinworms are relatively long, whitish worms with a very long, slender tail. They occur in the large intestine of the horse. The males are very small and are seldom found. The female may attain a length of three to six inches.

LIFE HISTORY The adult worm passes from the horse in the manure and deposits the eggs in the manure or becomes attached

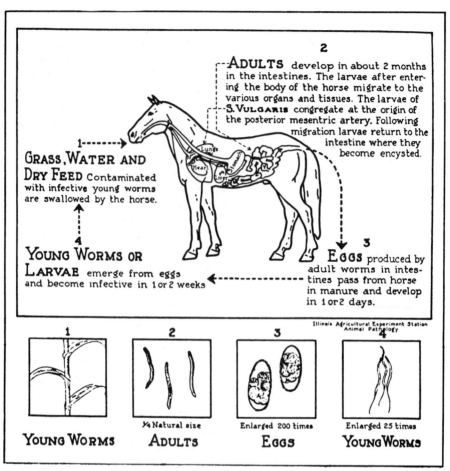

2

┌─ADULTS develop in about 2 months
│ in the intestines. The larvae after enter-
│ ing the body of the horse migrate to the
│ various organs and tissues. The larvae of
┌─┤─S. VULGARIS congregate at the origin of
│ │ the posterior mesentric artery. Following
│ │ migration larvae return to the
│ │ intestine where they
│ │ become encysted.

1------►
GRASS, WATER AND
DRY FEED Contaminated
with infective young worms
are swallowed by the horse.

4
YOUNG WORMS OR
LARVAE emerge from eggs
and become infective in 1 or 2 weeks ◄------------

3
EGGS produced by
adult worms in intes-
tines pass from horse
in manure and develop
in 1 or 2 days.

Illinois Agricultural Experiment Station
Animal Pathology

1   **2**   **3**   **4**

¼ Natural size   Enlarged 200 times   Enlarged 25 times

YOUNG WORMS   ADULTS   EGGS   YOUNG WORMS

*Life History of Palisade Worms of Horses. (1) Young worms (larvae)
are swallowed by the horse in feed and water. They travel to the various
body tissues and organs, such as the liver, pancreas, spleen, lungs, and
kidneys, and return to the intestines to develop into mature red worms.
(2) Adult worms lay eggs which pass out in the manure. (3) Within
one to two weeks, eggs develop into young worms, and when they are
swallowed by the horse they start the life cycle all over again. Courtesy
Dr. Robert Graham.*

near the anal opening and deposits the eggs in this region. The
egg are seen as a yellowish external incrustation. In either case the
eggs develop outside the body and under favorable conditions become infective in one to three days. Eggs are capable of producing
infection from one to four months after development. Infective eggs
may be taken into the body of the horse through infected water,
pasture, grain, or hay. The young worms reach the large intestine
and become adults in three or four months.

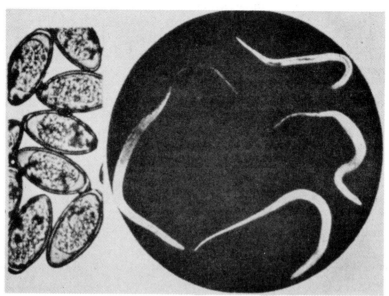

Pinworms (Oxyuris equi and eggs). The female worms are found in the large intestine of the horse. Passing out with the manure, they deposit their eggs with it or on the ground. Under favorable conditions the eggs become infective in a few days. Females attached to the anus may deposit eggs around the external anal region, causing intense pruritis. Horses will rub on any object available to relieve the itching sensation.
Courtesy Dr. Robert Graham.

SYMPTOMS   The attachment of the pinworms in the region of the anus and the egg incrustation produce an intense itching that causes the infected animal to rub its posterior parts against any object available. This may cause an eczematous inflammation. Pinworms may cause digestive disturbances, emaciation, and, in rare cases, anemia.

TREATMENT FOR PINWORMS.   Thiabendazole preparations (given for strongyle control) and various organophosphates are effective treatments to eliminate pinworms.

GENERAL PREVENTIVE MEASURES

The aim of all treatment and preventive measures is to break the life cycle of the parasites and to protect the horse from infestation. Cropping land, rotating pastures, mowing pastures, dragging pastures with a chain harrow to break up piles of manure, frequent cleaning of stables, proper disposal of manure, and confining horses after treatment for parasites help to reduce parasite troubles. Filthy stables, poorly drained barnyards and paddocks, low swampy pastures with slews and stagnant surface ponds increase parasite infestation.

The continuous feeding of horses on the same ground and the overstocking of pastures year after year may increase intestinal parasites in horses and be responsible for disappointing results. The denser the horse population on a farm the greater the parasite hazards and problems.

Though preventive measures are helpful, real effective parasite control depends upon treatment. All horsemen should practice regular, systematic treatment of horses to control parasites. Such a program is especially important for foals, yearlings, and two-year-olds.

For a parasite control program to be effective, every horse on the place should be dewormed on the same day at intervals of 6 to 8 weeks. At least four different classes of drugs should be used during the year to prevent the parasites from building up an immunity to one drug. Some drugs can be given in the form of pastes, powders, or pellets mixed with the grain fed to the horses. However, giving the dewormer by stomach tube, a dosing syringe, or a "balling gun" puts the medication into the stomach in high concentration so it can go through the digestive tract in full force.

Parasite control depends upon regular treatment with effective drugs.

A brief summary of the anthelmintic drugs available for deworming horses appears in the following tables.

Table 1.   Bot Control

Active Ingredient	Trade Name	Method of Administration
1. Carbon disulfide	————	Tube
2. Piperazine–carbon disulfide complex	a. Parvex	Tube
	b. Parvex Plus	Tube
3. Dichlorvos	a. Equigard	Feed
	b. Equigel	Intra-oral
4. Trichlorfon	a. Dyrex	Tube, feed, bolus
	b. Anthon	Feed
	c. Com Bot	Tube
	d. Equizole B	Tube, feed

Table 2. Ascarid Control

Active Ingredient	Trade Name	Method of Administration
1. Carbon disulfide	———	Tube
2. Piperazine	a. Various	Tube, feed
	b. Parvex	Tube
	c. Equizole A	Tube, feed
3. Dichlorvos	a. Equigard	Feed
	b. Equigel	Intra-oral
4. Trichlorfon	a. Dyrex	Tube, feed, bolus
	b. Anthon	Feed
	c. Com Bot	Tube
5. Mebendazole	a. Telmin	Tube, feed
	b. Telmin-SF	Intra-oral
6. Cambendazole	a. Camvet	Tube
7. Pyrantel	a. Strongid-T	Tube, feed, drench

Table 3. Strongyle Control

Active Ingredient	Trade Name	Method of Administration
1. Phenothiazine	a. Various	Low level in feed
2. Phenothiazine and piperazine mixtures	a. Parvex Plus	Tube
	b. Dyrex T.F.	Tube
3. Thiabendazole	a. Equizole	Tube, feed
	b. Equizole A	Tube, feed
	c. Equizole B	Tube, feed
4. Dichlorvos	a. Equigard	Feed
5. Pyrantel	a. Strongid	Feed
	b. Strongid-T	Tube, feed, drench
6. Mebendazole	a. Telmin	Tube, feed
	b. Telmin-SF	Intra-oral
7. Cambendazole	a. Camvet	Tube

Table 4. Pinworm Control

Active Ingredient	Trade Name	Method of Administration
1. Thiabendazole	a. Equizole	Tube, feed
	b. Equizole A	Tube, feed
	c. Equizole B	Tube, feed
2. Trichlorfon	a. Dyrex	Tube, feed, bolus
	b. Anthon	Feed
	c. Com Bot	Tube
3. Piperazine	a. Parvex	Tube
4. Dichlorvos	a. Equigard	Feed
5. Mebendazole	a. Telmin	Tube, feed
	b. Telmin-SF	Intra-oral
6. Cambendazole	a. Camvet	Tube

THE HORSE IN HEALTH

Good horsemen can recognize a horse in health, a condition of the body in which all functions are performed normally.

The experienced, observant horseman can quickly detect changes that indicate disease problems. Loss of appetite—failure to clean up the feed—is often the first sign of trouble. Other indications of disease include a rise in temperature, sweating, fast or labored breathing, increased pulse rate, coughing, nasal discharge, lameness, stiffness, swelling or heat in any part, listlessness and dejection, diarrhea, constipation, inflamed mucous membranes, discharge from the eyes, itching, loss of hair, and an unhealthy coat.

The peripheral pulse rate of a mature horse at rest is about 36 to 40 beats per minute. The pulse of a horse in intensive training and top condition for his job may stabilize at 30 or a bit lower.

The pulse can be felt at the artery that crosses the lower jaw bone in front of the large cheek muscle. The pulse can also be felt on the outside of the hind leg below the hock between the lateral splint bone and the cannon bone; on the foreleg over the sesamoid bones; and in the central artery that runs up the middle of the outside of the ear. After fast or hard exercise the pulse rate may be very high, 90 to 100 or more. In a well-conditioned horse the pulse returns to near-normal range 20 minutes to an hour after exercise stops.

The respiration rate of a mature horse at rest is from 8 to 16 breaths per minute. In hot, humid weather the resting respiration rate may reach 40 breaths per minute. The breathing should be regular, rhythmical, and noiseless. Following exercise, the respiration of a well-conditioned horse should return to normal within 30 minutes. The time will vary with climatic conditions. The respiration rate can be determined by watching the horse's nostrils, the movement of the flanks, or the steamy expiration of breath on a cold day.

The temperature of a mature horse at rest is about 100°F. It is taken with a veterinary rectal thermometer inserted into the anus for 3 minutes. In very hot weather and after exercise the temperature may be elevated one or two degrees. Mares in heat will register 101°F. or higher. Also, foals will have a temperature range one or two degrees above that of mature horses.

SOME COMMON DISEASES OF HORSES

The good horseman, working in cooperation with his veterinarian, can help to prevent or control several common diseases of horses.

Influenza. Influenza is the most highly contagious horse disease. It is caused by two specific viruses unrelated to the "flu" of other species. The viruses are transmitted by sneezing and coughing, and by means of the digestive tract. Influenza is most common in large groups of horses, especially among young horses. Therefore, epidemics may occur at race tracks, horse shows, and sales. Affected horses have a temperature of 103–106°F. and rather persistent coughs. They may be off feed and depressed. Complete rest is indicated.

If uncomplicated, influenza ends in 7 to 10 days. However, it is frequently followed by bacterial invasions that cause swelling of the lymph glands, snotty noses, pneumonia, and laryngitis. The mortality from flu is low, but the economic loss is great as a result of a setback in training and lost opportunities in competition and sales.

Such losses can be minimized—if not completely avoided—by vaccination, which gives immunity for 6 to 12 months. Some farms make a practice of vaccinating all horses semi-annually. Yearlings should be vaccinated before they are sent to sales or to winter training tracks.

Strangles. Strangles, or distemper, is an acute, contagious disease of young horses. It is characterized by mucopurulent inflammation of the nasal and pharyngeal mucosae and abscess formation at the regional lymph nodes. The organism *Streptococcus equi* is always present in nasal discharge and in pus from the swollen lymph nodes. Exposure to cold and wet, stress and fatigue from hauling long distances, and viral infections of the respiratory tract contribute to a horse's susceptibility. Therefore, strangles is most common where large numbers of horses are assembled: at race tracks, horse shows, rodeos, trail rides, and sale barns.

Affected horses have a temperature of 104–106°F. They refuse their feed and show depression. A copious nasal discharge develops, as well as a cough that may persist for weeks. The lymph nodes under the jaw swell and ultimately rupture to discharge a large amount of creamy pus. Care involves complete rest and treatment with penicillin and some other drugs. Mortality is very low, but economic loss may be great. Vaccination with *Streptococcus equi* bacterin, plus annual booster shots, may be given; however, this is not always very successful.

Equine viral rhinopneumonitis. Rhinopneumonitis is a mild, highly contagious respiratory disease that can result in drastic financial losses for the horse breeder. It is caused by equine herpes virus Type 1, which is maintained in the upper respiratory tract of carrier horses. This virus causes a fever, respiratory catarrh, runny noses, and coughs in young horses. Mares rarely show these symptoms, but the same virus causes pregnant mares to abort; the abortion usually occurs from the eighth to the eleventh month of pregnancy. Prenatally infected foals carried to full term usually die within a day of birth. Mares aborting from this cause usually are immune for two or three years and may be bred back without trouble.

However, a safe, effective, reliable vaccine is available, and it should be used on all horse breeding farms in areas where equine viral rhinopneumonitis has occurred.

Equine encephalomyelitis. Encephalomyelitis, or sleeping sickness, is an acute viral disease characterized by sudden onset, cerebral damage, and a very high mortality rate. It can also affect men, birds, and monkeys. Three strains of the virus are found in the United States: Eastern, Western, and Venezuelan. The disease is transmitted by blood-sucking insects (especially culex, aedes, and anopheles mosquitoes) and by chicken mites, lice, and ticks. The virus is maintained in nature by mosquitoes and certain birds. Therefore, the disease appears in the United States from June to November, and more frequently in areas with large mosquito and bird populations. It affects pastured horses more often than stabled horses. Affected horses have a high temperature, an irregular gait, and, if brain damage is extensive, rapidly developing incoordination and paralysis. The mortality rate is extremely high; over 90 per cent of the horses infected by the Eastern strain of the virus die.

A triple vaccine, effective against the Eastern, Western, and Venezuelan strains of sleeping sickness, is available. Immunity developing from vaccination lasts only one season. Therefore, all horses should be vaccinated annually against equine encephalomyelitis.

Tetanus. Tetanus, or lockjaw, is caused by the spore-bearing anaerobe *Clostridium tetani,* which is found in the soil and in the feces of animals, especially horses. The organism enters the horse's body by way of some penetrating injury from nails, splinters, wire, or accidental cuts. The bacterial infection remains localized, but the spores produce a potent exotoxin which, when absorbed and passed to the spinal cord, causes characteristic spasmodic muscular tension contractions of the voluntary muscles. The symptoms, which appear from one to several weeks after the injury, include tense jaws, extension of the head and neck, a typical sawbuck stance, stiff tail, difficult movement, fever and sweating. Over 80 per cent of affected horses die.

Because of this high mortality rate and the widespread occurrence of the tetanus organism, all horses should be permanently immunized against tetanus. Vaccination makes use of tetanus toxoid given in two doses three weeks apart. Annual booster shots should be given to maintain effective protection. Pregnant mares should receive their booster shots about one month before foaling. All foals should be immunized before weaning; they usually are vaccinated during their third and fourth months.

NONCOMMUNICABLE DISEASES

Most noncommunicable diseases of the horse develop as a result of poor animal management—injudicious feeding and watering, failure to control parasites, inadequate daily care, unsanitary quarters, and poor judgment in training, riding, or driving. Except for tetanus, most of these diseases cannot be prevented by vaccination. However, close daily inspection, cleanliness, and good general care and management can prevent many troubles.

The sensible trainer will not use a horse to the point of exhaustion. An unconditioned horse will not, for example, voluntarily go so hard and so fast in hot, humid weather that he suffers from overheating or heatstroke.

Probably the most common cause of colic, or bellyache, is infestation by internal parasites. Horses on farms with a regular worming program have very few cases of colic.

Laminitis, or founder, has a number of causes. Overeating grain, too much water when overheated, retention of the afterbirth following foaling, too fast or too much exercise on hard surfaces, all can bring on founder. The person in charge of the horse can prevent it in most cases.

The organism *Sphaeropherous necrophorus* causes thrush, a disease characterized by a foul-smelling black discharge from the frog of the foot. Horses that are kept in clean, dry stalls or paddocks, or on pasture, and that have their feet inspected regularly, do not develop thrush.

15

Horseshoes and Horseshoeing

The ideal foot for any horse or pony should be big in proportion to body weight or bulk, full and rounding at toe and quarters, wide and deep at the heel, with enough arch of sole and strength of hoof wall to guarantee long tenure of service in whatever area of activity the horse or pony is used.

During the heyday of the work horse business, flatness was the prevailing foot ailment of work horses whose job it was to earn their living on city streets. It was important therefore that the feet of these horses have sufficient concavity of sole and toughness of hoof wall to oppose flatness.

The feet of light-leg horses, unlike the feet of draft horses, are seldom troubled with flatness. Nevertheless, the feet of light-leg horses do have their prevailing ailments, the most common of which are contraction and navicular disease. Feet with narrow heels are predisposed to contraction. Hence light-leg horses of all kinds should stand on feet that are wide at the heels. Width of heel in the make-up of a horse's foot opposes contraction.

Of course, the wide-heeled horse is comparatively easy to shoe, because the inside and outside walls of his feet have sufficient flare to them to permit the driving of the nails with ease and safety. The narrow-heeled horse, on the other hand, with his upright hoof walls is one whose feet are very difficult to shoe and shoe properly.

THE SHOE AND THE HOOF WALL OF THE FOOT

A primary aim in shoeing horses of all kinds is to shape the shoe to fit the foot, rather than to whittle and rasp the foot to fit the shoe. It is not good practice to nail into place a shoe which is really too small for a horse's foot; then take the rasp and rasp away

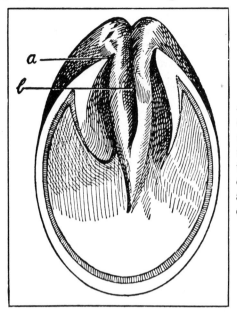

A narrow fore hoof with bilateral contraction of the rear quarters: a, spur of hoof wall which compresses the frog; b, very narrow cleft of frog due to compression. From Lungwitz and Adams, *Horse Shoeing,* courtesy J. B. Lippincott Company.

all of the protruding hoof wall about the exterior of the shoe. This may give the appearance of a more finished job, but in reality the practice results in cutting away the thickest portion of the hoof wall, which should be saved as a bearing surface to support weight. Not only does the hoof wall function in protecting the inner, more tender tissues of the foot; one of its primary purposes is to support the weight of the body. Hence the shoe should be shaped to fit the foot and the hoof wall should be saved for the weight-bearing function.

FACTORS DETERMINING THE KIND OF SHOE

The kind of shoe that a horse should wear depends upon the set or position of a horse's legs, the shape and position of his feet, the kind of service demanded of him, and the kind of ground or surface upon which he works.

In the old days, when work horses were employed in numbers on city streets, the kind of service of which a city horse was capable depended a great deal upon the paving materials used in the construction of city streets and the kind of shoes with which a horse was rigged. The farm work horse has always worked barefooted at many of his jobs in the field. The same horse on a teaming job over gravel roads would need to have his feet protected with shoes. Such a work horse could get along with the ordinary three-calk work shoe with a toe clip. The calks could be blunt when weather conditions were mild and the roads free from snow and ice. During the winter months, when ice and snow and sleet interfered, the same work horse would have to be shod with sharp calks or with never-slip calks which screwed into the web of the shoe and could be replaced when they became too worn and blunt to give a horse secure footing.

The shoes for trotters and pacers differ much more in design than do the shoes for any kind of work horse. Trotters and pacers work at speed and of course over all kinds of tracks. I have known of trotters rigged with smooth shoes in front that would scalp themselves worse on a track when the cushion was deep and soft and loose than they would when rigged with a rim or a three-calk shoe on their front feet. I have known of horses that were completely cured of the scalping and speedy-cutting faults by the use of shoes with low, sharp grab calks on them. Some horses can't go a step with a calk on the front shoe; others can't go their best without them. A trotter that glides along in front, making two distinct impressions with his front foot on the track every time he lands, will not do well wearing a calked shoe. The wide-webbed, thin, plain shoe suits him better. A calk will stop his slide, shorten his stride, interfere with his front action, throw him completely out of balance, and oftentimes make him so sore in his muscles that he will appear to have been foundered. These examples are cited to show why various designs in shoes are essential to meet the needs of horses that are required to do altogether different jobs.

SPECIFIC FEATURES OF THE SHOE

The front feet of a horse are more nearly circular or rounding at the toe and quarters than are the hind feet. Usually the front feet are wider at the heels than are the hind feet. The hind feet are more pointed at toe and quarters and are commonly more narrow at the heels than are the front feet. Hence the difference between a front shoe and a hind shoe is sharply defined and easily distinguishable. Since the outside wing or web of a hind shoe is always longer than the inside web, it is easy to distinguish the difference between the left and right rear shoes.

The hoof wall is thicker at the toe than at the heels of the foot; hence the web of the shoe is usually wider at the toe than at the heels. The shoe should be so placed upon the foot as to permit the hoof wall to function as a weight-bearing agency from toe to heel.

The wings of the front shoe should be long enough to reach the bulbs of the heel and provide support for the hoof wall, but not so long that a hind foot can come in contact with them and pull them off. Usually the wings of the hind shoes are a little longer than the wings of the front shoes. Especially is this true of the

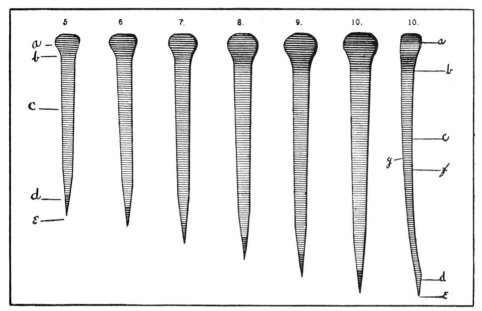

Machine-made horseshoe nails (natural size) with a low, wide head for a fullered shoe. Nail 10 is shown from one border, the others from the inner face of the nail: a, head; b, neck; c, shank; d, bevel; e, point; f, inner face; g, outer face. From Lungwitz and Adams, Horse Shoeing, courtesy J. B. Lippincott Company.

outside wing of the hind shoe, on which a low heel calk is sometimes used. This extra length of the outside wing of a hind shoe gives a little more support to a hind foot; the low heel calk raises the outside of the foot a little and tends to throw the hocks closer together to produce more collected action.

That part of the shoe which is in contact with the hoof wall should be horizontal. The web of the shoe should be wide enough to cover the hoof wall, the white line, and a small fringe of the outer edge of the sole. Shoes for large hoofs require a broader bearing surface than do shoes for small hoofs. The hoof surface of the shoe has to be concave or seated to relieve pressure on the sole of the foot, the degree of seating depending upon the shape of the sole of the foot. Shoes have to be seated but slightly if they are to be used on feet whose soles are strongly arched and very concave. The object of making a shoe concave is to prevent pressure upon the horny sole except at the outside margin of the sole. Undue pressure of a shoe upon the horny sole might result in bruises which could develop into corns.

The inner borders of a shoe should be fitted snugly. If his shoes are so fitted, it is more difficult for a horse, in shifting the position of his front feet, to catch the inner edge of a shoe on a supporting foot with the shoe of a shifting foot and literally tramp off his own shoes. This could happen in the case of hind feet also if the shoes are not snugly fitted along the inside borders of the feet. Moreover, interference, either slight or severe, is not so likely if the inside borders of shoes are snugly fitted. And if the inside borders of shoes are moderately rounded, open wounds are not so likely to result if interference occurs.

Fullering or creasing the ground surface of the wings of a shoe is not absolutely necessary, but it has several advantages; the crease in the wings of the shoe from toe to heels makes a shoe lighter in proportion to its size; it makes easier the uniform placement of the nail holes; and it roughens the ground surface of the shoe, thereby giving a better purchase upon any surface with which the shoe is in contact.

In every job of shoeing, the number, the depth, and the distribution or placement of the nail holes are very important. The nail holes must be so placed that nails can be driven to the hoof without being driven into the sensitive tissues of the feet, called driving the nails "too green." The nails should be driven in such a manner as to avoid the splitting of the hoof wall. The nail holes should be so punched as to permit the driving of the nails without interference with the expansive mechanisms of the feet. Finally, the nails should taper from the ground to the hoof surface, all of them driven at about the same angle so that when they are clinched none of them will have been driven too green and cause blood poison, nor will any of them have been drawn so tight as to cause painful compression.

In the case of shoes of medium weight, six nail holes are sufficient. With heavier shoes, especially those with toe and heel calks, eight nails may be necessary. The rear nail holes in front shoes are driven just slightly rearward of the center of the wings of the shoes. In hind shoes, the nail holes should be driven in the anterior two thirds of the wings of the shoes. A common rule is to drive the rear nails but slightly rearward of the middle of the wings of the shoes. The heels of the foot must have opportunity to expand as the foot touches the ground. If the nails are driven too far rearward, the heels are held too rigidly in place, there is no opportunity for the heels to expand, and the supporting structures are unduly abused because of maximum concussions. Nails should not be driven inside the white line of the foot, which is the junction between the hoof wall and the sole.

Clips are semicircular or semitriangular features of a shoe and anchor a shoe more securely on a horse's foot. Clips reduce to a

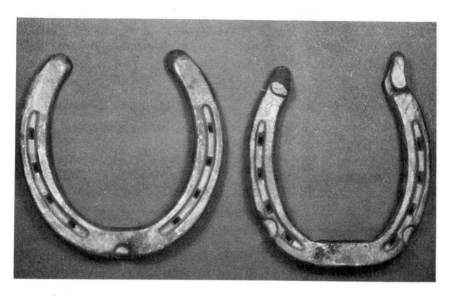

Typical shoes for hunters. The one on the left is a right hind shoe with squared toe, drawn side clips, and low heel calks. The front shoe on the right has a drawn toe clip. These shoes weigh about 10 ounces each. Photo by Gary Warzocka.

minimum the chances of a shoe's shifting position after it has been nailed to the foot. Both toe clips and side clips are in common use. It is common practice to place a side clip on that branch of the shoe which first meets the ground in locomotion. So placed, a clip helps the nails to keep the shoe firmly anchored in correct position.

Some clips are made by heating the web of the shoe at the toe or on the side and drawing a portion of the web upward from the outer edge of the shoe. Such clips are called drawn clips. Other clips are braised on or welded into position. There is a rule among blacksmiths that the height of a clip on flat shoes should at least equal the thickness of the shoe. On shoes that have toe and heel calks, the clips should be higher and stronger. Drawn clips make a neater, more finished job of shoeing than do welded clips.

SELECTING THE SHOES

There are a number of factors to consider in selecting the shoes with which a given horse should be rigged. The weight of the horse,

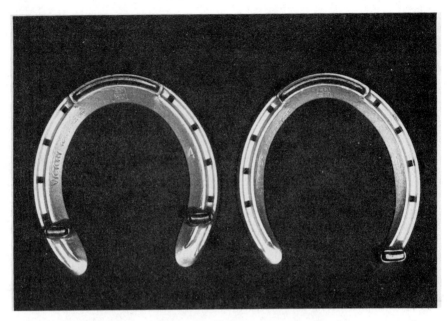

Aluminum racing plates with steel toe calks and heel calks set in. Front shoe on the left, left hind shoe on the right. Each shoe weighs about 3 ounces.
Photo by Gary Warzocka.

the shape of the hoofs, the set of his legs, the nature of his work, the footing over which he works, the gaits required, the texture of his feet—these are some of the factors upon which the selection of the shoes is based.

The length of the shoe in relationship to the length of the foot is very important. The usual practice is to choose a shoe that is ample in length, because, as the hoof wall grows, the shoe is carried forward with it. Furthermore, the rear quarters of the feet are gradually lowered because of the rubbing and wear of the rear hoof wall upon the wings of the shoe. As the foot grows and the shoe is carried forward, it is important that the tips of the wings of the shoe be sufficiently spread so as to prevent too much shoe contact with the sole of the foot and the resultant bruises of the sole which develop into corns.

In the case of work horses shod with the common three-calk work shoe, the wings of the shoe should extend backward far enough to furnish ample support to the bulbs of the heels.

In the case of light-leg horses whose job it is to work at speed, shoes should be fitted snugly. This is especially important for the

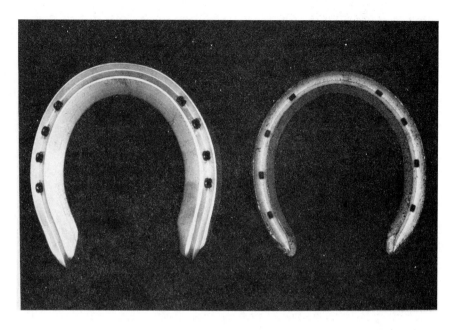

Broad aluminum racing plate on the left. Steel racing plate on the right. Each shoe weighs about 5 ounces. Photo by Gary Warzocka.

front shoes. If the wings of his front shoes are too long, any horse may be thrown off balance, mix his gaits, and catch his shoes and pull them off. The loss of a shoe may mean the loss of a race or the loss of an important class at a show. Furthermore, when a horse pulls a shoe, there is always the possibility that a large portion of the foot will be broken off and the horse will be temporarily unusable.

There is a wide range in the weight requirements of shoes for horses and ponies of various types. There is so much difference in the size and the action of horses that inevitably there is a wide range in the weight of the shoes they wear. A racing plate for a Thoroughbred may weigh only three or four ounces. The Scotchbottom show shoe for a drafter may weigh from three to three and a half pounds.

Many front shoes have some roll to the toe of the shoe at which point a horse's foot breaks over. The rolled toe results from a more or less pronounced upward turn of the toe of the shoe. The rolled toe or rolling motion shoe in front guarantees more nearly even wear on the shoe and also hastens the breaking over of the forefoot, thereby reducing the possibility of the defect in gait known as forging. If the front foot breaks over readily, a horse is less likely to strike the toe of a hind shoe against the extremities of a front shoe.

THE WHITE LINE A GUIDE TO THE BLACKSMITH

The white line of a horse's foot is the guide which the black-smith follows in driving the nails into the hoof wall. This line is the boundary line between the hoof wall and the sole of the foot. It corresponds to the quick of a fingernail or a toenail in man.

If nails are driven inside the white line, blood poison may result. Therefore the nail holes of the shoe should cover the white line of the foot; then the blacksmith can drive the nails as they should be driven and with comparative ease.

Usually, the last nail holes are driven slightly rearward of the center of the wings of the shoe. From the last nail holes rearward to the distal extremities of the shoe the wings of the shoe should widen gradually until at their extremities they project at each quarter slightly beyond the outside rim of the hoof wall. This extra width between the wings of the shoe will furnish the hoof wall at the heels with a supporting base upon which the hoof walls may expand as the foot comes in contact with the ground. Of course, the inner wing of the shoe, both front and hind, should fit the hoof wall more snugly to prevent interference and to keep a horse from tramping off his own shoes.

SHOES FOR TROTTERS AND PACERS

The purpose in shoeing all horses is to protect their feet and to make it possible for them to go in a balanced, coordinated fashion. In the case of trotters and pacers, as well as in the case of all show horses who work at speed and in form, the shoes may augment or retard performance.

If a trotting colt stands squarely on his legs and can go straight at the trot barefooted, his first shoes are usually absolutely plain, with the edges and heels well beveled off. The hind shoes can be smooth, plain, and without calks of any kind. But if a colt has a strong, bold way of going, with a tendency to go wide-gaited at the hocks, a very light swedged shoe can be used to good advantage, for the slight hold he will get with it will have a tendency to pull him together, to help him collect himself, and to give him confidence. Also, he will not tire so quickly, for it is in his hind legs that he gets his propelling power and it is there he will tire first.

The weight of the shoes for a trotting colt is simply a matter of judgment after having watched the colt move barefooted. If the colt is a high, natural moving colt in front, folds his knees satisfactorily, and strikes the ground lightly, shoe him with light, plain shoes chiefly to protect his feet. Square the toe of his front shoes slightly and bevel them off a little so as to reduce to a minimum the friction or resistance at the point where the breakover comes. By a light shoe is meant a shoe weighing four to six ounces. In preparing the foot do not dress it too close. Leave him enough hoof wall to take away the sting of the blow when the foot hits the ground. It is better to do this than to cut the hoof wall close and then use a leather or fiber pad to make up for the lack of natural horn.

If a colt's action is low, if he stubs his toes and is lacking in knee action, a heavy bar shoe made of half-round iron or steel may help him. Have the nail holes well countersunk so that there will be no projections of any kind, for the heavier shoe in front may cause him to scalp or speedy-cut himself or both.

A good plan, where considerable weight is necessary to make a colt "break loose" and go to trotting, is to use a rubber pad and a half round tip shoe, squared at the toe. A colt can carry more weight in rubber with less effort than he can in metal and there is a rebound to rubber that helps him to a full, round stroke or revolution.

When the object for which it is put on is attained, the weight should be taken off. In some cases it is necessary to reduce the weight gradually and carefully. But this does not always apply to colt trotters, for once the youngster discovers he can trot, that is, "finds his gait," so to speak, taking off a good portion of the weight at one time may not bother him. If he does miss it and shows you that he misses it by mixing and shuffling when he starts out, a heavier quarter boot or a light toe weight put on when you are about to step him up may be all that is needed to square him away.

I knew of a three-year-old trotting filly that for a period of two weeks carried twenty-six ounces on each front foot. After two weeks she had learned to break or fold her knees and was a good gaited trotter. The weight of her front shoes was reduced to ten ounces and she never missed the additional weight. She had learned to use her feet, had gotten the trotting gait fixed in her head, and went on to race successfully the next season in six-ounce shoes.

I also knew of an over-two walk-trot gelding that wore shoes weighing forty-six ounces on each front foot when in competition in the ring. When he was returned to his stall, the heavy shoes were removed, not to be replaced until time for the three-gaited stake the last of the week. This horse was shown successfully and won the three-gaited stake at the Kentucky State Fair. He carried more

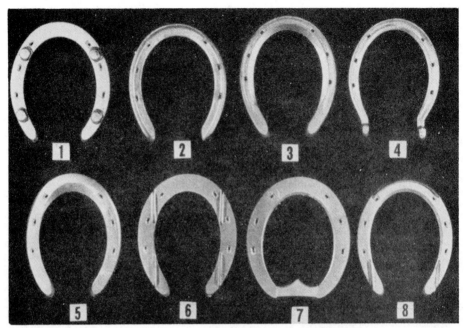

*Types of Shoes for Pacers and Trotters. 1, Memphis nub shoe; 2, rim
shoe (front or hind); 3, swedged shoe (front); 4, swedged shoe (hind);
5, scooped, rolled toe shoe; 6, four-calk shoe (front); 7, plain toe, bar shoe
(front); 8, three-calk pacing shoe.*

weight on his feet than any saddle horse I have ever known. Removing the heavy shoes between shows was a precaution against
bowed tendons. I mention this particular case because it shows
what a great range there is in the weights of shoes worn by horses.

If the trotting colt's hind toes are full and rounding in shape,
shoe him with a round-toed shoe. If his toes are narrow and a little
pointed, make the toe of the shoe square, but in order to get it
square do not sacrifice the toe of a foot which may be already too
short. If this be the case, let the shoe project on each side of the
toe a little, for it will do no harm. Colts with sharp, pointed hind
feet are predisposed to knuckle over. Knuckling is also attributed
to long toes and weak ankles, but in many cases it is caused by the
fact that foot and ankle rock sideways when breaking over, for a
horse's leg pivots on the point of a narrow rear toe. A hind shoe
squared at the toe gives a horse a good base to break over on and
may help the colt that is predisposed to knuckling.

If the prospective race colt is a pacer, he can be shod with a
light, swedged shoe in front. Fit the shoe snug at the heels, especially the inside heel, and bevel it off well so that it really looks like

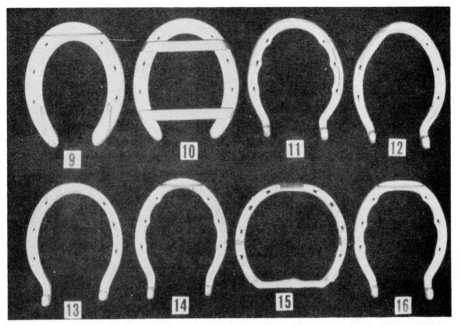

Types of Shoes for Pacers and Trotters (cont'd). 9, *three-calk trotting shoe;* 10, *Memphis bar shoe;* 11, *hind pacing shoe;* 12, *half-swedged oblique toe shoe;* 13, *half-swedged cross-firing shoe;* 14, *hind trotting shoe, full and rounding at the toe;* 15, *ice racing shoe (front);* 16, *hind trotting shoe, squared at the toe.*

a part of the foot. This is a precaution against the colt's hitting his rear shins or his hocks in passing or grabbing the shoe with the opposite hind foot if he cross-fires.

In shoeing the average pacing colt behind, lower the foot a trifle on the inside and use a half-swedged shoe, swedged on the outside, half round or plain on the inside. Set the shoe full on the outside, leaving on the outside wing at the heel a trail of half an inch turned slightly out, and fit the inside close and short.

Many young colt pacers are started with about five-ounce shoes in front and four ounces behind. As they improve and make speed, many times pacing colts gather speed more rapidly than do trotters. To steady them it may then be necessary to add a little toe weight or a pad in front, or use a heavier shoe. Sometimes it may be necessary to reduce the weight of their hind shoes slightly, but it is not a good plan to make any radical changes in dressing their feet.

Every ten days to two weeks, if in training, a colt's shoes should be removed and his feet leveled and dressed. If the feet must be cut down considerably and their angle changed, it is not safe to give the colt any fast work for a few days until ligaments and joints have become adjusted to the new conditions. It is possible to bow a tendon by cutting the feet down one day and giving a colt a stiff workout on the next.

THIN HOOF WALLS A PROBLEM IN SHOEING

Particular care should be exercised in the treatment of feet with a thin, delicate wall. Small nails should always be used. Although it may be necessary to use the coarse rasp on the bottom of the foot, it should never be used in finishing off the clinches. A fine, flat file will do the work much better without disfiguring the wall of the foot and without destroying its glazed surface to any extent and so making possible the evaporation of the moisture from the hoof wall. Dry hoof walls lose their toughness because dry tissues are brittle and break readily.

If the colt's foot is low at the heels and the wall is thin and weak, the proper shoe is the bar shoe. The frog in a foot of that kind is usually very prominent and if the colt happens to be the big, bold-gaited sort that hits the earth a hard blow at every stride, the frog should be protected with a bar, for there is always danger that a foot of that kind will spread enough under pressure to cause acute pain. This characteristic is more prevalent, however, among Thoroughbreds than among trotters and pacers, for the texture of the wall of the Thoroughbred's foot is finer than that of most harness horses. If the wall of a colt's foot is very thin at the heels and if, after being shod a few days, the foot begins to creep or expand over the edges of the shoe which has been fitted flush, it is a good idea to draw a clip up on each side of the shoe, back pretty well toward the heel. Every time the shoe is removed draw the bar a little if the heels of the foot seem the least bit pinched or cramped. There is a very little danger, however, of a foot of this kind becoming contracted.

SHOES FOR SADDLE HORSES

The shoes for three-gaited and five-gaited saddlers vary a great deal in design to suit the needs of horses whose natural aptitudes at the several gaits differ so widely. If a saddle horse can work his legs barefooted, the shoes he wears are generally plain in design and are worn mostly for protection. Usually shoes for saddle horses are comparatively light, short, and fitted snug to prevent forging, interfering, and pulling of the shoes.

The hoof surface of the shoes should be wide enough to support the hoof wall and to cover the white line and a small margin of the sole. Usually both front and hind shoes are fullered and concaved on the ground surface.

The wings of the front shoes should be long enough to give good support to the buttresses of the feet, yet snug enough at the heels to reduce the danger of being caught and torn off by a hind foot. Usually, the outer border of the shoe is beveled. This contributes to neatness of workmanship and gives a dressier appearance to the feet.

If heel calks are used, it is general practice to bevel them strongly downward and forward under the foot. This helps to prevent forging. The ground surface of the shoe at the toe may be plain and flat or it may be spoon-shaped, giving a horse's front foot a little better purchase on the ground and providing a kind of uphill point of turnover which forces a horse to use his knees. Also, the toe of a saddle horse shoe may be oval in design, providing a "roller" motion type of action in front in order to aid a horse in breaking over quickly at the toe. Some front shoes for saddle horses have additional weight in the web of the shoe at the toe. This helps a horse to lengthen his stride. Others have additional weight in the web at the rear extremities of the wings in order to help a saddle horse to break or lift his knees and thus add height to his stride.

Hind shoes for saddlers may have wings that project rearward of the heels one fourth to three eighths of an inch. The toe of a hind shoe should be blunt and either fairly well rounded or squared, with the rim of the hoof wall extending slightly beyond the rim of the shoe. The branches of hind shoes are usually of equal thickness. The height of the calks on hind shoes equals the thickness of the shoe. To prevent interference, the inside calk may be omitted and the inner wing of the shoe thickened, beveled, and fitted snug. Clips may be placed on the inner and outer toes. In the case of narrow feet, clips may be used on both front and hind shoes. Six or seven nails may be used.

The shoes for hunters that are ridden to hounds or in steeplechase events are not widely different from shoes worn on any good saddle hack or pleasure horse. The shoes for a hunter are usually lighter than most shoes for saddle horses because the hunter does not have to perform at different gaits. The hunter must gallop and jump. A plain swedged shoe with a drawn toe clip is used in front. The hunter's hind shoes often have a squared toe set back just a bit and both inner and outer toe clips drawn from the web of the shoe. The outer wing of the hind shoes may feature a trailing edge and a heel calk.

In the United States today almost all racing Thoroughbreds are

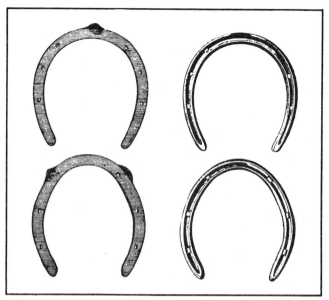

Shoes for Thoroughbreds. Above, left to right: A fore running plate: hoof surface, and ground surface. Below, left to right: A hind running plate: hoof surface and ground surface.

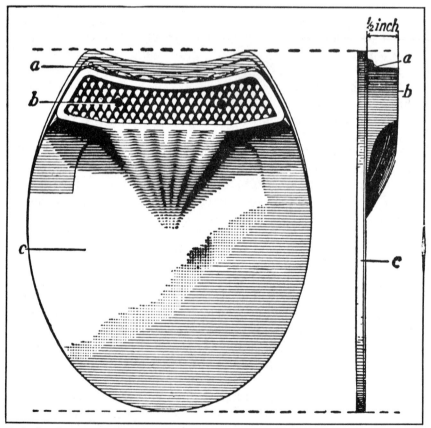

A light driving pad, gummed and stitched to a leather sole, seen from the ground surface and in profile. Used with a seven- to ten-ounce short shoe: a, stitching; b, rubber bar under buttress of foot and frog; c, leather sole. From Lungwitz and Adams, *Horse Shoeing,* courtesy J. B. Lippincott Company.

shod with light aluminum shoes weighing 3 to 5 ounces. Such shoes may be absolutely plain, or they may be swedged or have steel toe and/or heel calk inserts. The shoes of a race horse in training and competition are frequently reset, and the horse's feet are lightly trimmed.

SHOEING THE DRAFTER FOR SHOW

Scotch-bottom shoes are the show shoes most commonly seen on drafters. Both front and rear Scotch-bottom shoes are beveled at the rim all the way around in such a fashion as to permit the edges of the shoe to continue the slope of the hoof wall to the ground. The Scotch-bottom shoe, therefore, makes a drafter's foot look even larger than it is.

Scotch-bottom shoes for the front feet are made full and rounding at the toe and front quarters and have a toe clip to help anchor the shoe to the foot. Low, flat, heel calks may be used on the front shoes if a horse happens to be very shallow-footed.

Scotch-bottom shoes for the rear feet usually feature a heel calk on the outside wing of the shoe. These outside heel calks raise the outside buttress of the rear feet, tend to push the hocks closer together, and aid a horse in collecting himself on the move.

The inside branches of Scotch-bottom shoes on both front and rear feet should be fitted snug to keep a horse from treading on them and tramping them off. Scotch-bottom shoes for the hind feet also feature a toe clip which, along with the nails, helps to hold the shoe securely in position. Usually, the clips on both front and rear shoes are drawn upward from the outside web of the toe of the shoe. Drawn clips make a neater job of shoeing than do welded or braised clips.

POINTS FOR HORSE OWNERS TO CHECK

All horse owners should realize that shoes of any kind are unnatural for the horse. Horses that have sound feet with hoof walls of tough texture can be used barefooted for many jobs, if their feet are trimmed regularly every ten days. Horses have even been raced barefooted during a strike by race track blacksmiths.

However, if the horse is being used frequently, if shoes are needed to protect the hoof or to provide good traction, if shoes are needed to enhance the way of going of a show horse, if the surface on which the horse must be used wears down the hoof wall rapidly, then the horse must be shod.

The hoof wall grows at the rate of about one-third of an inch

Typical Scotch-bottom shoes for draft horses that are to be shown. The shoe at the right is a front shoe. The shoe at the left is a hind shoe. Note the fullness at the toe and front quarters of the shoe as well as the width at the heels. The rear nail holes are punched just slightly rearward of the center of the wings of the shoe. This permits expansion at the heels when the feet are on the ground. Notice that the front shoe has a drawn toe clip and that the hind shoe has a welded or brazed toe clip. The drawn clip makes the nicer job. The hind shoe weighs 48 ounces. The front shoe weighs 50 ounces. Photograph courtesy Photography Department, The Ohio State University

per month. Unshod hoofs grow faster than shod hoofs. The average pleasure mount should have his shoes removed, his feet trimmed, and the shoes re-set every six weeks. Most race horses in training have their shoes re-set quite frequently and the type of shoe changed, if necessary, according to the condition of the track on raceday.

The great majority of horse owners do not shoe their own horses. They hire a horse shoer to do the job. Nevertheless, every horse owner should have an intelligent understanding of the problems involved in order properly to evaluate the quality of service given by his farrier.

Dr. D. L. Proctor, member of a highly respected veterinary firm at Lexington, Kentucky recommends that the following points be checked when inspecting a horseshoeing job.

1. The two front feet should be the same size and have no flares or wings at the quarters. Likewise, the hind feet should be the same size.

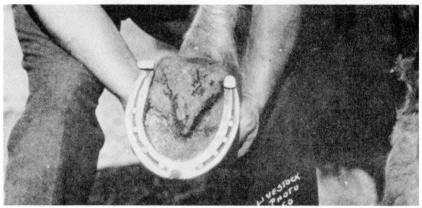

Scotch-bottom show shoe.
Front shoe above, hind shoe below. Note that the rear nails are driven just slightly rearward of the center of the wings of the shoe. Also note the drawn toe clip. Photograph courtesy Live Stock Photo Co.

2. The foot should be in balance, trimmed so the balance is maintained and the foot axis from the front and side corresponds to the direction of the bones of the foot.

3. Bars of the foot should *not* be pared away. Removing the bars weakens the foot and leads toward contraction of the heels.

4. The foot should be level and should hit the ground squarely when the horse walks.

5. The axis of the foot should be a prolongation of the axis of the pastern.

6. The nails and clinches should be evenly spaced and at a uniform height.

7. Clinches should be smooth and should not protrude.

8. The shoe should be shaped and fitted to the foot, not vice versa.

9. Proper expansion at the heels should be possible. The last nails should not be too far to the rear.

10. The buttress of the hoof—where bar and hoof wall join—should be covered by the heel of the shoe.

11. No air spaces should appear between the shoe and the hoof wall.

12. The sole of the foot should be pared enough and/or the shoe concaved to prevent pressure of the shoe upon the sole of the foot and the possible development of corns.

13. The hoof wall should not be rasped above the clinches. Rasping the hoof wall removes the periople. With the periople layer removed loss of moisture from the hoof wall occurs. Dryness leads to contraction of the wall and heel and to pinching of the sensitive tissues within the foot.

16

Equitation

Many volumes have been written on horsemanship from the days of Xenophon in the 5th century B.C. down to the present time. A single chapter in a text such as this can set forth only the major basic requirements for good horsemanship. Anyone who wants to become proficient in riding horses should take serious training under a competent riding instructor.

SEAT AND HANDS

Equitation, or horsemanship, is the art of riding a horse intelligently, gracefully, and well, with the greatest degree of comfort and enjoyment to both rider and horse. The two basic requirements for good horsemanship are a good seat and good hands. Good hands are important because they are one of the rider's means of control and communication. However, since one cannot have good hands without first having a strong, comfortable, supple, steady seat, the more fundamental requirement for riding in good form is a good seat.

The rider should sit balanced on the horse, in the lowest part of the saddle, leaving a space of at least a hand's breadth between his buttocks and the cantle. His body should be easily erect, balanced on a base consisting of seat, thighs, knees, and stirrups. The rider's back is straight, his waist relaxed, head erect, and shoulders square.

The seat and legs are close to the horse without pressure, knees down and closed against the saddle. The thighs, knees, and calves are in contact with the horse. The rider's lower legs are under his seat and rest lightly against the horse slightly behind the girth. The stirrup leathers should hang vertically. The ball of the rider's feet should be on the stirrups. His ankles should be well flexed, his heels down to the limit, his toes out slightly, at an angle best suited to his conformation. If the rider looked down, he would not see his toes. The stirrup leathers should be long enough so that the tread of the stirrup will strike at (or just below) the rider's ankle bone when the rider's legs are hanging naturally out of the stirrup.

The elbows bend slightly just forward of the body, but hang from the shoulders naturally. The forearms are extended to make a straight line from the elbows through the wrists and reins to the horse's mouth. The hands, separated evenly over and in front of the horse's withers, are closed lightly on the reins and feel the horse's mouth by flexing of the fingers.

The reins should be held in both hands not only for balance but also to obtain the best results from the horse. Sympathy, adaptability, and control should be evident in the hands. The hands should be held with the little fingers on the bottom, the thumbs on top, and the knuckles about 30 degrees inside the vertical.

Many hunters have a rather low head carriage. Therefore, hunter-seat riders carry their hands low, near the horse's withers. American Saddlebreds and others commonly shown by saddle-seat riders have a comparatively high head carriage. Their riders consequently hold their hands higher. However, both the hunter-seat rider and the saddle-seat rider have proper length of rein when their reins and forearms make a straight line from the bit to the rider's elbow.

The method of holding the reins is optional. However, one acceptable method of holding the reins of a double-reined bridle is as follows: the snaffle reins are passed under the little finger and the curb reins between the little finger and the ring finger. Both reins pass through the hands, come out over the forefinger, and are held in place by the thumb, with the bight falling to the off side.

Many good riders when riding with a single-reined bridle hold the rein between the little finger and the ring finger of each hand. The rein passes through the hand and is held by the thumb over the forefinger.

Every effort should be made to keep the fingers, hands, and wrists soft, pliable, flexible, and yielding to the horse's mouth. The wrists should work like a hinged door, and should give and take with the horse's head. The control of the horse should come largely from the movement of the fingers and wrists. The arms should remain quiet.

When light pressure on the reins is brought to bear and the horse responds, release should be instantaneous. If it is at all possible, the horse should be allowed to "float" in a half-inch area of

Hilda Gurney, Woodland Hill, California, riding her noted Dressage horse Keen. A four-time winner of the U.S. National Dressage Championship, Miss Gurney also won the Individual Silver Medal in the 1975 Pan-American Games at Mexico City and the Individual Gold Medal in the 1979 Pan-American Games in Puerto Rico. Photo by Gamecock, courtesy of the U.S.E.T.

on and off contact. The lightest touch does much to improve the over-all appearance and performance of the horse, and this relates instantly to the rider himself.

The basic position just described balances the rider on his seat in exactly the right spot on the horse's back, just to the rear of the withers. The rider's center of gravity is almost over the center of gravity in the horse. Therefore, the rider represents the least possible load to the horse and should feel himself "part of the horse."

The rider who has acquired this seat finds that a minimum use of the aids is necessary to get immediate and correct response from the horse at any gait. A good rider has a workmanlike appearance, light, supple seat and hands, and gives the impression of effective and easy control.

The aids for the rider are his legs, his seat, his back, his hands, his weight, and his voice. A very common fault of the beginning rider is failure to use his leg aids. The rider controls the horse's forehand with his hands and reins; he controls the horse's hindquarters by using his legs reinforced by his seat and back. Impulsion comes from the hindquarters. Therefore, the rider *must* use his legs, his seat, and his back to keep the horse in forward motion. The hands guide and control, release or retain the output of energy created by the legs.

If the horse is kept moving strongly forward, he cannot kick, or rear, or shy, or run backwards, or suddenly stop. All of these actions not only are unsettling to the rider but also are dangerous. All of them can be quite largely prevented by vigorous application of the leg aids.

Before a horseman can be said *to ride* he must have established a strong, supple seat entirely independent of the reins and stirrups. Then he can place his weight in direct relation to the point of balance or center of gravity of the horse, and can move his weight to influence that balance. He can ride in balance and can use his legs and arms not to preserve his own balance on the horse's back but to influence the action of the horse.

MOUNTING AND DISMOUNTING

There are two main ways of mounting and gathering up the reins preparatory to mounting. Both are considered good form, but the method always seen in the show-ring is as follows. The rider stands, half facing to the rear, opposite the horse's left shoulder. He takes the reins in the left hand, adjusts them so as to have gentle contact with the horse's mouth, places the left hand on the horse's withers with the bight of the reins falling to the off side.

He then grasps the stirrup with his right hand, places his left foot in the stirrup, brings the left knee against the saddle, and places his right hand upon the cantle of the saddle. Then, aided by his left foot in the stirrup and his grasp on the saddle, he rises by springing off his right leg, swings his right leg over the horse, and settles gently into the saddle. Last he puts his right foot in the stirrup and takes the reins in both hands.

A second method of mounting, one that is easier for most short or awkward people, follows these steps. The rider stands half facing to the front, opposite the left stirrup. He grasps the reins in his right hand with the bight of the reins falling to the off side. He then places his right hand on the pommel of the saddle and adjusts the reins so as to feel the horse's mouth lightly. With his left hand, he holds the stirrup and places his left foot in the stirrup. Then he grasps the horse's mane with his left hand, brings his left knee against the saddle, and raises his body erect in the stirrup. He then passes his right leg over the horse and sits lightly in the saddle. He puts his right foot in the stirrup and takes the reins in both hands.

The description of mounting takes much longer than the act itself. The important thing is to mount quickly, efficiently, and quietly while the horse remains still.

To dismount, the rider may either step down or slide down. However, it is safer to slide down because the left foot has been removed from the stirrup and the rider is free from the horse.

RIDING AT THE WALK

Whenever the rider wants to move out from the halt, he must first attract his horse's attention. This is called "gathering" the horse. The rider gathers his horse by settling in the saddle, by moving his hands a bit, and through his leg action getting the horse's legs so disposed under him that he can move readily. The rider simultaneously releases somewhat his hold on the horse's mouth and either presses with his calf or boots the horse lightly with his heel.

The rider is said to be "with his horse" or "in balance" whenever he so disposes his weight as to require the least muscular effort to remain in his seat, and when the weight distribution interferes least with the horse's movement and equilibrium. This condition of being "with the horse" is the keynote of good riding. The rider's balance should be entirely independent of the hands and reins. The rider must fit into the saddle and so be attached to the horse. Thus both rider and horse can move in rhythm, gracefully and comfortably.

When the horse is in motion the rider's upper body is inclined forward to a degree determined by the speed of the horse and the gait. This forward inclination should always be such that the rider remains in balance over his base of support and never gets "behind his horse." For unforeseen movements by the horse, such as shying or bolting, which tend to unbalance or unseat the rider, security is provided and balance retained by an increased grip of the legs.

At the walk the upper body is inclined forward only slightly more than at the halt. As a result the rider remains in balance. He does not slouch, lean back on the cantle, or get "behind his horse." The upper body should have the same erect, alert appearance as when halted. For good form, safety, and control, the rider should always keep his head and eyes up and look forward in the direction he is riding. He should not look down at his horse because looking down bends his back, disrupts his seat, and lessens his control. The rider should keep the horse up in the bridle and swinging along at a good brisk, flatfooted, ground-covering walk. To do this, the rider must use his seat and his waist. Thus, he has slight motion in the saddle. He cannot be stiff and rigid. His hands must follow the motion of the horse's head.

RIDING AT THE TROT

To trot his horse, the rider first takes a shorter hold on his reins. He then gives the horse a sufficiently firm signal with his leg to cause the horse to trot.

At the trot the rider's center of gravity undergoes more varied displacements than during any other gait. With this two-beat diagonal gait there is a decided impact that throws the rider from the saddle. The correct way to ride a trot is by posting. Posting can be described as "rocking" to the trot. More comfort for both horse and rider is achieved by the rider posting or rocking gently from the saddle and easing back into the saddle with the two beats of the trot. When his horse trots the rider's body is inclined forward a little more than at the walk.

The knees and thighs must at all times be in contact with the saddle if a secure seat is to be maintained. Posting should be a gently rolling motion in coordination with the horse's trot, not a forced, labored rising from the saddle to stand in the stirrups.

In show-ring competition in the United States riders are expected to post to the trot on the proper diagonal. This involves posting in rhythm with the horse's foreleg that is next to the rail. Thus, if riding to the left hand (counterclockwise), the rider should

Bruce Davidson riding his grey Thoroughbred, Might Tango, which won the Individual Gold Medal at Lexington, Ky., in 1978 in the first World Championship for a Three-Day Event competition ever held in the U.S.A. A member of the U.S. Equestrian Team for several years, Mr. Davidson also won the Individual Gold Medal in the World Championship held at Burghley, England, in 1974, and the U.S. Three-Day Event championship in 1975 and 1981. Photo by Milton C. Toby, courtesy of the U.S.E.T.

post with the horse's *right* foreleg. When the horse's right foreleg is advanced, the rider posts; when the right forefoot hits the ground the rider is in the saddle. Conversely, the rider posts with the horse's *left* foreleg when his horse is trotting in a clockwise direction around the ring. Posting on the proper diagonal tends to keep some horses more square and balanced in their trot, especially in a small enclosure.

When the horse trots the rider should try to keep his hands as steady and quiet as possible because at this gait the horse's head and neck remain steady. Some horses seek and need considerable support, especially at a fast trot.

RIDING AT THE CANTER

The canter is a restrained collected gallop, a three-beat gait. When riding at the canter the rider sits as close to the saddle as possible, with his knees, thighs, and seat in close contact with the saddle. The upper body should be relaxed but erect and not inclined forward quite as far as when the rider is posting to the trot. To regulate the speed and ride at a collected canter the rider must use his hands in rhythm with the horse and "take the horse back" gradually. Then the horse will canter in harmony with the rider's hands and not against them. No gait requires such light hands as does the canter.

The canter can be done on either the right lead or the left lead, that is, with either forefoot leading. If a horse is ridden in an enclosed ring, he should canter on the left lead when circling to the left and on the right lead when he is reversed. This is necessary for balance, comfort, and safety. Hence, in show-ring competition a horse cantering on the wrong lead is penalized in the judging.

The simplest method to take a canter on the left lead is as follows. When riding at the walk to the left hand the rider positions his horse at a slight angle to the rail. He then uses his right leg against the horse's side, shortens the right rein a bit, and lifts slightly at the same time. This is called using the lateral aids for the canter depart. To take the right lead the rider uses his left leg and left rein.

The well-trained horse, under an accomplished rider, is frequently put into the canter by use of diagonal aids. To take the left lead, for example, the rider lifts his left rein a trifle and applies tension to the right and rearward. At the same time he uses his right leg to the rear of the girth. Such rein action tends to lighten the horse's left shoulder and serves as a distinct and individual indication that the left lead is desired.

Speed is not a requisite of the canter. A horse that looks animated enough to run, but restrains himself at the will of the rider is performing properly. This happens when the horse hits the ground lightly in front, sustains much of his weight in the hindquarters, and canters at a rate of speed very little faster than a fast walk. The old horseman saying about "cantering all day in the shade of an apple tree" expressed the desire for a slow, restrained, "rocking chair" canter, easy on both horse and rider.

Although the rider may turn his horse either towards or away from the rail when he reverses direction, most show riders turn towards the rail. A good rider on a responsive horse will often execute the schooling figure known as a half-turn in reverse to change direction.

*The saddle seat. Miss Jennifer Miller, Bedford, Ind., saddle-seat equita-
tion champion of the 1968 National Horse Show at Madison Square
Garden. A pupil of Mrs. Helen Crabtree, Simpsonville, Ky., Miss Miller
is shown here on her three-gaited mount Easter Creation at the 1967
Rock Creek-Kentucky Home School Horse Show.* Unretouched photo by
Ralph Crane courtesy of Mr. M. L. Miller.

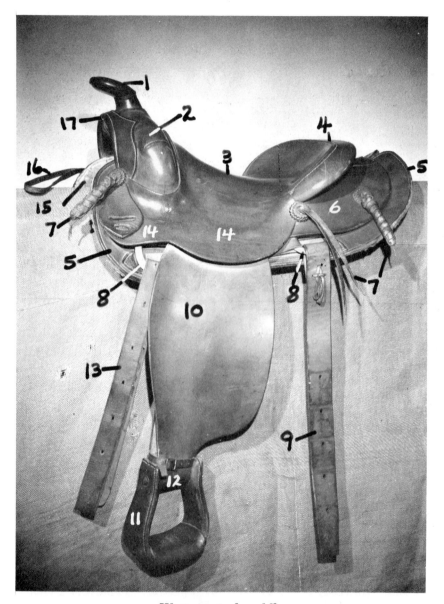

Western stock saddle

1. Horn
2. Fork
3. Seat
4. Cantle
5. Skirt
6. Back housing or back jockey
7. Lace strings
8. Dee rings
9. Leather flank girth
10. Fender or sudadero
11. Stirrup
12. Stirrup leather
13. Front tie strap or cinch strap
14. Front jockey and seat jockey, one piece
15. Wool lining
16. Rope strap
17. Pommel

Photo by Andy Tau, University of Missouri.

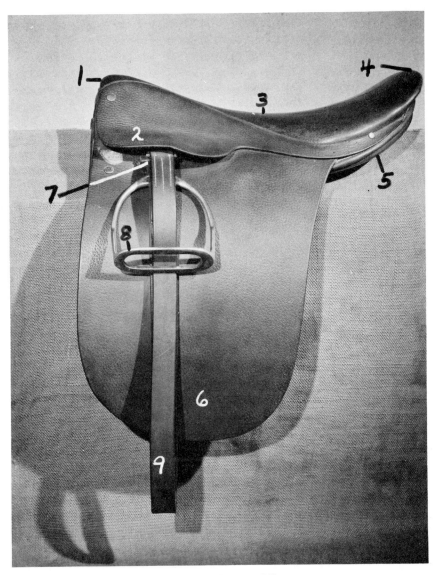

Flat English Saddle

1. Pommel	4. Cantle	7. Stirrup bar
2. Skirt	5. Panel	8. Tread of stirrup iron
3. Seat	6. Flap	9. Stirrup leather

Photo by Andy Tau, University of Missouri.

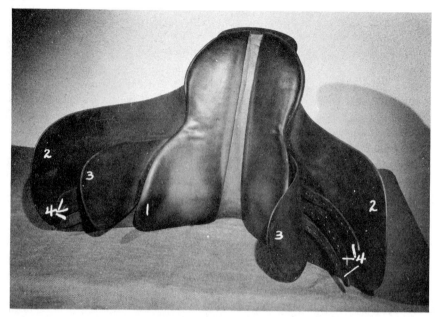

English Saddle, under side

1. Panel	3. Sweat flap
2. Flap	4. Billets for the girth

Photo by Andy Tau, University of Missouri.

RIDING AT THE GALLOP

In the United States the term canter is used to refer to a slow form of the gallop. The horse goes at a rate of speed no faster than he trots, and perhaps even more slowly. When the horse is allowed to gallop on he moves his legs the same way as at the canter. However, he takes a longer stride, hits the ground with greater force, and goes about twice as fast as he normally trots.

The rider on a cantering horse sits deep in the saddle and maintains contact with the saddle. He sits more nearly upright than at the posting trot.

At a gallop the rider should take up a balanced position by putting his weight on his stirrups and raising his buttocks a little out of the saddle and pushing them to the rear. His weight is brought more sharply forward at the waist. The reins, consequently, are held quite short but without restraining the motion of the horse's head. This balanced position takes some of the weight off

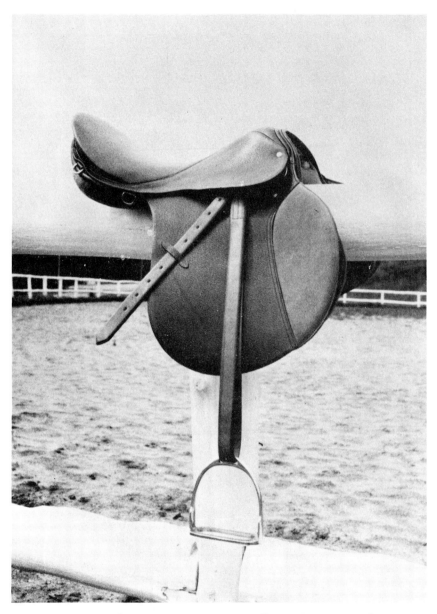

Forward seat saddle with padded knee rolls for hunting and jumping.
Photo by the author.

the horse's back and provides greater comfort for the rider when the horse is going at a strong gallop.

SADDLE-SEAT APPOINTMENTS

Riders and horses in show-ring competition should be **properly**

Hunting snaffle bridle with laced reins. Photo by the author.

One ear bridle often used on the working stock horse. Photo by Andy Tau, University of Missouri.

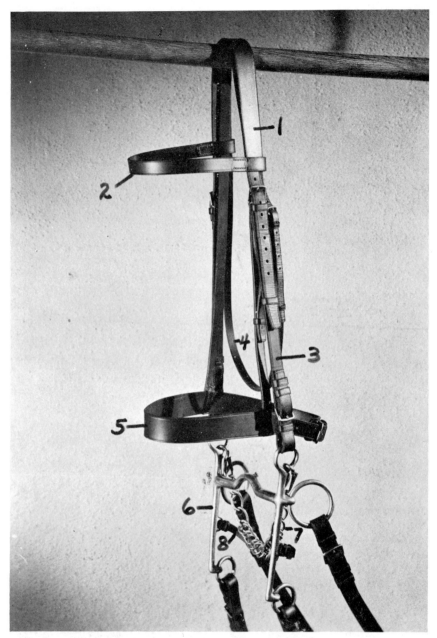

Pelham bridle. This double-reined bridle with some style of a Pelham curb bit is often used on pleasure riding horses, polo ponies, and hunters.

1. Crownpiece or
   headstall
2. Browband

3. Cheek piece
4. Throat latch
5. Caveson or
   noseband

6. Pelham curb bit
7. Curb chain
8. Lip strap

Photo by Andy Tau, University of Missouri.

1. Crown piece or
   headstall
2. Browband
3. Cheek pieces

4. Throat latch
5. Caveson or
   noseband
6. Weymouth
   curb bit

7. Snaffle bit
8. Curb rein
9. Snaffle rein
10. Curb chain
11. Lip strap

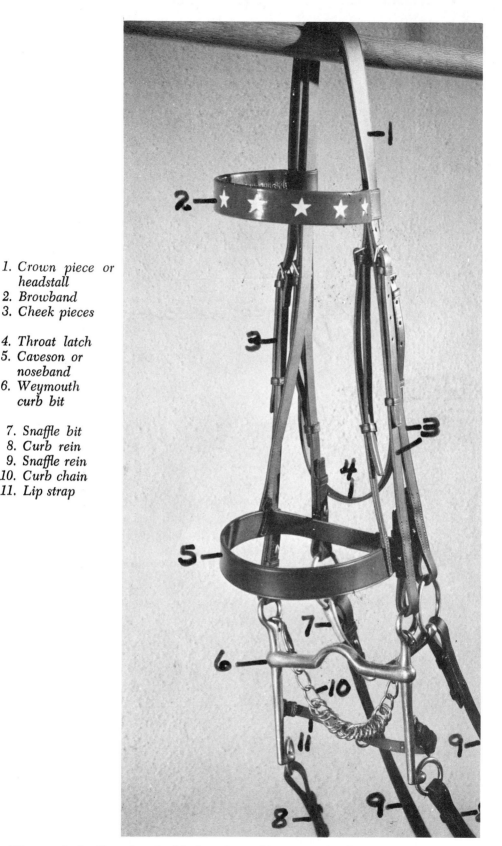

Weymouth bridle. This double-bitted, double-reined bridle is used for showing American Saddle Horses, Arabians, and Morgans under saddle.

Photo by Andy Tau, University of Missouri.

turned out. Neatness is the first requisite of a rider's attire.

For informal saddle-seat classes conservative and solid colors are required. Solid colors include a black, blue, gray, green, beige, or brown jacket with matching jodhpurs (white jacket in season) and derby or soft hat. Boots and breeches also are acceptable but they are not often seen in saddle seat classes.

Even more conservatism is required for evening wear. Solid colors include a dark gray, dark brown, dark blue, or black tuxedo-type jacket with collars and lapels of the same color, top hat, jodhpurs to match, and gloves. A dark-colored riding habit with appropriate accessories is also acceptable.

Horses in saddle-seat classes must be shown in full bridles. Weymouth bridles with both curb and snaffle bits are used. Martingales, or similar tie-downs, are prohibited. Saddles must be of the flat English type. Forward seat and Western saddles are prohibited. Spurs of the unrowelled type, whips, or crops are optional appointments.

HUNTER-SEAT APPOINTMENTS

Riders in hunter-seat classes should wear coats of any tweed or melton for hunting (conservative wash jackets in season), breeches (or jodhpurs), and boots. A dark blue or black hunting cap or a black or brown derby must be worn. Spurs of the unrowelled type, crops or bats are optional appointments.

Horses shown in hunter-seat classes may be brought out with snaffle bridles (with or without dropped nosebands), Pelham bridles, or full bridles. Martingales are prohibited in classes not to jump, but are optional in classes over jumps and in classes requiring both jumping and hacking. Forward seat saddles are used.

STOCK—SEAT APPOINTMENTS

Clothing must be workmanlike and neat. Riders should wear pants and a long-sleeved shirt, or a one-piece equitation suit with collar and cuffs. A belt under loops, Western hat, boots, chaps, and a necktie, kerchief, or bolo tie are required. Spurs are optional. Hair must be neat and securely fastened if long so as not to cover the rider's number.

The stock saddle must fit the rider. Any standard Western bit is acceptable, unless a certain kind is specified. A curb chain, if used, must be at least ½ inch in width and lie flat against the jaws of the horse. No wire, metal, or rawhide device is permissible in conjunction with a leather chin strap, which must be at least ½ inch in width.

Los Rancheros Visitadores, a group of California horsemen, shown here on one of their annual rides; they typify the spirit and love for horseback riding found in similar groups all over the United States. Photo courtesy Los Rancheros Visitadores.

Hackamores, tie-downs, running martingales, and drawreins are prohibited. If closed reins are used, hobbles must be carried, attached below the cantle on the near side of the saddle. If split reins are used and the horse is broken to ground tie, no hobbles are necessary. Bosals or cavesson type nosebands are prohibited. A lariat or reata must be carried attached to the fork of the saddle. Silver equipment, if used, is not given preference over good working track. The use of shoes other than standard horse shoes may be penalized. Shin or bell boots may be used only in Medal Classes.

CLASS ROUTINE

Horses in saddle-seat competition enter the show-ring at the trot and proceed to the left hand (counter-clockwise) around the ring. On the judge's command the entries go at least once around the ring at each gait. Then, on command, they reverse direction and repeat. The order to reverse may be executed either towards or away from the rail. The entries line up on command and any or all riders may be required to execute any appropriate tests included in the class requirements.

The saddle seat. Miss Lu Anthony of Oklahoma City, blue ribbon winner of the Equitation Stake at the Houston Pin Oak show in 1967, High Point Equitation Champion on the Southwest Circuit in 1967 after competing in the San Antonio, New Orleans, Oklahoma City, Tulsa, and Houston shows, and fourth in the Good Hands class at Louisville. Showring pictures are always taken when the horse's inside hind leg is raised. Consequently such pictures always show the rider at the height of his posting position. Nevertheless this photo does show an excellent position of the rider's thigh, knee, and lower leg, flexion of the ankle, and an evident soft touch on the reins. Miss Anthony received all her riding instruction from Harold Adams of Oklahoma City. Photo courtesy Lu Anthony

In hunter-seat classes not to jump, the contestants enter the show-ring and proceed to the left hand. At the judge's command they circle the ring at least once at each gait, then reverse and repeat. The order to reverse may be executed either towards or away from the rail. Light contact with the horse's mouth is required. Entries line up on command and any or all riders may be required to execute any appropriate tests included in the class requirements.

The saddle seat. Mrs. A. E. Knowlton, Emerald Farm, Delaware, Ohio riding the five-gaited mare Carolina Caroline with whom she won many ladies' classes. Note the erect but easy carriage of the rider's body, the firmness of her seat, the angle of the lower leg, and the flexion of the ankle and depression of the heel. Note also the short hold of the reins and the straight line along the snaffle rein to the rider's elbow. Photo by McClasky.

Horses in stock-seat equitation classes enter the ring at a walk. Contestants are judged at a walk, jog, and lope. They are worked both ways of the ring at each gait. The order to reverse may be executed by turning either toward or away from the rail. Following the group workout on the rail, each contestant performs individually by riding the pattern established for stock horses shown in the Western Division of a horse show. This pattern includes such maneuvers as changing leads while loping a figure eight, running and coming to a sliding stop, backing, and turning on the haunches. Such a test demonstrates not only the horse's handiness but also the rider's ability.

DRIVING

Driving a horse is excellent training for all riders. The driver does not have the problem of balancing himself on the horse's back.

Dierdre Pirie, Hamilton, Mass., driving her four-in-hand at Myopia in 1979, where she won the Presentation and Dressage phases of the driving competition. As an alternate member of the first U.S.E.T. Driving squad sent to a World Driving Championship, Mrs. Pirie was the only American driver to complete all phases of the World Driving Championship held at Windsor, England, in 1980. She finished 27th among 42 drivers from 11 nations. Photo by Ken Ettridge, courtesy of the U.S.E.T.

Thus he can use his hands independently. His only contact with the horse is through his hands on the reins to the bit in the horse's mouth. The driver learns how much can be accomplished by a light touch.

The contact between the driver's mind and the horse's mind depends on a communication system from the driver's hands to the sensitive structure of the horse's mouth. It can be gentle and like magic, or it can be rough and brutal. The key to the mouth of a horse can be found at the opposite end of the reins. This is a lesson all riders should learn. And driving helps to teach it.

The driver takes the reins in the left hand, the whip in the right. If the horse is hitched to a four-wheeled rig, the driver enters from the left side. The driver's seat is always on the right-hand side of the rig. After seating himself the driver should immediately adjust the reins.

The hunter seat. Miss Carol Hoffman riding Not Always. This consistent brown gelding won the American Horse Shows Assn. Horse of the Year award for Regular Working Hunters shown in 1966. He was owned by Miss Peggy Steinman, Lancaster, Penna. Photo by Budd.

The hunter seat. Eugene Cunningham, Warrenton, Va., riding his bay Thoroughbred gelding Cap and Gown. This horse was American Horse Shows Association high point winner as a Regular Conformation Hunter 1963-64-65. He was champion of the ten shows in which he competed in 1965. Note the excellent balance of the rider, the freedom of the horse's head, and the easy, seemingly effortless manner of jumping.
Photo by Freudy.

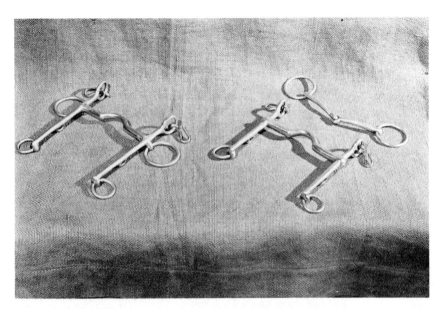

Riding bits. Left, Pelham curb bit with rings at end of mouthpiece and rings at lower end of cheekpieces for attaching two sets of reins. The hooks are points of attachment for the curb chain. The eyelets in the lower cheek pieces are for the lip strap. Right, Weymouth curb bit and snaffle bit used with it in a Weymouth bridle. Photo by Andy Tau, University of Missouri.

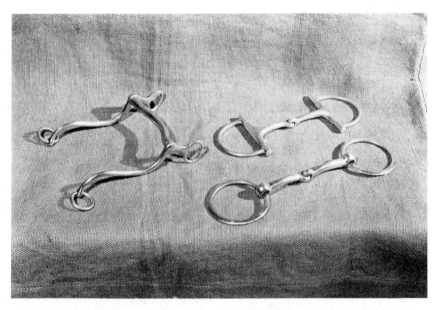

Riding bits. Left, a style of curb bit with S-shaped shanks frequently used on Tennessee Walking Horses. Right, two snaffle bits, the upper one a Dee bit often used on Thoroughbred race horses. The lower bit is a hunting snaffle with flat, round rings used on some hunters and race horses. Photo by Andy Tau, University of Missouri.

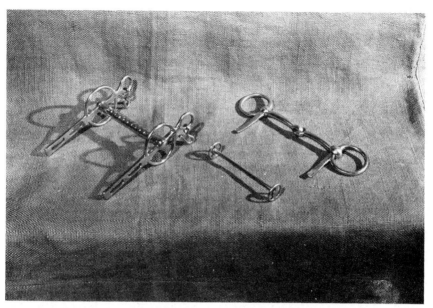

Driving bits. Left, Liverpool bit (a curb bit) used on Hackney horses and ponies and on three-gaited saddle horses when shown in harness. One side of the mouthpiece is smooth, one side is corrugated. The driving reins may be attached at any one of three places. Right, a half-cheek snaffle bit and small check bit. These bits are used on harness race horses, roadsters, and fine harness horses. The driving reins are attached to the snaffle bit, the overhead check rein to the check bit. Photo by Andy Tau, University of Missouri.

The best drivers in American show-rings drive under usual conditions with the left hand. The right hand holds the whip and takes up on the lines. The accepted procedure is to hold the reins in the left hand, the near (left) rein over the forefinger, and the off (right) rein between the middle and ring fingers. Thus the reins are separated by two fingers of the left hand. The reins should be kept even in length and just tight enough to feel the horse's mouth.

To start the horse a "cluck" is used and the left hand is dropped a little forward so the horse will feel free to start. If the driver wants to take a shorter grip on the reins, he grasps the reins with his right hand (to the rear of his left) and slides his left hand forward.

While driving, the right hand is carried lightly just forward of the left hand and is kept free for rein adjustment and use of the whip. The forearms should be carried horizontally about six inches from the body and at almost right angles to the reins. This position permits the greatest freedom of wrist and fingers and is conducive to a light hand. It prevents a continuous dragging pull on the horse's mouth.

To turn left the right hand is placed forward of the left on the near rein. A slight pull on the mouth of a well-trained horse completes the turn. To turn right the right hand is used on the off rein.

The whip should be carried at an angle above the horse and somewhat to the left. Only the thong is to be used.

The driver should sit well back in the seat in a comfortable position with his feet forward and well braced. He should always look straight forward to watch every move of the horse.

Close observation of the top drivers of Hackneys, Shetlands, fine harness horses, and other breeds shown in light harness will reveal that they concentrate all control in the left hand. Every variation in the gait of the horse is accompanied by a little slide forward or backward on the reins.

However, many people do drive with a rein in each hand. An acceptable manner of holding the reins is between the first finger and middle finger. The reins should be gripped by their edges, not on the flat side. The driver should strive always to keep a light, sensitive feel of the horse's mouth.

17

Selling Registered Horses

Earlier chapters in this book discussed judging and selecting horses, breeding, feeding, parasite and disease control, and other management problems. If a horseman has been a discriminating judge and has bred good horses of recognized bloodlines, if he has fed his horses well and kept them free from parasites and debilitating diseases, he will be able to sell the horses he produces.

Many thousands of horses are sold annually at private treaty and at public auctions. The buyers are looking for well-bred and well-made horses. If his pedigree gives a horse the right kind of identity and if the horse is a pleasing individual, he will appeal to prospective buyers. A Thoroughbred colt bred to run fast, a Standardbred trotter or pacer bred to go fast in harness, or a Saddlebred colt whose ances-

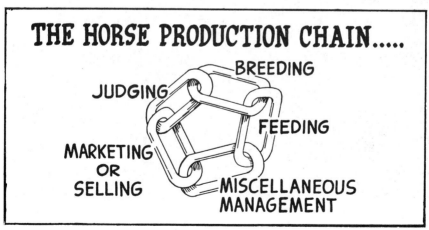

THE HORSE PRODUCTION CHAIN.....

BREEDING
JUDGING
FEEDING
MARKETING
OR
SELLING
MISCELLANEOUS
MANAGEMENT

"For," said the deacon, "it's mighty plain,
That the weakest link must stand the strain;
And the way to fix it, I'm not in jest,
Is to make that link as strong as the rest."

Sales ring at Saratoga. The yearling filly in the ring sold for $177,000 in the 1966 yearling sales. She was consigned by Whitney Stone, Morven Stud, Charlottesville, Va., and was bought by the Cragwood Stables of Charles W. Engelhard. She was sired by Sailor and was out of Levee by Hill Prince. Photo by Jim Sargent, courtesy Fasig-Tipton Co.

The top price of $3,500,000 at the 1981 Keeneland Summer Sale was brought by a colt consigned by the Windfields Farm. He was sired by Northern Dancer and was out of the 1970 Canadian Oaks winner South Ocean, thus was a brother to the Canadian champion Northernette and to Storm Bird, the 1980 two-year-old champion in England. He was bought by the British Bloodstock Agency (Ireland), Mr. Robert Sangster with European and American partners. Photo courtesy the Keeneland Association, by Bill Straus.

The top price at the 1981 Tattersalls Sale for Standardbred yearlings was $385,000. It was brought by this bay colt, bred and consigned by the Castleton Farm, Lexington, Ky. He was named Listening. This colt was sired by Bret Hanover, p, 4, T 1:53 ⅗, the former world champion pacer, and was out of the fast pacing mare Stand By, p, 3, T 1:58, the dam of four horses with 2:00 records. Photo by *Horseman & Fair World*.

A future Derby winner being sold at Keeneland. The Thoroughbred colt in the ring of the Keeneland Sales Pavilion at the 1967 yearling sale was consigned by Leslie Combs II, Spendthrift Farm. He was sold for $250,000 to Frank McMahon, Vancouver, B.C. Named Majestic Prince he won the Kentucky Derby and Preakness Stakes in 1969. He was sired by Raise a Native and was out of Gay Hostess by °Royal Charger. Photo by "Skeets" Meadors, courtesy Keeneland Assn.

tors have proven their worth as show horses will attract buyers and will almost sell themselves. The number of buyers seeking the best horses is always greater than the number of top horses.

SOME NOTED PUBLIC AUCTIONS

For many years the breeders of Thoroughbreds, Standardbreds, and American Saddlebred horses have patronized public auctions as a means of bringing sellers and buyers together. The annual sale of Thoroughbred yearlings at Saratoga Springs, New York, is a fine example. Held during the race meeting at Saratoga each August, this sale always features very choice, highly-selected consignments of Thoroughbred yearlings of the best breeding. Many noted market breeders such as the Newstead Farm, Upperville, Virginia; Mereworth Farm, Lexington, Kentucky; Windfields Farm, Chesapeake City, Maryland; and the Morven Stud, Charlottesville, Virginia, regularly send yearlings to this sale.

Prospective buyers looking over a yearling colt in the consignment from the Morven Stud, Charlottesville, Va. Mr. Whitney Stone, the owner, in the figured shirt. Photo by the author.

The Morven Stud of Whitney Stone consigned this dark chestnut son of Tom Fool to the 1967 Saratoga yearling sale. He brought $30,000 on the bid of Noble Gilmer. Photo by the author.

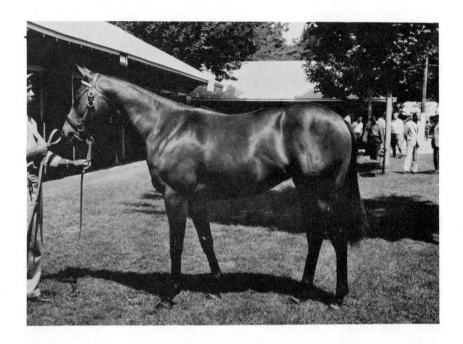

John E. duPont, Foxcatcher Farm, Newtown Square, Pa., gave $190,000 for this lovely filly at the 1967 Saratoga yearling sale. She was the first foal of the stakes-winning mare Blue Norther and was sired by Bold Ruler. She was consigned to the sale by the Jonabell Farm, Agent for her breeder, Mrs. William R. Hawn of Dallas, Texas. This filly had fine quality, balanced conformation, and an impeccable pedigree. She was presented in beautiful bloom. She sold herself. Her groom, Francis Wilson, is on the lead strap. Photo by the author.

The Keeneland Summer Sale, held each July at the Keeneland Race Track, Lexington, Kentucky, also offers highly-selected, well-bred, well-made, and well-fitted Thoroughbred yearlings from the leading nurseries. In addition to these two long-established sales, several other Thoroughbred auctions are held in the United States.

The figures in the following table indicate the high quality of the Thoroughbred yearlings sold at the Saratoga and Keeneland Summer Sales. The figures also show that prices for top Thoroughbreds rose faster than the inflation rate of the economy as a whole during the 1970s.

	Summer Sales Saratoga-Keeneland*		All Other Yearling Auctions*	
Year	No. Sold	Average	No. Sold	Average
1950	701	$ 4,950	1,016	$ 1,536
1960	549	11,503	1,308	2,815
1970	480	28,631	2,749	4,017
1980	520	160,427	6,559	19,318

*The Blood-Horse, Jan. 17, 1981

The world of racing and the world of breeding meet at the sales. Many prominent racing stables replenish their ranks by purchases of yearlings at auction.

Yearlings are sold "with their engagements." That is, if they have been made eligible for any stakes races, their eligibility is not affected by their sale. However, the new owner must pay any necessary additional fees to maintain the eligibility to compete in the stakes races.

After their sale, Thoroughbred yearlings are usually broke to saddle during the fall and put into light training. If they stay sound and develop well physically, they come to the races the following year as two-year-olds.

The biggest Standardbred sale in America is held early in November at Harrisburg, Pennsylvania. The Hanover Shoe Farm, perhaps the largest horse breeding establishment in the world, annually consigns its yearlings to this sale. In 1979 Hanover sold 180 yearlings at Harrisburg for $6,256,400—an average of $34,758.

Another big Standardbred sale is Tattersalls, held during the Lexington Trots every October at Lexington, Kentucky.

Standardbreds purchased at yearlings sales are broke to harness in the fall, jogged during the winter months, and go into more serious training for harness racing in the spring. Thus they get to the races as two-year-olds.

Auctions for horses of the pleasure riding breeds and for ponies are not usually so large as those for race horses. However, for Quarter Horses, the most numerous breed in America, there are a great many auctions all over the country. Many of these sales are sponsored by state or regional breeder organizations or held in conjunction with some horse show or race meeting.

The Heart of America Saddlebred Horse Sales, held twice a year at Kansas City, Missouri, and the semi-annual Tattersalls Sales at Lexington, Kentucky, are patronized more by trainers and dealers in American Saddlebreds than by breeders. The breeders of American Saddlebreds make most of their sales by private treaty.

Sales by private treaty are most commonly used by breeders of Arabians, Morgans, and Appaloosas. However, a few large breeders—such as Lasma Arabians, Scottsdale, Arizona—hold yearly auctions of the horses produced on their farms.

Horse shows have helped many breeders make sales. There are several reasons for this. First, the shows give a winning horse a chance to identify himself on a competitive basis as a top horse. Second, shows bring the breeder-exhibitor and the potential buyer together. The prospective buyer can inspect a large number of horses with a minimum expenditure of time and money. Third, the shows— local, state, and national—are among the most effective advertising agencies of good livestock; they furnish the breeders of top stock with an opportunity to identify themselves as leaders in their field.

Duke of York, champion of the weanling division of the American Saddle Horse Futurity at the Illinois State Fair. This colt had great style and finish, a smooth, balanced conformation, and an exciting trot. He had what it takes to win in tough Futurity competition. He was bred and shown by Asa Robison, Tremont, Ill., who is on the lead strap in this photo. Photo by Launspach, courtesy Asa Robison.

Furturity events have often benefited horse breeders. A "futurity" class at a horse show usually requires the nomination of in-foal mares whose foals, when dropped, are kept eligible by payment of entry fees to compete on show day as weanlings, yearlings, or two-year-olds, depending upon the specific rules that goven each futurity competition.

These futurity events have emphasized in the minds of the breeders the need to mate their mares to the best stallions available. Futurity shows have taught breeders to fit and train their colts well. The futurities have made strong appeal to the small breeder with only one or two colts because the futurity classes give him an excellent chance to advertise his breeding.

Without question, the shows are one of the best methods of advertising registered horses. But other methods are also very help-

This bay colt by Hail to Reason and out of Jolie Deja by *Djeddah brought $110,000 in the 1967 Keeneland Sale of Thoroughbred yearlings. Charles W. Englehard's Cragwood Stables bought the colt consigned by the Nuchols Bros.' Hurstland Farm, Midway, Ky. Charles Nuchols is in the checked shirt in this photo. Photo by "Skeets" Meadors courtesy Keeneland Assn.

ful. The local papers, breed publications, circulars, folders, booklets, catalogs, and billboard and roadside advertisements can be effective publicity agents. Of course, letters, photographs, and personal conferences may be decisive factors in the consummation of sales.

The treatment of the prospective buyer is most important. Courteous treatment and promptness in correspondence please customers. The horse breeder must sell himself before he can sell his horses.

The horse breeder must first have his offering well bred, well made, and fit and ready for sale. He should sell when he has a live customer. And, lastly, he should sell when he is making a profit. Any stud must be both productive and profitable if it is to endure for the benefit of the breeder and his breed.

Appendix

Appendix

Palomino	Palomino Horse Breeders of America P.O. Box 249 Mineral Wells, TX 76067
Percheron	Percheron Horse Association of America Route 1 Belmont, OH 43718
Pinto	Pinto Horse Association of America, Inc. 7525 Mission Gorge Road San Diego, CA 92120
Quarter Horse	American Quarter Horse Association 2736 West Tenth Street Amarillo, TX 79168
Shetland	American Shetland Pony Club Fowler, IN 47944
Shire	American Shire Horse Association 14410 High Bridge Road Monroe, WA 98272
Standardbred	United States Trotting Association 750 Michigan Avenue Columbus, OH 43215
Suffolk	American Suffolk Horse Association 15B Roden Wichita Falls, TX 76311
Tennessee Walking Horse	Tennessee Walking Horse Breeders' and Exhibitors' Association P.O. Box 286 Lewisburg, TN 37091
Thoroughbred	The Jockey Club 380 Madison Avenue New York, NY 10017
Welsh	Welsh Pony Society of America P.O. Box 2977 Winchester, VA 22601

HORSE AND PONY BREED
REGISTRATION ASSOCIATIONS

American Saddlebred Horse	American Saddlebred Horse Association, Inc. 929 South 4th Street Louisville, KY 40203
Appaloosa	Appaloosa Horse Club, Inc. P.O. Box 8403 Moscow, ID 83843
Arabian	Arabian Horse Registry of America, Inc. 3435 South Yosemite Street Denver, CO 80231
	International Arabian Horse Association (Half-Arabian and Anglo-Arabian Registries) P.O. Box 4502 Burbank, CA 91503
Belgian	Belgian Draft Horse Corporation of America P.O. Box 335 Wabash, IN 46992
Clydesdale	Clydesdale Breeders of the United States Route 1, Box 131 Pecatonica, IL 61063
Connemara	American Connemara Pony Society HoshieKon Farm Goshen, CT 06756
Hackney	American Hackney Horse Society P.O. Box 174 Pittsfield, IL 62363
Morgan	American Morgan Horse Association, Inc. P.O. Box 1 Westmoreland, NY 13490
Paint	American Paint Horse Association P.O. Box 18519 Fort Worth, TX 76118

HORSEMEN'S ASSOCIATIONS

The American Horse Council
1700 K Street, N.W., Suite 300
Washington, DC 20006

American Driving Society
79 Southgate Avenue
Hastings-on-Hudson, NY 10706

American Horse Shows Association, Inc.
598 Madison Avenue
New York, NY 10022

Carriage Association of America, Inc.
P.O. Box 3788
Portland, ME 04104

Masters of Foxhounds Association of America
112 Water Street
Boston, MA 02109

National Cutting Horse Association
P.O. Box 12155
Fort Worth, TX 76116

National Steeplechase and Hunt Association
Box 308
Elmont, L.I., NY 11003

North American Trail Ride Conference
1505 East San Martin Avenue
San Martin, CA 95046

Professional Horsemen's Association of America, Inc.
301 N. Union
Kennett Square, PA 19348

Professional Rodeo Cowboys Association
101 ProRodeo Drive
Colorado Springs, CO 80919

Thoroughbred Owners and Breeders Association
P.O. Box 358
Elmont, L.I., NY 11003

United States Combined Training Association
292 Bridge Street
South Hamilton, MA 01982

United States Dressage Federation
Box 80668
Lincoln, NE 68501

United States Equestrian Team, Inc.
292 Bridge Street
South Hamilton, MA 01982

United States Polo Association
1301 West 22d Street, Suite 706
Oak Brook, IL 60521

United States Pony Clubs, Inc.
303 South High Street
West Chester, PA 19380

Index

Index